BEING HUMAN IN A CONSUMER SOCIETY

Classical and Contemporary Social Theory

Series Editor: Stjepan G. Mestrovic, Texas A&M University, USA

Classical and Contemporary Social Theory publishes rigorous scholarly work that re-discovers the relevance of social theory for contemporary times, demonstrating the enduring importance of theory for modern social issues. The series covers social theory in a broad sense, inviting contributions on both 'classical' and modern theory, thus encompassing sociology, without being confined to a single discipline. As such, work from across the social sciences is welcome, provided that volumes address the social context of particular issues, subjects, or figures and offer new understandings of social reality and the contribution of a theorist or school to our understanding of it. The series considers significant new appraisals of established thinkers or schools, comparative works or contributions that discuss a particular social issue or phenomenon in relation to the work of specific theorists or theoretical approaches. Contributions are welcome that assess broad strands of thought within certain schools or across the work of a number of thinkers, but always with an eye toward contributing to contemporary understandings of social issues and contexts.

Also in the series

The Poetics of Crime:
Understanding and Researching Crime and Deviance Through Creative Sources
Edited by Michael Hviid Jacobsen
ISBN 978-1-4094-6995-7

Hegel's Phenomenology and Foucault's Genealogy
Evangelia Sembou
ISBN 978-1-4094-4308-7

The Making of a Postsecular Society:
A Durkheimian Approach to Memory, Pluralism and Religion in Turkey
Massimo Rosati
ISBN 978-1-4724-2312-2

Being Human in a Consumer Society

Edited by
ALEJANDRO NÉSTOR GARCÍA MARTÍNEZ
University of Navarra, Spain

LONDON AND NEW YORK

First published 2015 by Ashgate Publishing

2 Park Square, Milton Park, Abingdon, Oxfordshire OX14 4RN
52 Vanderbilt Avenue, New York, NY 10017

Routledge is an imprint of the Taylor & Francis Group, an informa business

First issued in paperback 2020

British Library Cataloguing in Publication Data
A catalogue record for this book is available from the British Library.

The Library of Congress has cataloged the printed edition as follows:
Being human in a consumer society / [edited] by Alejandro Néstor García Martínez.
      pages cm. — (Classical and contemporary social theory)
   Includes bibliographical references and index.
   ISBN 978-1-4724-4317-5 (hardback : alk. paper)
   1. Consumption (Economics)—Social aspects—Philosophy. 2. Consumers—Philosophy.
3. Economics—Sociological aspects—Philosophy. I. García Martínez, Alejandro Néstor,
1977–

   HC79.C6B39 2015
   339.4'7—dc23
                                                                    2014030029

ISBN 978-1-4724-4317-5 (hbk)
ISBN 978-0-367-59973-7 (pbk)

Contents

List of Figures and Tables   *vii*
Notes on Contributors   *ix*
Acknowledgements   *xiii*

Introduction: Why Consumption and What Society?   XV
Alejandro Néstor García Martínez

**PART I   BLURRING HUMAN BEINGS: STRUCTURAL
             CONSTRICTIONS IN CONSUMER SOCIETY**

1   Postemotional Law in Consumer Society   3
             Stjepan G. Mestrovic

2   The Dehumanized Consumer: Does the
             Prosumer Offer Some Hope?   25
             George Ritzer

3   Status Matters? The Contradictions Surrounding
             Conspicuous Consumption   41
             Colin Campbell

**PART II   CONSUMER CULTURE AS MEDIATION IN HUMAN
             RELATIONSHIPS**

4   The Two Faces of Consumerism: When Things
             Make Us (In)Human   69
             Pablo García-Ruiz

5   Accepting and Resisting Insecurity: Using Consumer
             Culture to Have it Both Ways?   87
             Allison J. Pugh

6   Conformity and Distinction in Scandinavia's
             Largest Department Store   103
             Karin M. Ekström

PART III FRAMING THE HUMAN BEING IN A CONSUMER SOCIETY

7 Reflections on the Cultural Commons 129
Talbot Brewer

8 On Being Human in a Consumer Society:
Fashion Skirts the Ethical Agenda 159
Efrat Tseëlon

9 Framing Humanity Consumerwise: Embodied Consumer
Selves and their Varieties 177
Roberta Sassatelli

Index *197*

List of Figures and Tables

Figures

6.1	Map of the Gekås Ullared location in Sweden	105
6.2	Entrance to Gekås Ullared	106
6.3	Queue to the store one Saturday morning in August 2009	109
6.4	Baskets in a shopping trolley	110
6.5	A couple of men waiting among the shopping trolleys outside the women's fitting room	113
6.6	Consumers learn to take a shopping trolley before entering the department store	115
6.7	Shopping trolley parking outside the fitting rooms	115
6.8	Shopping trolley with plastic film and aluminum foil	117
6.9	Shopping trolley with Hula Hoop and poster	117
6.10	The Shakti mat—conformity and/or distinction	119
6.11	Loss leaders at the entrance	119
6.12	Market in Strängnäs, October 2009. "Cheaper than at Ullared"	121
6.13	Father Christmases at Gekås Ullared in August—refined or coarse?	123
8.1	"It's depressing no longer being able to buy all those things we don't really need"	175

Tables

8.1	From profit to holistic vision	162
8.2	Eco challenges and partial solutions to the materials economy	170
8.3	Global average virtual water content of some selected products, per unit of product	171
8.4	Unexamined assumptions of ethical fashion	174

Notes on Contributors

Talbot Brewer is Professor and Chair of the Philosophy Department at the University of Virginia and a Faculty Fellow at the Institute for Advanced Studies in Culture. He specializes in ethics and political philosophy, with a special emphasis on moral psychology and Aristotelian normative ethics. He is the author of numerous articles, including "Virtues We Can Share: A Reading of Aristotle's Ethics" (*Ethics* 115, 2005), "Savoring Time: Desire, Pleasure and Wholehearted Activity" (*Ethical Theory and Moral Practice* 6, 2, 2003), "Two Kinds of Commitments (And Two Kinds of Social Groups)" (*Philosophy and Phenomenological Research* 66, 2003), and "Maxims and Virtues" (*The Philosophical Review* 3, 2002). He has also authored two books, the most recent of which is *The Retrieval of Ethics* (2009).

Colin Campbell is Emeritus Professor of Sociology at the University of York. He is the author of half a dozen books and over 100 articles dealing with issues in the sociology of religion, consumerism, cultural change, and sociological theory. He is probably best known as the author of *The Romantic Ethic and the Spirit of Modern Consumerism* (1987, 2005), while his other publications include *The Myth of Social Action* (1996), *The Easternization of the West* (2007), and *Toward A Sociology of Irreligion* (1971), a new edition of which was published in 2013.

Karin M. Ekström is Professor (Chair) in Marketing at University of Borås, Sweden. She is the initiator and former director of the Centre for Consumer Science (CFK), an interdisciplinary consumer research center. Her research interests are family consumption, consumer socialization, collecting, consumer's relations to artefacts, and the meaning(s) of consumption. She has edited several books most recently *Consumer Behaviour—A Nordic Perspective* (2010) and *Beyond the Consumption Bubble* with Kay Glans (2011). Recent journal articles include publications in the *Journal of Consumer Behaviour*, the *Journal of Macromarketing*, the *Journal of Marketing Management* and *Research in Consumer Behaviour*. Her most recent publication is "The Discovery of Relations to Artefacts in the Boundless Process of Moving" in *Coping with Excess; How Organizations, Communities and Individuals Manage Overflows* (edited by Barbara Czarniawska and Orvar Löfgren, 2013). She has studied reuse and recycling of clothes and textiles in a research project for the last three years. Her current research projects focus on culinary tourism and market orientation of art museums.

Alejandro Néstor García Martínez is Lecturer at the University of Navarra in Sociology, Social Theory, and Theory of Organizations. He also serves as a Research Fellow for the *Emotional Culture and Identity* project at the Institute for Culture and Society at the same university. He is the author of numerous articles and several books, including *Fashion and Social Distinction* (2007) and the edition of the monographic issue of *Anuario Filosófico* on "Consumption and Identity" (2010).

Pablo García-Ruiz is Associate Professor of Sociology at the University of Zaragoza (Spain), whose PhD in Philosophy (Social Theory) was awarded by the University of Navarra (1992). His research interests are the relationship between consumption projects and self-identity formation, and the role of consumption patterns in the emergence of new forms of citizenship. He is the author of some papers on topics such as "Consumption and Identity: A Relational Approach" (2010), and "Reflexive Consumers: Consumption as a Social Practice" (2010). His latest book came out in 2009, entitled *Rethinking Consumption*.

Stjepan G. Mestrovic is Professor of Sociology at Texas A&M University, USA. He is the author of Émile Durkheim and the Reformation of Sociology, *The Barbarian Temperament: Toward a Postmodern Critical Theory*, *Genocide After Emotion: The Postemotional Balkan War*, *Postemotional Society*, *Anthony Giddens: The Last Modernist*, *The Coming Fin de Siècle: An Application of Durkheim's Sociology to Modernity and Postmodernity*, and *Strike and Destroy: When Counter-Insurgency (COIN) Doctrine Met Hellraiser's Brigade*.

Allison J. Pugh is Associate Professor of Sociology at the University of Virginia and Honorary Research Fellow at the United States Study Center, at the University of Sydney at Camperdown, Australia. Her book *Longing and Belonging: Parents, Children, and Consumer Culture* (2009) won the 2010 William J. Goode award for the best book in family sociology. Her new book, *The Tumbleweed Society: Working and Caring in an Age of Insecurity* (2015), looks at how unrequited commitment at work shapes how insecure workers view their obligations at home. Research interests include inequality, culture, work, intimacy, childhood, and how empathy and knowledge are related.

George Ritzer is Distinguished University Professor at the University of Maryland. His best-known work is *The McDonaldization of Society* currently in its 7th edition (with an 8th edition forthcoming). It has been translated into 15 languages. He has published many other books that have themselves been frequently translated (a total of about 20 languages). In addition, Ritzer has published many widely cited scholarly articles and often-translated textbooks, several of which have gone through multiple editions. His current scholarly work focuses on the issue of prosumption.

Roberta Sassatelli is Associate Professor of Sociology at the University of Milan (Italy). She has previously taught at the University of East Anglia (Norwich, UK) and the University of Bologna (I). Her research focuses on the theory of consumer action, the sociology of consumer practices, and the politics of contemporary consumer culture as well as theories of embodiment, sexuality and gender studies. She has done empirical research on ethical consumption, the commercialization of sport and leisure, consumption and class boundaries, and commodities and the sexualization of the body. She also works on cultural theory and visual studies. Among her recent books in English are *Consumer Culture: History, Theory and Politics* (2007) and *Fitness Culture: Gyms and the Commercialisation of Discipline and Fun* (2010, paperback edition 2014). She has been visiting fellow at Caltech (US), Birkbeck College (UK) and Une (Australia).

Efrat Tseëlon is trained in social psychology and cultural analysis and holds the Chair of Fashion Theory at the School of Design, University of Leeds. Since receiving her PhD from Oxford on *Communicating via Clothing* she has been developing a critical perspective on the study of fashion, beauty, and the body.

She has contributed to fashion scholarship in extending the research agenda from designer fashion to ordinary clothes, shifting the focus from a stereotypical approach of ceremonial costumes to a wardrobe approach of everyday clothes.

Her research focus covers societal practices, cultural objects and representations, and individual cognitions. She is the editor in chief of *Critical Studies in Fashion & Beauty*, and is the author of numerous publications on topics as diverse as the study of beauty as stigma, clothing as an instrument of gender construction, authenticity as a critical factor in distinguishing art from fashion, masquerade as a technology of identity, and fashion ethics as ideological discourse, among others.

Acknowledgements

As editor of this book, I would like to express my gratitude to Social Trends Institute for its generous support of the 2011 conference (Being Human in a Consumer Society) from which many of the essays contained in this volume were drawn. In particular, I would like to thank Carlos Cavallé, president of Social Trends Institute, and Tracey O'Donnell, secretary general of Social Trends Institute, for their support of that initial conference and the publication of its proceedings. I give special thanks to Christa Byker and Lynden Parry for their help in the organization of the conference and the collegial atmosphere they provided for us in Barcelona. My deepest gratitude goes to Neil Jordan and Ashgate for assistance in bringing this volume to publication. Finally, I wish to thank all those who participated in the 2011 conference for three days of informative and enlightening discussion that has helped to shape the present publication.

A Note on Social Trends Institute

Social Trends Institute (STI) is a nonprofit research center that offers institutional and financial support to academics of all fields who seek to make sense of emerging social trends and their effects on human communities. STI focuses its research on four subject areas: family, bioethics, culture and lifestyles, and corporate governance. STI organizes experts' meetings, which bring scholars together to present and discuss each other's original research in an academic forum. These meetings are not open to the public and are intended to foster open intellectual dialogue between scholars from all over the world, of various academic backgrounds, disciplines, and beliefs. Often, STI helps to publish a collection of the conference papers in a single volume, revised and reviewed in light of the meeting's discussion. STI's sole aim is to promote research and scholarship of the highest academic standards. In so doing, STI hopes to make a scholarly contribution to fostering understanding of the varying and complex social trends that are intertwined with the modern world. STI is committed, then, to that which makes such scholarship possible: intellectual freedom, openness to a diversity of viewpoints, and a shared commitment to serve our common humanity.

Introduction:
Why Consumption and What Society?

Alejandro Néstor García Martínez

Consumption is a key element of contemporary society. The consequences of consumption culture and its social structure for human beings are manifold and, quite often, ambivalent. All of them seem to be rooted in the paradoxical nature of consumption itself: on the one hand, the structure of consumer society drives production, generates employment and wealth, and brings about cultural changes. On the other hand, these powerful and extensive capacities rest on seemingly capricious and changing consumer wants, desires or needs.

This basic discontinuity between social structure and individual motivations is the starting point for many approaches to consumption and consumer culture. But building on it further, the social position and agency of human beings within consumer society are usually considered through two different perspectives. For some structuralist approaches, the human being is seen as an individual explicitly or symbolically dominated by social structures, which impel him or her to particular patterns of consumption and so to specific lifestyles. Phenomenologist and postmodern approaches, on the contrary, study the diverse forms of consumption as expressions of individual autonomy and how those practices suit or further the individual's quest for identity. Both approaches are founded on a specific and latent view of human beings: either as a subject whose consumer choices are largely reflected in the dominant needs or rules created and favored by social structures; or as an entirely autonomous subject who chooses in line with wholly undetermined wants and desires, which—in turn—express the "authentic self."

In this context, structural tensions and cultural paradoxes based on the discontinuity between motivations and social constraints are numerous. Generally speaking, it is possible to identify a specific cultural pattern that tends to encourage viewing society solely as a space for experiential consumption, where everything can be (potentially) consumed, even the human person themself. However, at the same time, there are some objects that resist or can be withdrawn from this consumption logic because they retain some level of significance beyond their viability for consumption. This significance arises from a concrete relationship with the object or from a relational context in which the object is embedded (for example an object with an attached affective meaning, moral principles, solidification of cultural values, ideologies and so on).

In connection to this, the problem of identity—personal or collective—acquires special relevance in consumer societies. Consumption is not only an instrumental action, aiming towards the acquisition of status, pleasure, or particular mental states, but is also an expressive or relational action through which people define, reproduce, and construct their identities and lifestyles. Identity is *reproduced*, for example, when consumption is dependent upon social position, where the motivations for consumption are grounded in social emulation, distinction or envy. By contrast, the *construction* of identity is made manifest when identity is conceived of as the result of an unrestrained personal quest. In this case, one's self-motivations are considered to be *de facto* unconditioned by social constraints. Individual consumption, viewed through this lens, appears as a wholly individual and essentially self-referential activity, which leads to the primacy of a type of experiential or emotional consumption.

Key Questions

The reflection that guides all chapters included in this book can be formulated as significant questions, such as:

- What significant cultural or structural transformations can be identified in consumer society, in comparison to earlier societies?
- In discussing consumption, what is the relation between individual motivations and structural constraints? How can these two concepts be linked in order to understand consumer society and its dynamics?
- What processes and tendencies have been—and still are—relevant for the consolidation of a culture of consumption? How does consumption culture affect our understanding of the nature of human beings and praxis?
- To what extent does the culture of consumption spread to other social spheres, affecting social relationships? What are the limits, if any, of this extension?
- In what ways can a culture of consumption lead to isolation, individualization or commodification of human beings?

Structure of the Book

Part I, entitled "Blurring Human Beings: Structural Constrictions in Consumer Society", focuses more specifically on those structural constrictions that seem to determine human choices and, eventually, become symbolic domination, often via hidden mechanisms (the "illusion" of freedom, for example), through which social structures and certain cultural values exercise their manipulative function.

But, as has been said above, the structural consequences of consumption and consumer culture for human beings cannot explain alone the complexity of contemporary societies. Consumers' praxis is embodied in significant relationships, with material culture and other people. Structures, relationships, and culture are intertwined. This is why Part II, "Consumer Culture as Mediation in Human Relationships", tries to explore these connections with a more optimistic view of the place and possibilities of human beings in consumer societies, introducing more phenomenological and relational aspects involved in consumers' behavior.

So, how can we frame the position of human beings in consumer culture? From different points of view and also from diverse academic fields (political philosophy, fashion studies and a sociological perspective), Part III, "Framing the Human Being in a Consumer Society", suggests the idea of understanding consumer culture as "lived culture." In doing so, it also offers a rich analytical framework for understanding that very lived culture by differentiating between the symbolic and cultural aspects diffused socially through commercial advertising, in addition to many other channels. At the same time this analytical proposal devotes attention to embodied dispositions; to practices situated in particular contexts; to the reflexivity, agency or "subjective creativity" that also appears in consumer choices; and finally to the social structure that crosses and is shaped in various ways by those choices.

As a whole, this book offers an interdisciplinary approach to some normative questions related to the good life and human flourishing in consumer societies. Chapters are ordered in order to take into account the structural conditions that consumer culture imposes (Part I), but also try to leave some ground to human autonomy through the connections between those structural conditions and human relationships as a cultural context for human praxis (Part II). Finally, these reflections conclude with some more general approaches and an analytical framework for understanding consumer culture and human praxis (Part III).

PART I
Blurring Human Beings:
Structural Constrictions in
Consumer Society

Chapter 1

Postemotional Law in Consumer Society

Stjepan G. Mestrovic

Introduction

Thorstein Veblen's key points regarding the position of the consumer in relation to capitalist social structure seem to be as true today as they were approximately a century ago. In meticulous detail, Veblen documented the exploitation of the "common man" by the "robber barons" of his era. His overall argument seems to have been that modern society is really a latter-day barbarism, or a new version of feudal society which compels the common man to take on the role of the serf in relation to corporations as the leisure class. To phrase the matter another way, the common man becomes the prey to the government-corporate structure conceived as a predator. In Veblen's words:

> As it finds expression in the life of the barbarian, prowess manifests itself in two main directions—force and fraud. In varying degrees these two forms of expression are similarly present in modern warfare, in the pecuniary occupations, and in sports and games. (Veblen [1899] 1967, 273)

It is more true than it was a century ago that force and fraud characterize contemporary warfare, economic markets and the business professions, advertising, sports, gambling, and other institutions that are modeled on war, money-making, and sports. As I write this chapter, the world is "recovering" from the "Great Recession." Today's equivalents of Veblen's robber barons on Wall Street were bailed out by the government while the common man gets little to no relief in terms of his or her financial debt, home foreclosures, or other private, financial catastrophes. State governments are all in financial crisis and are resolving these crises through slashing budgets by cutting salaries and benefits for teachers, policemen, firemen, and other social roles that fit Veblen's characterization of the common man. The situation in the European Union is similar to that of the US, with various EU countries taking on the role of individual states in the US. This phenomenon—the government aiding big business while declining to rescue the common man—has become the object of mockery and humor on *The Daily Show*, *The Colbert Report*, and other comedy television shows. But it has not become an object of academic study in or on Veblen's terms.

C. Wright Mills ([1959] 1967) hailed Veblen as the greatest American social critic.[1] Veblen has influenced sociology and social thought primarily through his terms "conspicuous consumption" and the related terms, conspicuous waste and leisure. In *Consumer Society*, Jean Baudrillard (1998) uses Veblen—among other theorists—to extend the idea of consumerism to include the consumption of ideas and collective representations, which is a prelude to Baudrillard's version of postmodernism as the rootless circulation of ideas. In *The Lonely Crowd*, David Riesman (1950) drew upon Veblen (again, among other theorists) to develop the concept of the hypersensitive "other-directed type" who applies "conspicuous consumption" to all aspects of social life, not just economic acquisition or the desire for pecuniary gain. The other-directed type wants to be seen, noticed, and *liked* much more than the previous tradition-directed and inner-directed types. Another important distinction seems to be that the inner-directed consumer was motivated primarily by status whereas the other-directed consumer is motivated more by superficial affection and emotion from the peer group. And even when the other-directed type consumes or strives after pecuniary gain, he or she is always attuned to the opinions of the peer group. Directly or indirectly, Veblen influenced an entire generation of sociologists in the 1950s and 1960s to focus on the consumer, peer groups, conformity, the problem of authenticity, and issues related to narcissism. From Erich Fromm's (1955) writings on the marketing type to Christopher Lasch's (1979) *The Culture of Narcissism*, one may find strands of Veblen's influence. In a word, the dominant lesson drawn from Veblen seems to have been that the consumer is a narcissist of some sort.

However, Veblen's powerful claims that the corporate-government social structure is essentially barbaric has been overlooked or otherwise ignored. Veblen's disturbing message is that all modern social institutions are fundamentally predatory. Veblen writes:

> The predatory phase of culture is attained only when the predatory attitude has become the habitual and accredited spiritual attitude for the members of the group; when the fight has become the dominant note in the current theory of life; when the common-sense appreciation of men and things has come to be an appreciation with a view to combat. ([1899] 1967, 19)

Riesman asked, regarding Veblen's work, "Who is the real barbarian?" I believe the question ought to be modified as follows: "Who is the real narcissist?" Is it the consumer who buys primarily to please the peer group, who markets his or her self on the personality market, and who goes into debt in order to achieve conspicuousness? Or is it the "captain of industry" (the contemporary CEO) who manipulates the system and the consumer into conspicuous consumption?

---

1   See also other works by Mills on white-collar workers and the power elite which draw implicitly or explicitly on Veblen's theory (Mills [1951] 2002, [1956] 2000). See also Kerr (2009) for an extended discussion.

Other questions and issues follow from these: What is the emotional labor required to achieve, maintain, resist, and even escape this narcissism on the part of the consumer as well as the social structure? How does the common man and woman succumb to predatory culture? How can the common man and woman escape the postemotional predicaments of falling prey to predatory culture against his or her better and more altruistic instincts?

There are many definitions and understandings of what it means to "be human." On one end of the continuum one finds various doctrines that promote rugged individualism, survival of the fittest, and variations of narcissism that include lack of social responsibility, lack of empathy for others, and a desire to outshine all others. Ayn Rand's writings enshrine variants of these doctrines in literature, and far right political parties often include elements of them in political parties. On the other end of the continuum one finds doctrines that promote altruism, cooperation, understanding, sympathy for one's fellows (and animals), and social responsibility. But my overall point in this chapter is that it is not a matter of choosing one over the other, and that neither exists in a pure form. Rather, the two extreme points of view are conjoined in what I call a postemotional bind such that one's sense of virtue (the yearning for truth, patriotism, social responsibility and so on) are co-opted by a predatory culture in pursuit of antithetical aims. My goal in this chapter is to offer a modest sketch of what I mean by these claims, which may or may not be pursued in a future project.

Postemotional Society and the Issues of Being Human

Any answers to the questions I have posed above are bound to be as complex as the questions themselves. But contemporary sociology as well as society seems to have opted for the facile explanation that we have overcome the "constraints" of previous generations as well as social theories. Anthony Giddens (1990) proposes that the knowing agent is at all times enabled as well as constrained, and always has "choices" available to him or her.[2] (It is ironic that the same time that he promotes choice and agency, Giddens depicts modernity as a "juggernaut" that crushes everything and everyone in its path.) Giddens criticizes earlier social theorists, particularly structuralists such as Durkheim and Parsons for allegedly turning the human agent into an overly-constrained "cultural dope." The word "choice" has also permeated popular culture and advertising. Supposedly, the contemporary consumer has unprecedented choices in deciding upon phenomena ranging from Internet sites and brands of toothpaste to marriage partners and politics. But if we turn to the everyday life of the common man, it becomes apparent immediately that the doctrine of choice is specious. While it seems, on the surface, that the contemporary agent has unprecedented choices, one has to dig deeper to perceive

---

2   For an extended critique of Giddens, see Mestrovic 1998.

the continuation of old restraints. The human agent is often forced into making choice he or she does not choose in the fullest sense of the term.

For example, the consumer has no choice regarding the choices that were made by managers, advertisers, and corporations for what he or she may choose in a supermarket. Choices on the Internet are constrained by market principles of who pays for the privilege of being placed toward the top of the list on Google and other search engines. What Veblen termed fraud or chicanery are omnipresent in most transactions that involve the consumer. For example, one must invariably sign a contract in order to purchase a cell phone, appliances, automobiles, homes, access to web sites, as well as gain access to credit cards. Most often, the purchase of a consumer good, such as a cell phone or cell phone contract, is predicated on having credit, so that the consumer is constrained by several contracts simultaneously. The contracts are always lengthy, complicated, and, to the common man—incomprehensible. One does not need to conduct a sociological study to conclude that most people, most of the time, click "I agree" to terms and conditions without reading them fully. If one were to read them fully, one would often find that he or she gives up rights and privileges to a corporate entity, much as Veblen predicted. The products themselves have obsolescence built in to them so that the consumer will be compelled to repeat the purchase in a relatively short while. It is true that in the US and the EU, efforts have been made by consumer protection agencies to protect the consumer from fraud and usury, but despite legislation, the everyday situation has not enabled the consumer appreciably. In summary, the only real choice the consumer is often given is whether or not to "opt out" of an agreement or transaction.

I propose that the situation for the common person is not one of constraint versus freedom, but one of constraint under the illusion of freedom. I refer to this state of affairs as postemotional society (Mestrovic 1997). The word "postemotional" is awkward, because it does not imply a lack of emotions. On the contrary, it assumes a plethora of emotions which are subjected to chicanery and manipulation by one's self as well as social structure. Thus, postemotionalism involves an obfuscation of facts through the use of displaced emotions from history, and the manipulation of emotionally charged collective representations of reality on the part of individuals as well as the culture industry. "A working definition of postemotionalism might be that it is a neo-Orwellian mechanism found in Western societies in which the culture industry markets and manipulates dead emotions from history that are selectively and synthetically attached to current events" (Mestrovic 1997, 11). Postemotionalism always involves confusion, hypocrisies, nostalgia, ironies, paradoxes, and neo-Orwellian manipulation such that $2 + 2$ do *not* equal 4. (The main character in Orwell's novel, *1984*, maintains that he is spiritually free so long as he knows that $2 + 2$ equals 4.)

Postemotionalism overlaps with postmodern approaches, but is distinct from them. Both postmodernism and postemotionalism as modes of analysis emphasize the importance of simulacra and hyperreality. However, postmodernism tends to view society as a rootless circulation of fictions (Baudrillard 1986), and these fictions are mostly cognitive, whereas postemotionalism finds compulsive and emotional (albeit, displaced) patterns in the circulating fictions. A postemotional approach to consumerism and choice (or any other phenomenon) makes widespread use of what David Riesman ([1950] 1992, 196) called "fake sincerity," and is itself the outgrowth of what he called other-directed social character. As such, postemotional rituals, politics, and culture in general must be distinguished from more sincere and genuinely emotional responses to events. In other words, postemotionalism is not like the tradition-directed society's revivification of customs and celebrations that is described by Emile Durkheim ([1912] 1965) and it is not like the inner-directed society's internalization of ideas that were sincere enough to last for at least a lifetime that is described by Riesman.

Examples of political postemotionalism range from the Serbs invoking a grievance from the year 1389 in order to justify their violence in Yugoslavia in the 1990s, Greece using the memory of Alexander the Great in order to block the existence of Macedonia in the 1990s, to France and England still nursing their wounds at losing their Empires by reminding the world that they were the founders of civilization and the Enlightenment (Mestrovic 1997). Similarly, the USA used the moral code of the Puritans—who were expelled over 500 years ago from Europe to the North American continent—as the "beacon of democracy set upon a hill" depicted by Alexis de Tocqueville's *Democracy in America* to justify war against Iraq when the real enemy was Osama Bin Laden. But it seems that few people read the unabridged version of Tocqueville's classic, which deals with slavery and extermination of Native Americans ([1845] 2003, 370–485).

It is beyond the scope of this chapter to offer anything like a full explication of postemotionalism as a theory, which is derived from Durkheim, Veblen, Riesman, and the pragmatists such as William James ([1884] 1997) and John Dewey. Perhaps an illustration from literature will be helpful in capturing the practical reality of postemotionalism. Dostoevsky's protagonist in *Notes From the Underground* is angry at his boss for humiliating him, and nurses a grudge over the course of several years. When he finally confronts and assaults his boss in public, years after the insult had passed and had been forgotten, everyone thinks that the protagonist has simply gone mad. No one can make the emotional connection between the protagonist's emotions and the object of his emotions. I am suggesting that similar problems in connecting emotions and behaviors occur on a societal level, as illustrated by the above examples concerning the siege of Sarajevo in 1992 and the Battle of Kosovo in 1389. As we turn to the issues of consumerism, humanity, and choice, similar problems will be uncovered. I will elaborate on Veblen's insight that the doctrine of "choice" is rooted in the historical past which involves England, the Puritans, and theorists such as John Locke, Thomas Jefferson, and other prophets of the doctrine of Natural Law. Veblen notes, but does not elaborate, on the fact that the age of Enlightenment which produced the above-mentioned philosophers of liberty was also the age of witch hunts, slavery, and religious persecutions. But discrepancies of this sort are precisely what must be confronted and understood if social life is to make emotional sense. Like Dostoevsky's protagonist, like the leaders of the Belgrade regime who attacked Sarajevo in 1992, and like other examples of postemotional types, the modern consumer is blind to his or her being prey to the robber barons because of the widespread emotional misconnection to a historical period of alleged freedom and choice.

Postemotional Society and George Ritzer's *McDonaldization of Society*

Despite the limitations of space, I will touch briefly on the similarities and differences between Ritzer's complex argument in his *McDonaldization of Society* (1992) and my argument in *Postemotional Society*, with an eye on the overall theme of being human in consumer society. I explicitly draw upon Ritzer's work in my book on postemotionalism, which I sometimes paraphrase as the McDonaldization of emotions. It is not immediately clear what either Ritzer or I might mean or imply with this phrase, the McDonaldization of emotions, because both of us take complex stances toward the social theorists we use for our own theoretical scaffolding. The main difference between Ritzer's approach and mine is obvious: he primarily extends the thought of Max Weber while I primarily extend the thought of Emile Durkheim. I say primarily, because both of us are aware of and use a host of other theorists. Even in this regard, there is a parallel, in that one could argue that both Weber and Durkheim were concerned with the overall theme of "disenchantment" in modern societies. For Weber, charisma retreats in the face of rational-legal authority, and leads to the iron cage of modernity. For Durkheim, the "sacred" is the site of *emotional* attachment to persons, places, things, and ideas that are treated with awe and respect. Durkheim is aware that "sacred" names, holidays, rivers, trees, and a plethora of other "collective representations" are disappearing as modernity advances, and that, literally, formerly "sacred" representations become increasingly "profane"—which is to say, the social world becomes increasingly disenchanted, ordinary, and pedestrian.

But here again, Weber and Durkheim diverge. Weber is a pessimist, and offers no clues as to how we may exit the iron cage. Durkheim seems to be more optimistic, in that he leaves open the possibility that successive waves of "collective effervescence" will re-enchant the world. Formerly "profane" phenomena are "revivified" and made "sacred" anew, even if they are not the same sacred objects, ideas, and representations from previous generations. To phrase the issue differently, Weber seems to follow Nietzsche in condemning the Enlightenment as a trap which disenchants the world and disembowels charisma (Weber's rough equivalent of Durkheim's "sacredness"). Durkheim is also critical of modernity and Enlightenment narratives—after all, his book, *Suicide*, basically shows that civilized peoples are weakened with regard to the "will to life" in contrast to our ancestors. But overall, Durkheim is an optimist who believed that genuine, or at least new, forms of Enlightenment will emerge and that society's capacity to reinvent the sacred is infinite.

Ritzer's take on McDonaldization is also complex, yet essentially Weberian. Some of Ritzer's readers misread him as championing the alleged rationality, efficiency, predictability, and control that are the heart of McDonaldization. But he insists that he is a critic of these tendencies, and that his overall argument is that excessive rationality leads, paradoxically, to irrationality. Like Weber, Ritzer does not point to the exits that might lead out of McDonaldization, even though he does suggest home-spun suggestions for fighting the iron cage privately, suggestions such as "eat at a Mom and Pop restaurant." The problem is that Mom and Pop restaurants are disappearing all over the world and are being replaced with restaurant chains, and much the same is true for other sites of enchantment/sacredness—they are all subject to the seemingly inexorable law of disenchantment and the profaning of the sacred.

I am sometimes asked whether "postemotionalism" is simply another name for propaganda or manipulations of the individuals by governments and corporations. I always answer in the negative, but this does not mean that the questioner is convinced. My point is that while I agree with Weber's and Ritzer's social criticisms, I do adopt the Durkheimian optimism which they do not. By this I mean that governments, corporations, or other manipulation-systems are themselves invested with "sacredness" and enchantment. People develop patriotism and fierce emotional loyalties to corporate brands that are not the mere result of propaganda and manipulation. Rather, individuals bring self-manipulation to the table, and are expressing the Durkheimian law that societies must have some sort of "sacredness" and emotional connection to collective representations in order to exist.

Where is this discussion going with regard to the law and consumerism? The gist of my argument is that persons are McDonaldized, manipulated, used in the ways that Veblen described, and otherwise exploited by governments and corporations because of their social, emotional capacity to enchant the world. The "post" aspect in this emotional re-enchantment of the world lies in the rational disconnection between what persons and societies regard as sacred and exploitative governments and corporations regard as profane. More precisely, with regard to theme of this chapter, I expand upon Veblen's observation that modern persons allow themselves to be exploited because they are emotionally and sincerely attached to the beliefs that they live in an enlightened, free society.

Reformulating Veblen's Depiction of the Role of Law and Lawyers in Consumerism

Riesman is right to characterize Veblen's attitude toward lawyers as the view that they are "wordy, abstract fellows given to chicanery in aid of business sabotage" (Riesman [1953] 1995, 94). No doubt Riesman is referring to Veblen's essay "On Sabotage," in which he claims that the captains of industry routinely slow down production or use other means to subvert responsible production of goods and services in order to secure pecuniary advantages and profits. Other scholars have commented on Veblen's negative depiction of lawyers and law as extensions of the barbaric temperament, as persons and an institution bent mostly on pointless litigation and pecuniary gain for the robber barons. Geis quotes Veblen: "law schools belong in the modern university no more than a school of fencing or dancing" (Geis 1957, 62). Veblen's most searing treatise on law and lawyers is found in Chapter 8 of his *Theory of Business Enterprise* (1904). It is true that he lumps lawyers with other predators in modern society, but he raises issues that have been overlooked by scholars. Veblen holds that "modern institutions rest, in great part, on business principles" (Veblen 1904, 268). From education to law, modern institutions are geared toward the profit/loss model derived from business, and are bent on pecuniary gain above all other cultural values. In addition, Veblen observes that business and law—among other modern institutions—uphold the doctrine of Natural Law which emphasizes freedom and choice. Herein lies the rub. The doctrine of Natural Law holds that all men and women are equal and free yet modern institutions ranging from the government to the courts typically side with big corporations against the little man or woman. According to Veblen, "a constitutional government is a business government" (285) and "representative government means, chiefly, representation of business interests" (286). A "divergence" is established between the interests of the common man caught up in everyday life versus the interests of government and corporations to exploit the common man using chicanery and force. According to Veblen, the common man goes along with this exploitation based upon some "metaphysical" belief that gains by corporations at his or her expense somehow serve the common good or the aggregate. A more recent version of Veblen's depiction is Ronald Reagan's "trickle-down theory" of economics, which holds that the enormous wealth of capitalists in the upper strata of society will somehow improve the lot of the common man. Another common saying that captures this folk philosophy is: "What is good for Wall Street is good for Main Street."

It is important to note that across all of his writings, Veblen points to the North-West corner of Europe, especially England, in the seventeenth and eighteenth centuries as the epicenter of a momentous shift in cultural values. But whereas most academics and teachers in secondary and elementary schools depict this shift as a turn toward freedom, individualism, and Enlightenment, Veblen depicts it as a turn toward a new form of barbarism, one that relies more on "chicanery" than brute force. Again, I believe it is more fruitful to explore the tension between these opposing views rather than choose sides with one interpretation versus the other.

Links to the Durkheimian Tradition and Jean Piaget

A final link is necessary to flesh out the postemotional import of Veblen's observations, and link them to contemporary trends in consumerism. Like Durkheim and his followers, Veblen believed that remnants of the historical past always coexist in the present. For Durkheim, vestiges of mechanical solidarity survive into organic solidarity. For Veblen, barbaric *habits* from the age of feudalism survive into present-day democracy. Neither theorist explains how the past co-exists with the present, and this is what I am attempting to do with the concept of postemotionalism. But we shall return to this issue later. For now, let us fill in the gaps in Veblen's theoretical perspective on law, lawyers, and consumers.

Durkheim's disciple, Paul Fauconnet (1928), published *La Responsabilité*, which was intended to be co-authored with Durkheim, and which nonetheless elaborates upon Durkheim's theory of law embedded in *The Division of Labor* ([1893] 1984). The key points in Fauconnet's analysis are these: the law is derived from religion and therefore is always characterized by an aura of "sacredness." In other words, peoples in all societies tend to approach the law with an attitude of respect (an attitude which Veblen mocks as metaphysical or honorific). Traditional societies tended to focus more on collective and "objective" morality whereas modern societies tend to focus more on individual and "subjective" morality. By collective morality, Fauconnet meant that responsibility and punishment in traditional societies were routinely meted out to entire families, villages, tribes, and even nations for a transgression committed by an individual. Both Fauconnet and Durkheim refer to the Bible as illustration of this point (in addition to references from ancient Babylonian, Roman, and Greek laws): God routinely punishes entire cities for the sins of an individual or a few individuals. The subjective intentions of the sinner or transgressor did not matter. Crime is "objective" if it involves the transgression of a law or taboo regardless of the reasons the transgression had, including ignorance of the law.

By contrast, modern, enlightened societies shift from ascribing responsibility to collectivities to ascribing responsibility solely to an individual transgressor. According to Fauconnet, the subjective perspectives of the sinner or transgressor slowly but surely come to matter in matters of law and morality. Many mitigating factors come to play a role in diminishing the transgressor's responsibility: mental illness, childhood, the subjective history of his or her bad childhood, and so on. Fauconnet adds two caveats to his overall theory of the development of the law. The first is that it is a grand theory which applies to all cases involving law and morality, not only those which are strictly judicial or involve police, investigations, judges, and imprisonment. For example, Fauconnet refers to the "court of public opinion" which sometimes diverges from formal judicial rulings based upon an understanding of subjective factors. He also refers to the family and to religious organizations as also undergoing this shift from mechanical to organic, objective to subjective morality, and notions of responsibility. Second, Fauconnet warns that ancient, mechanical, collective, and objective notions of law do not disappear in modern societies, but are merely transformed. Modern persons are subjected to more, not less, "objective" crimes than the traditional type. Fauconnet cites the area of negligence law as an example. Modern persons are subject to being charged for negligence for a wide variety of "objective" reasons and failures to comply with social norms, much more than the relatively few and well-defined taboos in ancient societies. Fauconnet ends his book with the admonition that any doctrine of purely individual choice or responsibility is deceptive, because ancient ideas of morality and justice are always present in the background of social life.

In *The Moral Judgment of the Child*, Jean Piaget (1997) draws upon Durkheim and Fauconnet to develop a psychology of the moral development of children that is more like a sociology of children. To be precise, he refers to "child societies" which involve adults as well as children in a sort of replication of Durkheim's mechanical solidarity. In families, the parents are "the law," surely the first form of law and morality that the child experiences. Piaget explicitly mirrors Fauconnet in claiming that the child under age 12 uses "objective" morality while the child over the age of 12 begins to develop "subjective" morality. One of the many examples which Piaget uses to illustrate this point is helpful in making the transition to our larger discussion of consumers, choice, and morality. Piaget describes a vignette he read to an eight-year-old child about another child who walks into a room and accidentally breaks a cup. Piaget asked the child what the parent should do. The child answered that the parent should slap the child as punishment. The more cups the child breaks, the more he or she should be punished. Children over the age of 12 do not give this reply. They express the view that the child should be allowed to explain the circumstances of the transgression and to seek understanding with the parent and cooperation on the punishment. The ideas of cooperation and understanding are the hallmarks of "subjective" morality, according to Piaget, and are also the hallmarks of modern, enlightened societies characterized by organic solidarity according to the Durkheimians. The connection to the discussion at hand is that banks and corporations often tend to treat the modern adult as if he or she were a child under the age of 12. True, bankers and corporate representatives do not slap the adult for transgressions. Nevertheless, they do tend to punish, impose fines, and otherwise ascribe "objective" responsibility for an act regardless of circumstances or motives by the agent in the transgression of paying bills on time, filling out paperwork, seeking to escape the length of a contract on a cell phone, and so on. We shall illustrate this point later in the chapter.

Because Piaget has been "objectively" taken over by departments of psychology, it is worth quoting his deep and "subjective" affiliations with sociology. Academic disciplines seem to be as subject to Fauconnet's and Piaget's observations as other social institutions: psychology and sociology rarely seek "cooperation" and "understanding" between their respective points of view. For example, Piaget writes:

> No one has felt more deeply than Durkheim nor submitted to a more searching analysis the development and disappearance of obligatory conformity ... Now, does this analysis apply to our children's societies? In many respects, undoubtedly, it does. There is certainly a resemblance between segmented or mechanical solidarity and the societies formed by children of 5 to 8. As in the organized clan so in these groups, the individual does not count. (Piaget 1997, 102)

Elsewhere Piaget writes that "the main factor in the obligatory conformity of very young children is nothing but respect for age—respect for older children, and, above all, respect for adults" (103). Piaget points to a movement by young children and young societies from conceptualizations of justice as "expiation" to justice as "reciprocity" (227). Like the Durkheimians, Piaget envisioned the morality of the future as "a morality of forgiveness and understanding" (232), not expiation and vengeance. In the remainder of his book, Piaget struggles with the issues put forth by Fauconnet, which I have listed above. The issues are important, but were unresolved by Piaget and Fauconnet, and remain unresolved to this day. Some of these issues are: Are modern societies truly progressing toward a culture of understanding, forgiveness, cooperation, and autonomy? Or are modern societies still constrained by childish and ancient notions of expiation, revenge, conformity, and obedience? A third possibility is the one that I call postemotional: modern societies use the rhetoric of freedom, understanding, forgiveness, cooperation and autonomy (choice) all the while they are still guided, to a large extent in the area of consumerism, by ideas of punishment, conformity, and obedience to authority. The postemotional aspect is the *chicanery* or manipulation of implying, pointing to, or otherwise referring, directly or indirectly, to a "metaphysical" or mythical historical era of natural rights, freedom and autonomy to rationalize and justify the punitive and "objective" attitudes which dominate contemporary, predatory culture.

An Illustration from a Credit Card Company Contract

As an illustration of the above points, I would like to quote from a nine-page contract with a credit card company. It is a contract issued *after* the US Congress mandated revisions to such contracts which were largely felt to be unjust and usurious. Although I refer to it as a contract, one of the first peculiarities to note is that the contract is entered into agreement by the consumer each and every time he or she uses the credit card. Along the lines of Veblen's predictions, the contract grants rights to the corporation as if it were an adult or other respected authority and the consumer were a child who must accept any and all changes to the contract. The consumer has only one real choice if he or she disagrees, and that is the right to "opt out." Baudrillard (1986) observed in his book, *America*, that this attitude is captured with the "must exit" sign on freeways. One *must* comply or one *must* opt out and exit—but there is no middle ground. The contract begins as follows:

> We want to help you understand how your charge card works. This includes changes we're required to make because of new federal regulations that impact late payment fees, returned payment fees, and Penalty APRs. These changes are summarized in the table below. We're also pleased to let you know we've written your Cardmember Agreement so it's simpler and easier to use and understand.

The contract states that the penalty APR will apply if the consumer makes one or more late payments or makes a payment that is returned. There are no provisions for any sort of subjective reasons as to why a payment may be late, ranging from illness to accidents and snowstorms and blizzards that might delay postal delivery. The criteria are purely objective, like Piaget's vignette of the child who breaks the cup: if you're late, you get punished. Moreover, the consumer does not have to have subjective knowledge of all the elements or any changes to the agreement:

> Any supplements or amendments are also part of the Agreement. When you use the Account (or you sign or keep the card), you agree to the terms of the Agreement. We may change this Agreement, subject to applicable law. We may do this in response to the business, legal or competitive environment. Changes to some terms may require 45 days advance notice, and we will tell you in the notice if you have the right to reject a change.

Thus, the consumer's role in the purported agreement—which is not an agreement at all in the common sense understanding of this term—is to comply with any future changes in the agreement for any reason. This is a far cry from Giddens's depiction of the knowledgeable and enabled agent. But it is worth noting that this authoritarian attitude is couched in the language of rights and the law of contract. In a postemotional sense, the consumer has a right to be manipulated into an agreement he or she never formally agrees to, other than the assumed agreement by using the credit card, because of the sanctity of the idea of contract law in Western history. Veblen is undoubtedly correct that the only constraint on the corporation, namely, "applicable law," is written in favor of the corporations. The corporation will even decide whether the consumer has the right to reject a change. The agreement continues:

> We decide whether to approve a charge based on how you spend and pay on this Account and other accounts you have with us and our affiliates. We also consider your credit history and your personal resources that we know about [...] We may cancel your Account, suspend the ability to make charges, cancel or suspend any feature on your Account and notify merchants that your Account has been cancelled or suspended. If we do any of these, you must still pay us for all charges under the terms of this Agreement. *We may do any of these things at our discretion, even if you pay on time and your Account is not in default.* (Emphasis added)

It is one thing to punish the consumer for an "objective" transgression. This is a logic comprehensible even to a child or a person from a tradition-directed society. But note that the corporation gives itself the power, under "applicable law," to take punitive actions even if the consumer was "good" and did not make any transgressions under the agreement. Veblen's theory of the business enterprise would explain this clause on the grounds that the corporation is legally justified to protect its property as it sees fit. The agreement continues:

> You agree that we may obtain credit reports about you, investigate your ability
> to pay, and obtain information about you from other sources. And you agree
> that we may use such information for *any* purposes, subject to applicable law.
> You agree that we may give information about your Account to credit reporting
> agencies. We may tell a credit reporting agency if you fail to comply with any
> term of this Agreement. This may have a negative impact on your credit record.
> (Emphasis added)

Again, it is worth noting that the corporation tells the consumer that he or she
agrees—even if he or she does not agree, and certainly there is no element of
compromise or understanding in the agreement—that the corporation may use
information about the consumer for "any" purposes, not just some purposes
specific to pecuniary transactions. The notion of "any" purpose is vague and also
limitless. This clause, among others, truly places the corporation in the position
of an all-powerful adult or authority figure, and further reduces the status of the
consumer to that of a child. Moreover, a negative report to a reporting agency will
have an impact on the consumer's ability to provide for his or her family, and is
an indirect form of collective responsibility, which is another throwback to the
historical past. Finally, the agreement reads:

> We have the right to add, modify or delete any benefit or service of your Account
> at our discretion […] We may choose to delay enforcing or to not exercise
> rights under this Agreement. If we do this, we do not waive our rights to exercise
> or enforce them on any other occasion.

Other examples from everyday life can be added to this illustration. The purported
free agent consumer must comply fully and obey instantly any instructions from
airline personnel when flying. Except for the omnipresent choice of opting out,
he or she must comply with whatever the government or a particular corporation
puts into any contract for any service or purchase, from buying a cell phone to
using a government campground. The idealistic and purportedly Enlightenment-
based notions of cooperation, understanding, autonomy, and harmony put forth by
the Durkheimians and Fauconnet do not resonate with the everyday reality of the
consumer making purchases, all of which are under the terms of "applicable law."
On the other hand, Veblen's depiction of the law as an extension of the business
enterprise does seem to resonate with everyday experience. Finally, the concept of
postemotional society may be helpful in explaining how these two contradictory
notions of social life co-exist: educated, informed adults in democratic societies
allow themselves to be treated like children in relation to the law and corporations
because they are postemotionally committed to an idealized vision of the historical
past as guaranteeing their natural rights.

Emotional Dissonance in Postemotional Societies

The illustrations used thus far in this discussion may give the wrong impression that we are discussing the actions of individual consumers of material goods or pecuniary gain. In other words, the word, consumer, is typically associated with economic functions. But we have seen that Veblen argued that all of modern culture and all modern social institutions are increasingly being modeled on the business model and pecuniary standards. Thus, we should extend the concepts of consumer and consumption to include the consumption of education, information, personalities, goods from the profession of medicine, law, and other cultural "goods." In the remainder of this chapter, we shall examine whether the concept of postemotional law applies to these extended realms of consumption. I am not using the term "law" in the restricted sense of what is taught in law schools, but in the wider sense of notions of morality, justice, responsibility and concepts related to law in culture as a whole.

Both Durkheim and Veblen isolated the economic sphere as the most important part of modern but not traditional societies; as influencing all other social institutions; and as most vulnerable to anomie (for Durkheim) and the "predatory instinct" (for Veblen). For example, both thinkers agree that in modern societies, the market mentality is far more influential than religious, family, traditional, educational or any other social institution. In fact, all these other, traditional social institutions gradually come to be run as if they were businesses or corporations, so that their traditional functions become less important at the same time that they take on the characteristics of business. Thus, Durkheim writes in *Professional Ethics and Civic Morals*: "This lack of organization in the business professions has one consequence of the greatest moment: that is, that in this whole sphere of social life, no professional ethics exist" ([1950] 1983, 9). He is referring to the obvious fact, still extant today, that business "professionals" are motivated primarily by pecuniary gain, self-interest, and unchecked ambition—and far less by notions of social responsibility, empathy, and cooperation. An excellent illustration of this from popular culture is found in the film *Wall Street*, wherein the main protagonist, Gordon Gekko, declares "Greed is good." In the sequel to this film, Gekko declares, "Greed has now been declared legal." Durkheim writes: "This amoral character of economic life amounts to a public danger" (12). Durkheim makes it clear that this immoral, anomic tendency in economic life is "contagious" and spills over into other areas of society that are supposed to be altruistic and concerned with general well-being. For example, he writes, regarding scientific research: "Even science has hardly any prestige in the eyes of the present day, except in so far as it may serve what is materially useful, that is to say, serve for the most part the business professions" (11).

It is amazing that Durkheim wrote the above line, because it comes across as something that Veblen would have written. Veblen illustrates Durkheim's concerns especially in his book, *Higher Learning in America* (1918), in which Veblen points out that schools and universities increasingly take on the predatory habits of the business world: administrators become more important than teachers, evaluations are based upon machine-like evaluations, the institutions are run for a profit, promotions and graduations are based upon competition much more than cooperation, and so on. All of his observations are relevant to understanding contemporary schools and universities. For example, football teams are emphasized over libraries because they bring in more money, and are also based upon predatory values; professors live in a "publish or perish" atmosphere; teachers must bring in "research grants" or other external money in order to be valued and promoted, because mere teaching is not considered "honorific"; when a university researcher wins a government grant, he or she *must* turn over up to half of the grant to the university—much like "agreements" between consumers and credit card holders dictate what rights the consumer must grant to the corporation; most science graduates in the United States take jobs that involve research for corporations or the government in some fashion, and much of this research is devoted to making weapons or developing psychological and other techniques for waging war. Mills was right to connect Veblen's writings to the hidden realities of the military–industrial complex and the power elite. I leave it to the reader to find other contemporary examples of Veblen's insights.

The link to postemotionalism is that even if the scientist, student, professor, or other consumer of knowledge honestly believes that he or she is pursuing truth, service to humanity, or other socially responsible cause, the overall predatory culture compels him or her to "sell out" sooner or later. Of course, the consumer of knowledge always has the choice to "opt out" of the competition for status and gain, but the more important point is that status and gain are linked to predatory and pecuniary values. In other words, if one wishes to succeed in the field of education, one must eventually—even if reluctantly—take on the role of the predator to some extent. In Veblen's terminology, there is a "divergence" between the agent's professed motivation and the real motivation, which is compelled by the culture as a whole.

The parallel books in Durkheim's opus are *Moral Education* ([1925] 1961) and *The Evolution of Educational Thought* ([1938] 1977). In both works, Durkheim decries the anomie that has been imported from the business world into schools, which leads to lack of emotional attachment, lack of discipline, and lack of moral teachings that are necessary for societies to function. Let us be clear that Veblen thought that education *should* promote what he called "idle curiosity." Similarly, Durkheim believed that education should promote "spontaneous" emotional attachments to one's country, family, and workplace, and that these attachments were the basis for what he called "morality." Both scholars lament that an over-emphasis on narrow, "machine-like" intellectualism leads to anomic or predatory variations of education and approaches to social life in general. Thus, Veblen writes: "So it has come about that modern civilization is in a very special degree a culture of intellectual powers, in the narrower sense of the term, in contrast with the emotional traits of human nature" (in Mestrovic 2003, 56). Again, the parallels to Durkheim are that in *Suicide*, he argues that modern education leads to anomie and higher suicide rates, and that in *The Division of Labor*, he argues that civilization in general leads to decreased unhappiness and increased social problems of many sorts.

Again, the important point is that neither Durkheim nor Veblen attempted to explain *how* predatory and anomic tendencies on the one hand, are reconciled by the individual or society with altruistic and emotionally compassionate (what Veblen called "peaceable") traits on the other. If it is true that we are all taught that education and civilization are inherently good phenomena, it is difficult to reconcile the emotional attachment to these beliefs with the fact that the consumption of education and civilization leads to unhappiness-producing emotional states. The postemotional aspect of this discrepancy or divergence is that the agent has a difficult time connecting these opposing states of emotional attachment to ideas as objects of consumption. In addition to the well-known concept of cognitive dissonance, it may be helpful to refer to this unpleasant state of affairs as "emotional dissonance."

It is important to avoid imposing an artificial taxonomy onto the writings of Durkheim and Veblen. In truth, both scholars offer similar grand theories in each and every one of their books, which, in turn, touch upon a multitude of topics and cultural patterns simultaneously. They implicitly promote Darwin's model of survival through cooperation at all times, and just as consistently, they criticize anomic and predatory perversions of Darwin's model. It is important to keep in mind that the idea of the cooperative or cooperating consumer is fundamentally different from the idea of the isolated consumer who thinks primarily of his or her own pecuniary benefit. For example, Durkheim repeats his overall argument in *Suicide* that "in one sphere of social life, however—the sphere of trade and industry—it [anomie] is actually in a chronic state" ([1897] 1951, 254). But he applies this insight to a host of other areas and institutions in social life which promote unbridled consumerism, ranging from a "thirst for novelties" to dissatisfaction with one's marriage partner. In all these cases, "inextinguishable thirst is constantly renewed torture" (247). The business model, which enshrines Nietzsche's maxim of the will to power—that an increase in wants and desires is good in itself—spills over into other arenas of social life: "A thirst arises for novelties, unfamiliar pleasures, nameless sensations, all of which lose their savor once known" (256). In general, Durkheim holds to Darwin's maxim that "no living being can be happy or even exist unless his needs are sufficiently proportions to his means" (246). But herein lies the rub: the modern world is more oriented toward Nietzschean *wants* as opposed to Darwinian *needs*. It is beyond the scope of this chapter to do justice to Durkheim's deep and complex discussion of human and animal nature versus modern, anomic perversions of human needs in *Suicide*, *The Division of Labor*, *Professional Ethics*, and other books. I urge the reader to read these discussions in the context of interpreting Darwin as the champion of natural justice based upon cooperation, not Spencer's version. In general, Durkheim's conclusion still rings true today: "Government, instead of regulating economic life, has become its tool and servant" (255). This line, too, could have been written by Veblen. In fact, Veblen wrote similar lines, as we have already seen.

Like Durkheim, Veblen was essentially writing the same book throughout his many books. Each of his books touches on a multitude of topics ranging from pets, religion, sports, war, education and so on because he consistently follows the same model. Following Darwin, Veblen seems to agree that for animals as well as humans in traditional societies, the distance between *needs* and *wants* is very small. Animals and traditional humans generally want what they need, and therefore do not waste. The development of the brain and its mental functions gives rise to the "need" for prestige associated with conspicuously wasteful and therefore "honorific"[3] objects of desire. It is important to reflect carefully on Veblen's precise definition of "waste" in *The Theory of the Leisure Class:* "It is here called 'waste' because this expenditure does not serve human life or human well-being on the whole, not because it is waste or misdirection of effort or expenditure as viewed from the standpoint of the *individual consumer* who chooses it" (Veblen [1899] 1967, 98, emphasis added).

Clearly, Veblen's assessment has a Durkheimian as well as Darwinian tone to it. Veblen seems to be claiming that the conspicuous consumption, conspicuous leisure, and conspicuous waste—all of which are interrelated for him—that characterize all aspects of modern life are harmful to human life on the whole. Conspicuous consumption and waste may benefit the individual consumer, but they cause harm to society because society depends upon cooperation, not narcissism. Veblen is more concerned with the general lack of "cooperation" involved in "wasting" effort and expenditure on "useless" behaviors and goods than with how such activities might benefit an individual's will to power. Thus, the rampant consumerism involved in the useless consumption of fine cigars, whiskies, beer, silk stockings, pets, and other "honorific" goods all signify the eruption of the "predatory instinct" for Veblen. Overall, his moralism and insistence on living a life wherein wants and needs are in sync with each other is very similar to Durkheim's sense of morality. Note that by "morality" they are implying a compassionate, caring, altruistic concern for the welfare of all human life, not just one's self. One might say that they were promoters of "responsible consumerism," a consumerism that is mindful of the needs of other individuals, their society, and other societies.

But the postemotional aspect to this portion of the discussion is that narcissistic consumerism is aligned in modern, anomic, predatory cultures with the doctrine of Natural Rights: each individual has the right to choose to consume all the luxuries he or she can afford. Following Veblen's trajectory, it is one's patriotic duty to consume, even if the consumption is wasteful, because such consumption supposedly serves the common good. An illustration of Veblen's point is that President George W. Bush urged all Americans to shop immediately following the attacks on 9/11.

---

3   It is important to note that Veblen uses "honorific" as a synonym for predatory and aggressive: "A honorific act is in the last analysis little if anything else than a recognized successful act of aggression" (Veblen [1899] 1967, 17).

Furthermore, Veblen emphasizes the conspicuous nature of consumption. Fine foods, wines, and other consumer goods must be seen by others in order to give one fleeting satisfaction. Without a doubt, Veblen was describing collective narcissism, and foreshadowing Riesman's other-directed type, who is always and at all times keenly aware of the gaze of others in everything they do (Mestrovic 2003). The important point is that Veblen links the waste of conspicuous consumption in everyday life to similar behaviors by corporations. In his other books, he criticizes salesmanship, advertising, the use of credit, and "sabotage" in industry as common practices that are wasteful in his sense of the term (detrimental to humanity as a whole). Each and every one of these insights is more relevant today than in his time. For example, he forecast correctly that "salesmanship" would expand into the realm of the predatory class getting "something for nothing," which is evidenced by high-tech trades on stock exchanges which create huge profits but zero value due to the use of computers. Veblen could not have known that computers would be able to buy and sell stocks in fractions of seconds with the sole aim of making a profit that old-fashioned trades could not achieve. But he was right about the principle of "salesmanship," in its broadest sense, as obtaining benefits through exaggerating future earning power, qualities in a product, or the use of other half-truths and spin. (His word for these quasi-fraudulent practices was "chicanery.") He was right to point out that advertisements take up more space in newspapers than actual news stories without adding value to society. He was correct that the use of credit creates false value and benefits the "captains of industry" at the cost of exploiting the masses, who are perceived as the prey. Nowadays, banks charge interest rates that have surpassed traditional understandings of usury. Veblen understood "sabotage" as the willful refusal to exert effort by labor as well as corporations with the aim of harming the other side. It seems impossible to imagine animals using "sabotage" in this sense, or it serving any useful functions in terms of Darwinian survival. But it is abundantly clear that corporations, oil cartels and other "captains of industry" deliberately withhold production for the sake of profit as a routine part of business practices. I leave it to the reader to find other illustrations of Veblen's points.

All social phenomena are connected to all other social phenomena for Durkheim and Veblen, with an anomic and predatory business culture at the apex. Similarly, they treat warfare as both the conventional understanding of war and also as an extended practice in all social institutions. I urge the reader to self-consciously seek out Durkheim's use of "warfare" with reference to business and labor, in families, among families (as in the vendetta), and other refractions of vengeance. Durkheim cites the Bible to illustrate the "eye for an eye, tooth for a tooth" mentality which does *not* disappear in modern societies. For Durkheim, the "forced" division of labor is a form of violence and warfare that occurs daily in the modern workplace. Durkheim writes: "For the division of labor to engender solidarity, it is thus not sufficient for everyone to have his task; it must also be agreeable to him" (Durkheim [1893] 1984, 311). One should perform the thought-experiment of wondering how many contemporary workers feel that their jobs and work environments are agreeable or disagreeable to them, in all sense of those terms. Durkheim insists that, ideally, the worker "is not therefore a machine who repeats movements the sense of which he does not perceive" (308).

In this regard, too, the worker is caught up in a postemotional dissonance. He or she has been taught that it is a moral, social, and personal duty toward one's family and one's sense of fulfillment to choose and pursue a career that is enabling. In this sense, the modern person in a democratic society is a consumer of career choices. But numerous studies in organizational literature have shown that workers feel dissatisfied, burned-out, and above all, stressed as a result of their jobs. It is difficult for them to opt out and exit the stressful situation when they are postemotionally attached to the "sacred" ideas that it is their moral duty to find a career that makes them happy.

Similarly, Veblen links warfare to a host of other social institutions, all of which are subsumed under the predatory instinct. For example, he describes the close alignment of religions with war by referring to "the barbarian conception of the divinity as a warlike chieftain inclined to an overbearing manner of government" ([1899] 1967, 303). He illustrates this with a popular American religious hymn: "Mine eyes have seen the glory of the coming of the Lord; He is trampling out the vintage where the grapes of wrath are stored; He hath loosed the fateful lightning of his terrible swift sword; His truth is marching on" (304). Furthermore, he connects warfare to predatory habits in sports, business, fashion, and other aspects of social life. For example, he observes that military uniforms are "useless" for combat but that they exhibit "conspicuous consumption" and prestige by virtue of polished brass buttons, medals, ornamental caps, and other details that reflect the "useless" yet conspicuously expensive business suit.

In general, Veblen literally depicts warfare—in both senses, as orthodox war and as a general tendency in predatory culture—as madness. Referring to the First World War, Veblen wrote: "The current situation in America is by way of being something of a psychiatric clinic" (in Mestrovic 2003, 129). His several books on Imperial Germany and Japan (1939), and *The Nature of Peace* (1917), focus on the irrationality of war by virtue of its antithesis to the need for cooperation that is the fundamental basis for human survival. For example, Veblen writes: "Taken in the large, the common defense of any given nation becomes a detail of the competitive struggle between rival nationalities animated with a common spirit of patriotic enterprise and led by authorities constituted for this competitive purpose" (in Mestrovic 2003, 110).

For this reason, Veblen abhorred all patriotism as "useless" and potentially dangerous, because it keeps the population ready for war at any time. Similarly, Durkheim decried "narrow nationalism" ([1893] 1984, 222) whose only logical outcome was war.

But again, both thinkers seem to ignore the emotional labor the individual living in predatory culture must perform in order to cope with this dissonance. Patriotism impels individuals to support society's warlike aims, even when wars are perceived to be wasteful and useless means for achieving political aims.

One's emotional and genuine attachment to one's country leads to the postemotional splitting wherein one supports policies to which one is not emotionally attached.

Conclusion

In this brief analysis, I have attempted to extend the conceptualization of the consumer as one who consumes all sorts of intangible goods in modern society, from education to popular culture and politics. I have extended the concept of the law to include the court of public opinion and the judgments of what is moral, just, and responsible from cultural perspectives. Veblen's pessimistic take on modern societies as barbaric was contrasted with Durkheim's, Piaget's, and Fauconnet's more hopeful and optimistic assessments of social evolution as one of uneven progress toward an idealized state of cooperation, autonomy, and understanding. My contribution to this discussion has been to apply the concept of postemotional society to the issues of consumerism and what it means to be human. Postemotional society is one in which cultural values derived from the historical Enlightenment are misused and manipulated via sophisticated chicanery to achieve aims which are "objective," authoritarian, and predatory. Far from being a simple matter of propaganda, the evil of postemotionalism is that the individual manipulates his or her self into going along with predatory, barbaric culture. Contemplating an exit from this state of affairs is a challenging task because of multiple layers of fake sincerity, emotional dissonance, and complex divergences across many areas of social life.

References

Baudrillard, Jean. 1986. *America.* London: Routledge.

Baudrillard, Jean. 1998. *Consumer Society.* London: Routledge.

Durkheim, Emile. [1893] 1984. *The Division of Labour in Society.* New York: Free Press.

Durkheim, Emile. [1897] 1951. *Suicide: A Study in Sociology.* New York: Free Press.

Durkheim, Emile. [1912] 1965. *The Elementary Forms of the Religious Life.* New York: Free Press.

Durkheim, Emile. [1925] 1961. *Moral Education.* Glencoe: Free Press.

Durkheim, Emile. [1938] 1977. *The Evolution of Educational Thought.* London: Routledge.

Durkheim, Emile. [1950] 1983. *Professional Ethics and Civic Morals.* London: Routledge.

Fauconnet, Paul. 1928. *La Responsabilité.* Paris: Felix Alcan.

Fromm, Erich. 1955. *The Sane Society.* New York: Fawcett.

Geis, Gilbert. 1957. "Thorstein Veblen on Legal Education." *Journal of Legal Education* 10: 62–73.

Giddens, Anthony. 1990. *The Consequences of Modernity.* Stanford: Stanford University Press.

James, William. [1884] 1997. *The Meaning of Truth.* Amherst: Prometheus Books.

Kerr, Keith. 2009. *Postmodern Cowboy: C. Wright Mills and a New 21st-Century Sociology.* Boulder, CO: Paradigm.

Lasch, Christopher. 1979. *The Culture of Narcissism.* New York: Basic Books.

Mestrovic, Stjepan. 1997. *Postemotional Society.* London: Sage.

Mestrovic, Stjepan. 1998. *Anthony Giddens: The Last Modernist.* London: Routledge.

Mestrovic, Stjepan. 2003. *Thorstein Veblen on Theory, Culture and Society.* London: Sage.

Mills, C. Wright. [1951] 2002. *White Collar: The American Middle Class.* New York: Oxford University Press.

Mills, C. Wright. [1956] 2000. *The Power Elite.* New York: Oxford University Press.

Mills, C. Wright. [1959] 1967. *The Sociological Imagination.* New York: Oxford University Press.

Piaget, Jean. 1997. *The Moral Judgment of the Child.* New York: Free Press.

Riesman, David. [1950] 1992. *The Lonely Crowd.* New Haven: Yale University Press.

Riesman, David. [1953] 1995. *Thorstein Veblen.* New Brunswick, NJ: Transaction.

Ritzer, George. 1992. *The McDonaldization of Society.* London: Sage.

Tocqueville, Alexis. [1845] 2003. *Democracy in America.* New York: Penguin.

Veblen, Thorstein. [1899] 1967. *The Theory of the Leisure Class.* New York: Penguin.

Veblen, Thorstein. 1904. *The Theory of the Business Enterprise.* New York: Macmillan.

Veblen, Thorstein. 1917. *The Nature of Peace.* New York: Macmillan.

Veblen, Thorstein. 1918. *Higher Learning in America.* New York: Macmillan.

Veblen, Thorstein. 1939. *Imperial Germany and the Industrial Revolution.* New York: Macmillan.

Chapter 2

The Dehumanized Consumer:
Does the Prosumer Offer Some Hope?

George Ritzer

Introduction

Let me begin with a provisional view, if not a definition, of what it means to be human, at least for the purposes of this analysis. To be human is to have control, to have power, over one's life; including the social settings in which one finds oneself. The thinking of Michel de Certeau (1984) is important here, especially the view that actors are poets or their own affairs and trailblazers in formally rational systems. In a more negative sense this chapter is rooted in Max Weber's ([1921] 1968) work on *de*humanization, especially as it is caused by rationalized structures, as well as Karl Marx's ([1867] 1967) view that the structures of capitalism serve to destroy the natural interconnectedness that characterizes humans fully able to be dehumanized. The issue of concern here is whether it is possible for people to express their species being. Humanization and dehumanization constitute a continuum. No one is totally in control or totally controlled; totally humanized or become more fully human, to be less controlled by larger structures, especially in contemporary consumer society.

Surprisingly, being human in the seemingly free—and freewheeling—consumer society is no easy matter. This is true not only for those who work in such a society, especially in low-level service occupations, but contrary to conventional wisdom it is also true for consumers of the goods and services on offer. We have little difficulty understanding the great efforts that have been made to create structures of consumption that serve, perhaps unintentionally, to limit the humanity, to dehumanize, those who work there, especially those who stand at or near the bottom of the occupational hierarchy (Marx [1867] 1967; Ehrenreich 2008). After all, as Marx understood a century and a half ago, capitalism is impelled in various ways to increase its control over the proletariat and in the process to exploit, immiserate, alienate, and dehumanize those who labor in the system. While today there are fewer production workers of the kind Marx analyzed, at least in the developed world, the same basic processes he analyzed are now affecting the increasing number of service workers found in consumer society.

However, it is much harder to accept the view that at least some of those processes are also being directed at, and affecting, consumers. After all, from many perspectives—economics, marketing, and even sociology to some degree—

the consumer is "king" and the system is ostensibly set up to cater to "king consumer" (Slater 1997). Any king, including a consumer king, has power; is in control of his settings rather than being controlled by them. There is some truth to such a perspective on the consumer, especially as it applies to more affluent consumers. However, there is another side to this and this chapter will focus on it.

Much of my work has dealt with efforts which, intentionally or not, serve to control and dehumanize—not humanize—the consumer. In this context, humanization involves efforts by the consumer to gain greater control by avoiding, evading, or completely overturning the structures created by such efforts. However, my recent work (Ritzer 2010, 2014; Ritzer and Jurgenson 2010; Ritzer, Dean, and Jurgenson 2012) has shifted in the direction of a focus on the prosumer rather than the consumer, especially on the Internet and Web 2.0 (for example, Facebook, Wikipedia, blogs). Prosumption is the interrelated process of production and consumption. The prosumer consumes that which he or she produces and/or produces that which he/she consumes. The issue to be addressed here is whether the prosumer is more likely to be human, less likely to be dehumanized, than the consumer.

While the prosumer on Web 2.0 is something new, the fact is that people have always been prosumers (for example, as peasants raising and eating their own produce in pre-industrial society; Ritzer 2014). However, even outside the Internet we spend more time these days—compared to the industrial era—as prosumers in supermarkets, fast food restaurants and the like where we increasingly produce as we consume. However, it is on the Internet that the prosumer has truly blossomed. In fact, those who focus on the prosumer and the Internet sometimes argue that the prosumer is becoming so important there that we are witnessing the demise of the consumer. Most extremely, Shirky[1] goes so far as to say that the consumer is dead and that the Internet "heralds the disappearance of the consumer altogether." And he concludes by arguing that there "are no more consumers … we are all producers now." While there is some truth to this argument, it is put in indefensibly stark terms by Shirky (and others) because he is operating with a polar sense of both consumers and producers. While I do not accept this argument, the growth of the prosumer could lead, at least theoretically, to greater humanization (although I will deal with limits to this argument below and at the close of this chapter). Prosumption yields power to the actor including more power both to produce and over the process of consumption. Power is humanizing (although it can be, and has been, used in inhuman ways) and therefore what serves to dehumanize consumers is their lack, or loss, of power.

However, there is another perspective on all of this. That is, prosumers are often induced, if not forced into, productive "work." In this way, prosumption itself is dehumanized and prosumers are not only controlled, but exploited and alienated. Nonetheless, while they may be controlled, exploited and alienated, prosumers generally appear to like what they do; they do not "seem" to be aware of any

---

1   http://www.shirky.com/. Accessed September 15, 2014.

of these things. Does this mean that they are more humanized than producers or consumers? Or merely that they are less conscious of their exploitation, alienation and lack of control; of their dehumanization?

The discussion that follows is divided into two sections. In the first I deal with my work on the dehumanization of the consumer. In the second section, I discuss the issue of whether the prosumer offers hope for greater humanization.

Dehumanizing the Consumer

The Fast Food Restaurant

I first dealt with this issue in *The McDonaldization of Society* ([1993] 2013). In its broadest terms, the book is about the application of Max Weber's theory of rationalization to the world of consumption, specifically the settings in which consumption occurs. The argument is that many of those consumption settings, with the fast food restaurant as a paradigm, have rationalized in much the same way that bureaucracies, or later factories, had rationalized. However, it is a huge step from rationalizing production settings to rationalizing consumption settings, although it is important to note that consumption settings are also production settings that encompass rationalized work, just as production settings also involve rationalized consumption (for example, workers "consuming" raw materials in the process of production; in this sense production workers are also prosumers). Workers are paid employees in either type of setting and therefore the owner is free, within limits set by the government, labor unions, and the like, to rationalize the work setting to a high degree in order to maximize efficiency, productivity, and profitability. However, it is another matter when what is involved is rationalizing these contexts in ways that affect the way people consume. Rationalization is ultimately about control and since consumers are not paid, it would seem that they are free to avoid or reject completely such control. Thus, the rationalization of consumption cannot be as heavy handed as the rationalization of production. Even where it is, it needs to be hidden and sugar coated so that consumers are largely unaware of the process and the ways in which control is being exercised over them. However, whether or not it is concealed and sugar coated, it is control and therefore tends to dehumanize the consumption process.

Weber famously associated increasing rationalization with the creation of an "iron cage." Rationalizing societies as a whole, as well specific structures such as bureaucracies and factories (and fast food restaurants), can be seen as iron cages, as well part of a larger, more all-encompassing iron cage. The implication of the iron-cage imagery is, of course, that people will become increasingly less free as the process of rationalization proceeds. In the work world this led, historically, to protests over the control exercised over factory workers and bureaucrats. However, the idea that the freedom of consumers was being limited by the process of rationalization ran counter to the general economic and lay arguments that consumers are free to do as they wish with their time and money (assuming they have enough money to consume). Thus, it is hard to think of consumers as being locked into iron cages, but that is exactly the conclusion to be derived from the logic and reality of the rationalization process and its extension into the process of consumption in consumption settings.

One aspect of the process of rationalization, or McDonaldization, is the replacement of human with non-human technologies (see also Campbell 2005). While human technologies are controlled by people, non-human technologies are not only beyond peoples' control, but they exercise control over people. In the work world, the assembly line and the bureaucracy are examples of non-human technologies that exercise control over people. In the fast food restaurant one example of such a non-human technology, as it relates primarily to consumers, is the drive-through window. While consumers are free to avoid it and park their cars and enter the restaurant, once they commit themselves to the drive-through they are locked into a kind of self-propelled conveyor belt that they cannot leave until they obtain and pay for their food. Once the food is safely in their car, they are likely committed to eating it there (or to taking it home). Not insignificantly from the perspective of the fast food restaurant, they not only leave with their food but also with what will ultimately become their debris. Not only is the restaurant relieved of the task of dealing with the garbage, but that task is passed on to the consumer who must find a way of disposing of it without being paid for the work involved. Consumers are generally unaware of the way the drive-through window leads them to do what the fast food restaurant wants them to do, including serving as unpaid disposers of trash.

I emphasize, as did Weber, the irrationalities of rationality; the irrationalities associated with rationalization. One of the main irrationalities of rationality is dehumanization. Rationalized settings are not only dehumanized settings in which to work, but the same argument applies to consumption. For example, it could be argued that genuinely human consumption allows for lots of individual choice rather than few alternatives determined by those who control a chain of fast food restaurants. Another is having the option as a consumer of a leisurely meal, rather than eating hastily as dictated by fast food restaurants. The latter, of course, is a concern of the Slow Food Movement which, above all else, struggles for humanized consumption which among many other things might, at least at times, mean the possibility of a leisurely meal. However, by its very nature and name, the fast food restaurant stands opposed to the whole idea of a leisurely meal and would be forced to close its doors if most of its customers chose to spend hours at the relatively few tables slowly munching on drying hamburgers or cooling fries (or in Starbucks nursing a cup of coffee). The relatively low prices at fast food restaurants mean that they must do a large volume of business. That means moving people in and out of the restaurant as quickly as possible without making such an objective obvious to them. This helps to explain the attraction of the drive-through window which not only speeds up the movement of customers, but has the added benefit of discouraging them from ever entering the restaurant and thereby occupying tables. Furthermore, eating while driving or while parked in the restaurant's adjacent parking lot is a highly dehumanized way of dining.

The Cathedrals of Consumption

In my later work I built on my interest in the fast food restaurant to deal with a larger set of consumption sites (which includes the fast food restaurant) that I called the "cathedrals of consumption" (Ritzer [1999] 2010). The major cathedrals of consumption are shopping malls, casino-hotels, cruise ships and theme parks such as Disney World. At one level, these, like fast food restaurants, are highly rationalized with the result that they seek to exercise similar levels of control over consumers. At another level, however, the challenge is to first lure enough consumers to these sites so that these controls can be exercised in ways that lead consumers to engage not only in consumption, but hyperconsumption—consuming more than they need, want, or in many cases can pay for. The focus below will be on the control exercised over consumers after they have been lured to a cathedral of consumption.

It should come as no surprise that the cathedrals of consumption are highly rationalized and that they are continually seeking to ratchet up the level of rationalization. They employ huge numbers of people—for example, some of the new mega-cruise ships employ and house 2,000 to 3,000 workers—and their work needs to be rationalized. The fact that they need to deal with masses of passengers—think of the 6,000 people who need to be fed several, if not many, times a day on a mega-cruise ship—means that workers' dealings with customers need to be similarly rationalized. However, in many ways, the more necessary—and daunting—task involves the rationalization of the behavior of consumers in such cathedrals of consumption as the cruise ship. Chaos, anger, and perhaps outright rebellion would ensue among consumers if on a cruise, for example, their meals were not served on time, if there was a shortage of desired foods, or, heaven forefend, the bar ran out of liquor or the casino cashiers lacked sufficient cash. These, however, are things that the management can control (even though there are occasional disasters, especially on cruise ships [Weaver 2011]) rather easily. However, the biggest challenge in the cathedrals of consumption (and elsewhere) is the control over consumers.

That control is exercised in various ways, but most importantly through a variety of structures that lead consumers to behave in desired ways without them realizing that constraints are being exercised over them. For example:

In Las Vegas casinos, the few remaining nickel slot machines are usually placed in hard to get to corners where gamblers in search of them are forced to pass by—if they are able to resist—the lure of far greater payoffs from higher-cost machines.

In airports, wherever possible, gift shops are located on departing passengers' right as they head to the gate with fast food restaurants on the left. The reasoning is that passengers are more likely to cross the aisle in order to get food; they might pass up the gift shop if it is not conveniently placed on the right.

At the Gap, the much sought after denims are positioned at the back of the store, forcing customers to pass by all of the other goods in order to get to them.

In Disneyland and Disney World, visitors enter and exit through a mini-mall, Main Street, so that purchases can be made both on entering and leaving. Similarly, at the cathedral in Canterbury, England, visitors must leave through the gift shop, which sells a wide variety of souvenirs and *not* just those related to the cathedral specifically and religion in general.

Walt Disney believed that you needed to construct "weinies" in order to attract consumers and to lead them in the direction that you want them to go. In the context of Disney World, weinies are highly visible attractions (mountains, castles, and the like) to which virtually all visitors will find themselves drawn. Thus, visitors move in the directions that Disney management wants them to move and they do so without anyone telling them where they should go and how they should get there. This allows for the efficient movement of large numbers of visitors who pay a high price of admission to the park. Furthermore, they are led to pass by many kiosks, shops, restaurants, and the like where they can spend money.

In shopping malls, the number of exits is often deliberately limited to keep people in the mall; escalators tend to be placed at the end of corridors to force people to walk their length; fountains and benches are carefully positioned to entice shoppers into stores.

IKEA is intentionally constructed like a maze so that customers wander about, lost at least part of the time, therefore spending far more time (and money) there than they had planned. In addition, regular customers know this and are apt to put items in their cart as they move about because they cannot be sure they will be able to find their way back to the spot if they decide later that they want to purchase those items.[2] Like shopping malls, Disney World and Las Vegas casinos, IKEA is designed to make sure you feel it is nearly impossible to leave (or at least spend lots more time than you planned there).

At warehouse stores such as Sam's Club and Costco, food and other goods are sold in large quantities or multipacks so that people often end up buying more than they intended. One customer might say: "Look, you just see it and then you use it. I don't need 24 batteries, but, oh well, it's here and it's cheap and I'll use it— eventually." In addition, consumers are channeled past long rows of seemingly bargain-priced non-food items before even getting to the food area. Many of these items find their way into customers' carts.

Although an older means of consumption, the supermarket continues to be important and is especially revealing in terms of control and the techniques used to lead customers to do what is desired of them: the flower (or bakery) section is often the first one encountered in a supermarket. It is designed to tickle consumers' sensations, produce a positive image for the market, and weaken consumers' resolve. The best place to display food is at the head and foot of each aisle. Food displayed in those places ("end caps") can easily double or triple in sales. More generally, sales increase for items displayed at eye level or at the beginning of

---

2   www.dailymail.co.uk/femail/article-1349831/Ikea-design-stores-mazes-stop-shopper, by James Tozer. Accessed September 19, 2014.

an aisle. Foods oriented to children are usually placed lower on shelves. This allows children not only to see the products but also to pick them up and plead with a parent to purchase them. Dairy is generally on one side, produce on the other, with meat in the back. To get all the basics, customers must work their way through much of the store and past its array of merchandise. Stacking cartons of merchandise in the aisles can slow shoppers down and cause them to peruse the shelves more. They also present a warehouse image that conveys a sense of bargain pricing.

There are many such examples, but the central point is that the means of consumption (both new and old) were, and continue to be, structured in such a way as to control people and, among other things, to induce them to buy more than they intended.

The novelist Émile Zola saw the department store as a "selling machine." It is clear that the newer means of consumption are far more sophisticated and effective selling machines than their predecessors. As machines, as non-human technologies, they tend to control and thereby to dehumanize the consumer.

The cathedrals of consumption are dehumanizing in another way. They increasingly tend to offer the same or similar products to consumers who, while they have the illusion of great choice, in fact must choose among products that I have described as "nothing." While a wide range of products (and services) that can be thought of as nothing are available to consumers, consumers have less and less possibility consuming "something."

The Globalization of Nothing

Within the process of globalization, we can distinguish between glocalization and grobalization. There is no question that glocalization is an important part of globalization, but *grobalization*, coined in my book *The Globalization of Nothing* (Ritzer [2004] 2007), is a much-needed companion to the notion of glocalization. Grobalization focuses on the imperialistic ambitions of nations, corporations, organizations, and the like and their desire, indeed their need, to impose themselves on various geographic areas throughout the world. Their main interest is in seeing their power, influence, and in some cases profits grow (hence the term *gro*balization) throughout the world.

Grobalization leads to a variety of ideas that are largely antithetical to the basic ideas associated with glocalization. Rather than emphasizing the great diversity among various glocalized locales, grobalization leads to the view that at least some aspects of the world are growing increasingly similar. While it is recognized that there are differences within and between areas of the world, what is emphasized is their increasing similarity. This focus, of course, heightens the fears of those who are concerned about the increasing homogenization associated with globalization. In contrast to the view associated with glocalization, individuals and groups throughout the world are seen as having relatively little ability to adapt, innovate, and maneuver within a grobalized world. Grobalization theory thus sees larger structures and forces overwhelming the ability of individuals and groups to create themselves and their worlds. In other words, it sees these forces as controlling and dehumanizing.

In yet another stark contrast, grobalization tends to involve social processes that are largely unidirectional and deterministic. That is, forces flow from the global to the local, and there is little or no possibility of the local (or local actors) having any significant impact on the global. As a result, the global is generally seen as largely determining what transpires at the local level; the impact of the global is not contingent on what transpires at the local level or on how the local reacts to the global. Grobalization thus overpowers the local. It also limits the ability of the local to act and react, let alone to act reflexively back on the grobal.

From the perspective of grobalization, then, global forces are seen as largely determining what individual(s) and groups think and do throughout the world. It could be argued that, in the main, grobalization is a dehumanizing force in the sense that it imposes itself on consumers (and others).

A second key concept in the *Globalization of Nothing* is *nothing* which is defined as a "social form that is generally centrally conceived, controlled and comparatively devoid of distinctive substantive content" (Ritzer [2004] 2007, xi). It should be abundantly clear that any McDonaldized system, with the fast food restaurant being a prime example, would be a major form and purveyor of nothing. However, it is important to point out that there are many other examples of nothing that have little or no direct relationship to McDonaldization.

Let us look at the example of a chain of fast food restaurants from the viewpoint of the basic components of our definition of nothing. First, as parts of chains, fast food restaurants are, virtually by definition, *centrally conceived.* That is, those who created the chain and are associated with its central offices conceived of the chain originally and are continually involved in its reconceptualization. For their part, owners and managers of local chain restaurants do little or no conceptualizing on their own. Indeed, they have bought the rights to the franchise, and continue to pay a percentage of their profits for it, because they want those with the demonstrated knowledge and expertise to do the conceptualizing. This relative absence of independent conceptualization at the level of the local franchise is one of the reasons we can think of the franchise as nothing.

We are led to a similar view when we turn to the second aspect of our definition of nothing—*centralized control.* Just as those in the central office do the conceptualization for the local franchises, they also exert great control over them. Indeed, to some degree, such control is derived from the fact that conceptualization is in the hands of the central office; the act of conceptualizing and reconceptualizing the franchise yields a significant amount of control. However, control is exercised by the central office over the franchises in more direct ways as well. For example, it may get a percentage of a local franchise's profits, and if its cut is down because profits are down, the central office may put pressure on the local franchise to alter its procedures to increase profitability. The central office may also deploy inspectors to make periodic and unannounced visits to local franchises.

Those franchises found not to be operating the way they are supposed to will come under pressure to bring their operations in line with company standards. Those that do not are likely to suffer adverse consequences, including the ultimate punishment of the loss of the franchise. Thus, local franchises can also be seen as nothing because they do not control their own destinies.

The third aspect of the definition of nothing is that it involves social forms largely *lacking in distinctive content.* This is essentially true by definition for chains of franchised fast food restaurants. That is, the whole idea is to create restaurants that are virtual clones of one another. To put it another way, the goal is to produce restaurants that are as much alike one another as possible—they generally look much the same from the outside, they are structured similarly within, the same foods are served, workers act and interact in much the same way, and so on. There is little that distinguishes one outlet of a chain of fast food restaurants from all the others.

There is thus a near perfect fit between the definition of nothing offered above and a chain of fast food restaurants. However, this is a rather extreme view since, in a sense, "nothing is nothing." In other words, all social forms (including fast food restaurants) have characteristics that deviate from the extreme form of nothing. That is, they involve some local conceptualization and control, and each one has at least some distinctive elements. To put this another way, all social forms have some elements of somethingness. Consequently, we need to think not only in terms of nothing but also in terms of something, as well as a something–nothing continuum.

This leads us to a definition of *something* as "a social form that is generally indigenously conceived, controlled, and comparatively rich in distinctive substantive content." This definition makes it clear that neither nothing nor something exists independently of the other; each makes sense only when paired with, and contrasted to, the other.

If a fast food restaurant is an example of nothing, then a meal cooked at home from scratch would be an example of something. The meal is conceived by the individual cook and not by a central office. Control rests in the hands of that cook. Finally, that which the cook prepares is rich in distinctive content and different from that prepared by other cooks, even those who prepare the same meals.

While nothing and something are presented as if they are a dichotomy, we really need to think in terms of a continuum from something to nothing, and that is precisely the way the concepts are employed here—as the two poles of that continuum. Although a fast food restaurant falls toward the nothing end of the continuum, every fast food restaurant has at least some elements different from all others; each has some elements of somethingness associated with it. Conversely, while every home-cooked meal is distinctive, it is likely to have at least some elements in common with other meals (for example, they all may rely on a common cookbook, pre-prepared ingredients, or recipe) and therefore have some elements of nothingness. No social form exists at the extreme nothing or something pole of the continuum; they all fall somewhere between the two.

However, it remains the case that some lie closer to the nothing end of the continuum, whereas others lie more toward the something end. In terms of our interests here, fast food restaurants, and more generally all McDonaldized systems, fall toward the nothing end of the something–nothing continuum.

An example of the grobalization of nothing is a meal at McDonald's. There is little or nothing distinctive about any given McDonald's restaurant, the food served there, the people who work in these settings, and the "services" they offer. And, of course, there has been a very aggressive effort to expand the presence of McDonald's throughout much of the world. The global expansion of McDonald's (and other fast food chains) exemplifies the grobalization of nothing.

The grobalization of nothing tends to be dehumanizing. First, there is the effort to impose nothing on consumers wherever they may be in the world and such imposition limits choice and thereby dehumanizes consumers. Second, what is imposed most often is nothing. On one level that is dehumanizing because it limits choice; there is less and less chance of consuming something. More importantly, the nature of nothing is dehumanizing since it is centrally conceived, controlled and lacking indistinctive content. That means consumers are dehumanized because they are not able to do the conceptualization, what they consume is controlled by those in some central office, and they cannot express themselves in what they consume because they are consuming pretty much what most others consume.

In sum, most of my previous work on fast food restaurants, other cathedrals of consumption, and the globalization of nothing point toward the increasing dehumanization of the consumer.

Is There Hope for Increased Humanization in the Increasingly Omnipresent Prosumer?

The term prosumer is generally attributed to Alvin Toffler (1980) who devoted considerable attention to it in *The Third Wave*. Toffler argued that prosumption was predominant in pre-industrial societies; what he called the "first wave." It was followed by a "second wave" of marketization that drove "a wedge into society, that separated these two functions, thereby giving birth to what we now call producers and consumers" (266). Thus, the primordial economic form is neither production nor consumption, but rather it is prosumption. However, in Toffler's view, contemporary society is moving away from the aberrant separation of production and consumption and towards a "third wave" that, in part, signals their reintegration in "the rise of the prosumer" (265). While the prosumer in the first wave was poverty based (Toffler and Toffler 2006, 193), the third-wave prosumer is more defined by the advanced technologies that make prosumption increasingly likely and today's prosumer less likely to be impoverished.

Similarly, I argued (Ritzer 2010) that it was the industrial revolution that, at least to some extent, separated production and consumption. Unlike Toffler, I contend that even at the height of the industrial revolution production and consumption were never fully distinct (producers consumed raw materials; consumers produced their meals). The major social theorists of production (for example, Marx) and consumption (for example, Baudrillard [1970] 1997) distinguished too strongly between these two spheres; they can be said to have suffered from either a productivist and or a consumptionist bias. I reject this false binary and argue, instead, that the focus should *always* have been on the prosumer.

It is only recently that prosumption has become an important topic in the literature. Writing on business issues, Prahalad and Ramaswamy (2004) discuss this trend under the label of "value co-creation." Arvidsson (2005) sees consumers doing the immaterial labor that creates brand-value. Campbell's (2005) craft consumers often produce craft products out of an array of goods created for other reasons and uses. Tapscott and Williams (2006) see the prosumer as a part of a new "wikinomic" model where businesses put consumers to work. These models, as well as the whole idea of relying on consumers to produce, are criticized by Andrew Keen (2007) in *Cult of the Amateur* for, among other things, undermining professionals (for example, reporters) and their organizations (for example, newspapers). Beer and Burrows (2007) see new relations between production and consumption emerging online, especially on Web 2.0, a topic elaborated on below. Watson and Shove (2008) focus on DIY and the interaction between prosumers, practices, instruction manuals, objects, and the like. Humphreys and Grayson (2008) discuss prosumption in relation to Marxian theory arguing that only those who produce exchange value for companies are truly prosumers. Zwick et al. (2008) see new possibilities for value creation in prosumers who are, in effect, charged for the work that they do. Zwick and Knott (2009) see prosumers as producing the databases through which they are exploited. Ritzer and Jurgenson (2010) theorized the emergence of a new form of capitalism in the epoch of the prosumer marked by "free" products and services, unpaid labor, and abundance rather than scarcity. Jurgenson (2010) argues that prosumption online marks a reversal of the historic trend toward increasing rationalization in favor of a *de*McDonaldization of at least the Internet. In slightly different terms, Bruns (2008) focuses on the "produser," the productive consumer. While similar to prosumption, the idea of the produser replicates the productivist bias in this context by emphasizing the productive role of the produser and ignoring the produser's role as a consumer.

In the *McDonaldization of Society* I discussed the ways in which consumers have been put to work in the fast food industry; the "diner" at a fast food restaurant, the consumer of that food, is also, at least to some degree, a producer of the meal. Among other things, diners are expected to serve as their own waiters carrying their meals to their tables or back to their cars, sandwich makers (by adding fixings like tomatoes, lettuce, and onions in some chains), salad makers (by creating their own salads at the salad bar), and bus persons (by disposing of their own debris after the meal is finished).

While there were precursors to this trend toward putting the consumer to work—turning them into prosumers—in, for example, supermarkets, it accelerated in the wake of the birth of the fast food restaurant in the mid-1950s. Among the examples are: pumping one's own gasoline at the filling station; serving as a bank teller at the ATM machine; working at the checkout counter at the supermarket by scanning one's own food, bagging it, and paying for it by credit card; using electronic kiosks to check into hotels and at airports, and to purchase movie tickets and so on. Co-creating a variety of experiences such as moving oneself through Disney World and its many attractions or serving as an "actor" in the theatre "staged" by Starbucks designed to create the image of an old-fashioned coffee house (Ritzer [1993] 2013); or using do-it-yourself medical technologies (for example, blood pressure monitors, blood glucose monitors, pregnancy tests) that allow patients to perform tasks formerly performed by paid medical professionals without recompense.

Then there is a wide range of subtler and less material examples of prosumption. Much of what transpires online, especially on Web 2.0, is generated by the user. It is on Web 2.0 that there has been a dramatic explosion in prosumption. Web 2.0 is contrasted to Web 1.0 (for example, AOL, Yahoo), which was (and still is) more provider—than user—generated. Web 2.0 is defined by the ability of consumers to produce content collaboratively whereas most of what it exists on Web 1.0 is produced by the provider. Examples of Web 2.0 include:

- Wikipedia, where users generate articles and continually edit, update, and comment on them.
- Facebook, MySpace, and other social networking websites, where users create profiles composed of videos, photos, and text, interact with one another, and build communities.
- Google, where users' choices are analyzed using Google's indexing logarithm to create hierarchies of most visited Internet sites.
- Folksomies derived from categories created by users.
- Second Life, where users create the characters, communities, and the entire virtual environment.
- The blogosphere, blogs (Web logs), microblogging (Twitter) and the comments on them produced by those who consume them.
- eBay and Craigslist, where consumers rather than retailers create the market.
- YouTube and Flickr, where mostly amateurs upload and download videos and photographs.
- Current TV, where viewers create much of the programming, submit it via the Internet, and decide which submissions are aired.
- Linux, a free, collaboratively-built, open-source operating system, and other open-source software applications, like Mozilla Firefox, that are created and maintained by those who use them.
- Amazon, where consumers do all the work involved in ordering products and writing the reviews, and the users' buying habits and site navigation are documented to recommend products.
- Yelp!, where users create an online city guide by ranking, reviewing and discussing various locations and activities in their area.
- The GeoWeb, which consists of online maps where, increasingly, users are creating and augmenting content with Google, Microsoft, and Yahoo tools.

Google Maps users, for example, can fix errors; add the locations of businesses; upload photos; link Wikipedia articles to, and blog about their experiences with, or reviews of, places on the map, thereby creating social communities. Additionally, new "location awareness" tools, often used in conjunction with "smart" cell phones with GPS technology, allow users to track where they are at any given moment and upload this information to websites such as Facebook, Twitter or one's blog. Some examples include Google Latitude, Yahoo's Fire Eagle, and the Loopt mobile phone application.

Prosumption was clearly not invented on Web 2.0, but given the massive involvement in, and popularity of, many of these developments (for example, social networking sites), it can be argued that it is currently both the most prevalent location of prosumption and its most important facilitator. The growing experience with prosumption will inevitably spill over into material settings. New settings that depend on evolving forms of prosumption will be created and one-time consumers will be increasingly adept at, and comfortable with, prosumption. In fact, it seems likely that today's and tomorrow's consumers will demand more and more prosumption.

If we assume that the consumer is, and in fact has always been, a prosumer and that consumers will increasingly be prosumers, does looking at the consumer in this way offer hope for greater humanization? The most general answer, I think is that the more the consumer produces, the more the consumer is a prosumer, the greater the degree of humanization. Production implies greater control and power than does consumption and with that greater power prosumers will be able, if they wish, to humanize their environments to a greater degree. This stands in contrast to the consumer, at least in its extreme form, which implies passivity and control by a range of external forces (the structures of the cathedrals of consumption, advertisers and so on). The more consumers are prosumers, the more they produce, the more human they will be able to make their lives.

Of course, assembly-line workers and counter staff at fast food restaurants engage in production, but they clearly have little power or ability to control their work settings. However, the consumers who produce—prosumers—are in a very different position because they cannot be controlled as easily by those who run a given setting. This, in combination with the increasing ability to produce, will give the con(pro)sumers greater power than the kinds of production workers mentioned above.

The ability to humanize their lives, especially those aspects that relate to consumption, will depend to a great extent on whether it occurs in the material or the digital world (even though in many ways those worlds are converging [Jenkins 2006]). In the material world of fast food restaurants, IKEA, cruise ships, and the like, the nature of those physical structures, and the fact that they are owned by profit-making organizations, is likely to limit the ability of prosumers to humanize them. Of course, to the degree that prosumers take it upon themselves to humanize these worlds, or apply pressure to humanize them, those who run these structures will modify them to meet at least some of these demands. However, while the cathedrals of consumption will in the future be more likely to humanize their settings, there are limits to this, especially its impact on profits.

It is a very different matter on the Internet. For one thing, there is the experience of dealing with many sites or Internet-based phenomena (such as Linux, Firefox, Wikipedia) that are totally constructed by prosumers. These experiences are likely to spur further interest in prosumption not only on the Internet, but in the material world. Then there are the Web 2.0 sites devoted to consumption. While the underlying structures of these sites are prestructured, usually by profit-making organizations (for example, Amazon.com, eBay), much of the content on these sites is "user-generated," that is, generated by the consumers (users). Because of their power to create the content on these sites, prosumers have the ability to make them more "human." In any case, the mere fact that they, rather than some corporate employee, are generating the site means that it is, almost by definition, more human. However, the fact that they are owned and controlled by profit-making organizations will limit the power of the prosumer and their ability to humanize the sites.

There is another way to interpret what is taking place on the Internet, especially those sites controlled by profit-making organizations, which sees it as *less* rather than more humanizing. This relates to the fact that not only are many things on the web available free of charge (Anderson 2009), but prosumers do many tasks there for which they are not paid. For example, the prosumer on Amazon not only does all of the work involved in ordering a book (or any other product), but also might write reviews, create lists of recommendations, and so on. In the material world, a book shop would have had to pay an employee to do this work, but in the digital world of Amazon prosumers do it free of charge. Looked at from a Marxian point of view, if book store owners in a capitalist system exploit their workers by paying them less than they produce, what does this say about the prosumers on Amazon who are paid *nothing* for their work? It could be argued that this, in fact, ratchets up exploitation to an unprecedented level. Instead of getting productive work at little cost, entrepreneurs are now able to get it at no cost.

What does this have to do with humanization? Marx, of course, saw exploitative systems where workers were paid less than they deserved (actually *all* productive systems in capitalism) as alienating. Alienation ultimately means that workers are separated from that which makes them human (their species being). Being separated from that which makes us human is another way of saying dehumanization. Thus, by that logic prosuming for nothing on Amazon is dehumanizing, especially because in the process those on the top of that profit-making organization, including billionaire Jeff Bezos, control the actions of prosumers and are profiting from prosumers' free labor.

However, a more human form of con/prosumption is made possible on other sites on the Internet which are non-capitalistic in nature. The following are some examples: Wikipedia where one is free to consume text (and produce it) without enriching anyone else (at least economically). Open source software such as Linux which can be used free of charge (in contrast to Microsoft Explorer) and can be expanded upon if one has the programming skills. Peer-to-peer file sharing. Web sites licensed by Creative Commons which allow prosumers to share, reuse and remix content (Bruns 2008, 236).

It is on sites such as these that consumption, conceived of there as part of, and inseparable from, prosumption, is humanized to the greatest degree.

While the Internet, especially Web 2.0, makes the humanization of con/prosumption much more likely, in the end it comes down to the issue of capitalistic control. However, even on non-capitalistic sites, there is a struggle between those in control and prosumers. For example, the founder of Wikipedia, Jimmy Wales, exercises control over the site as does the hierarchy of mostly unpaid administrators who have come to play an increasing role in what does or does not appear on the site. Nonetheless, capitalism has been kept at bay in the sites mentioned above with the result that greater humanization is possible. Much less humanization exists on those web sites under capitalist control. Furthermore, there is an ongoing struggle on the Internet between the capitalists and the cyberlibertarians who want the Internet to be true to its original vision and be free of external control. While the struggle is ongoing, it is difficult to argue against the power of the capitalist. Therefore while prosumers have a greater ability than consumers to humanize their environments, in the long run it is difficult to bet against increasing efforts to dehumanize the con/prosumer even on the Internet.

References

Anderson, C. 2009. *Free: The Future of a Radical Price.* New York: Hyperion.

Arvidsson, A. 2005. "Brands: A Critical Perspective." *Journal of Consumer Culture* 5, 2: 235–58.

Baudrillard, J. [1970] 1997. *The Consumer Society.* London: Sage.

Beer, D. and R. Burrows. 2007. "Sociology and, of and in Web 2.0: Some Initial Considerations." *Sociological Research Online* 12, 5. Accessed October 7, 2014. http://www.socresonline.org.uk/12/5/17.html.

Bruns, A. 2008. *Blogs, Wikipedia, Second Life and Beyond: From Production to Produsage.* New York: Peter Lang.

Campbell, C. 2005. "The Craft Consumer." *Journal of Consumer Culture* 5, 1: 23–42.

De Certeau, M. 1984. *The Practice of Everyday Life.* Berkeley: University of California Press.

Ehrenreich, B. 2008. *Nickel and Dimed: On (Not) Getting By in America.* New York: Holt.

Humphreys, A. and K. Grayson. 2008. "The Intersecting Roles of Consumer and Producer: A Critical Perspective on Co-Production, Co-Creation and Prosumption." *Sociology Compass* 2: 963–80.

Jenkins, H. 2006. *Convergence Culture: Where Old and New Media Collide.* New York: New York University Press.

Jurgenson, N. 2010. "The De-McDonaldization of the Internet." In *McDonaldization: The Reader*, 3rd Edition, edited by G. Ritzer, 159–70. Thousand Oaks, CA: Pine Forge Press.

Keen, A. 2007. *The Cult of the Amateur: How Today's Internet is Killing Our Culture*. New York: Doubleday.

Marx, K. [1867] 1967. *Capital: A Critique of Political Economy*, vol. 1. New York: International Publishers.

Prahalad, C.K. and V. Ramaswamy. 2004. "Co-Creation Experiences: The Next Practice in Value Creation." *Journal of Interactive Marketing* 18, 3: 5–14.

Ritzer, G. [1993] 2013. *The McDonaldization of Society: Twentieth Anniversary Edition*. Thousand Oaks, CA: Pine Forge Press.

Ritzer, G. [1999] 2010. *Enchanting a Disenchanted World: Revolutionizing the Means of Consumption*. Thousand Oaks, CA: Pine Forge Press.

Ritzer, G. [2004] 2007. *The Globalization of Nothing*. Thousand Oaks, CA: Pine Forge Press.

Ritzer, G. 2010. "Focusing on the Prosumer: On Correcting an Error in the History of Social Theory." In *Prosumer Revisited*, edited by Birgit Blattel-Mink and Kai-Uwe Hellman, 61–79. Wiesbaden: VS Verlag.

Ritzer, G. 2014. "Prosumption: Evolution, Revolution or Eternal Return of the Same?" *Journal of Consumer Culture* 14, 1: 3–24.

Ritzer, G., and N. Jurgenson. 2010. "Production, Consumption, Prosumption: The Nature of Capitalism in the Age of the Digital 'Prosumer.'" *Journal of Consumer Culture* 10: 13–36.

Ritzer, G., Paul Dean and N. Jurgenson. 2012. "The Coming Age of the Prosumer." *American Behavioral Scientist* 56: 379–98.

Slater, D. 1997. *Consumer Culture and Modernity*. London: Polity Press.

Tapscott, D. and A.D. Williams. 2006. *Wikinomics: How Mass Collaboration Changes Everything*. New York: Portfolio.

Toffler, A. 1980. *The Third Wave*. New York: William Morrow and Co.

Toffler, A. and H. Toffler. 2006. *Revolutionary Wealth*. New York: Knopf.

Watson, M. and E. Shove. 2008. "Product, Competence, Project and Practice: DIY and the Dynamics of Craft Consumption." *Journal of Consumer Culture* 8, 1: 69–89.

Weaver, A. 2011. "The McDonaldization Thesis and Cruise Tourism." In *McDonaldization: The Reader*, 3rd ed., edited by George Ritzer, 241–56. Thousand Oaks, CA: Pine Forge Press.

Weber, M. [1921] 1968. *Economy and Society*. Totowa, NJ: Bedminster Press.

Zwick, D., S.K. Bonsu, and A. Darmody. 2008. "Putting Consumers to Work: Co-creation and New Marketing Govern-mentality." *Journal of Consumer Culture* 8: 163–96.

Zwick, D. and D. Knott. 2009. "Manufacturing Customers: The Database as New Means of Production." *Journal of Consumer Culture* 9: 221–47.

Chapter 3

Status Matters? The Contradictions Surrounding Conspicuous Consumption

Colin Campbell

Introduction

In August 2008 Apple produced a new app, in reality a glorified screensaver, for its iPhone called "I Am Rich." This consisted of a glowing red gem on a user's iPhone screen alongside of which are the words "I Am Rich" with "Category Lifestyle" underneath and the price of the app, which was $999.99. The official description of this product on the Apple website described it as follows: "The red icon on your iPhone or iPod Touch always reminds you (and others when you show them) that you were able to afford this. It's a work of art with no hidden function at all." As the commentary on the Fox News item that reported this put it, "The app displays a glowing red gem on a user's iPhone screen for the sole purpose of proving to onlookers one is of the moneyed class. That's all it does" (Fox News 2008). In the event this app only remained available for a few days before it was withdrawn from sale, by which time a mere eight people had bought one, although many more clicked on the sale site apparently under the impression that it was a joke.

Now what is interesting about this story is that the app in question was clearly targeted at conspicuous consumers, that is, at people whose concern is to enhance their social status in the eyes of others by demonstrating their purchasing power, and hence by inference their wealth. Indeed, as the Fox commentary noted, the app had no other purpose. Given the popular belief that conspicuous consumption is a widespread feature of contemporary society this app should have been a success. But it wasn't. This suggests two possibilities. The first is that most people in contemporary society are not actually engaged in conspicuous consumption, and the widespread belief that they are is something of a myth. The second is that most people are engaged in conspicuous consumption but do not wish to admit that they are, and hence the reason the "I am Rich" app failed to attract buyers was not because consumers did not wish to advertise their wealth but because they did not want to be seen to have deliberately decided to advertise their wealth; an interpretation that is consistent with the long-standing assumption that consumers who conspicuously consume have a tendency to deny that this is indeed what they are doing.

This latter interpretation raises some intriguing and difficult questions for the sociologist of consumption, the first of which is the problem of how to distinguish between the two groups of individuals who deny engaging in this form of activity, that is, between those who are not engaged in it, and those who are but who do not wish to admit that they are. What criterion, or distinguishing feature of their behavior, could we turn to that would successfully distinguish between these two groups? But then there is also the question of what to do if we find that there are people willing to admit to engaging in conspicuous consumption (after all eight people did buy the "I Am Rich" app). Do we simply take their admission at face value? There would seem to be no particularly good reason for not doing so and yet this leads to the bizarre position of treating consumers' confessions and their denials as equally indicative of conspicuous consumption. Not only would this seem illogical but it tends to make the claim that everyone in contemporary society is engaged in conspicuous consumption an un-falsifiable thesis. So perhaps, for the sake of consistency, we should assume that if people actually admit to doing it then the probability is that they are not? The only alternative would appear be to assume that there are two classes of conspicuous consumers, the honest and the dishonest, an intriguing thesis but one that would require the development of a new theory, one capable of explaining the reasons for the two categories.

These then are just some of the questions prompted by the story of the "I am Rich" app, questions I would like to explore in this chapter—questions that really come down to the crucial issue of what evidence is needed in order to be able to conclude that people are engaged in conspicuous consumption. But first I need to consider why these questions are important, and how they are connected to the concept of a human society.

Consumption and Sustainability

The assumption I am starting with is that a human society is a civilized and liberal one, which by definition would also be one in which people would be engaged in sustainable consumption, that is, consumption that meets the needs of those alive today without compromising the ability of future generations to meet their needs. Unfortunately it cannot be said that the consumption habits of the majority of the people in the developed world, and it must be said increasingly in the developing world, pass this crucial test. For most consumers in these societies now consume at levels that not only threaten to permanently de-stabilize the earth's climate but are also likely to deplete the planet's limited stock of natural resources, leaving little or nothing for future generations. There is, in consequence, an urgent need to persuade people to consume fewer goods and services than they do at present if these very real dangers are to be avoided. However, if this is to happen—that is if people are to be persuaded to consume less—then it is obviously first necessary to understand what it is that drives them to consume at the currently high levels.

There is probably no single answer to this question, as consumption is a term that covers a wide variety of human activities, each of which could be prompted by a different motive or guided by a different intention. However, as suggested above, there is one theory as to why people consume excessively that is not only regularly encountered in the media but which also has a largely taken-for-granted status as valid in the popular mind, and this is the theory of conspicuous consumption. According to this theory people in contemporary society consume excessively because they are engaged in what in popular parlance is called "keeping up with the Joneses," which is to say they consume as they do principally out of a concern with status. If this is indeed the case then there is real cause for concern, because status competition is by definition a zero-sum game, that is to say, the amount of high status that exists is necessarily fixed and cannot be increased. If therefore the principal reason consumers purchase more and more goods is in order to enhance their status the prospects are not good, and not simply for future generations. For this is also a somewhat self-defeating exercise for consumers themselves. Many who try to enhance their status are by necessity doomed to fail and will, as a consequence, be left feeling worse off than if they hadn't tried. But then in addition those who succeed in enhancing their status are likely to do so only temporarily, as very soon others will catch up with them, so that whatever satisfaction they might gain from their high status may only be temporary, while even if it lasts it is likely to be associated with anxiety about its possible loss. If therefore it really is the case that contemporary consumption is driven by status concerns, the prospects of realizing the ideal of a human society are not good. If however this is not the case and some other mechanism is responsible for the current phenomenon of over-consumption then perhaps there is more reason to be optimistic. This chapter will thus concentrate on the key question of whether it is indeed the case that the primary driver of modern consumer behavior is the individual's need to engage in conspicuous consumption. And intriguingly, as soon as we ask this question we encounter a contradiction, for while the general view in society at large is that conspicuous consumption is both prevalent and significant the view among sociologists of consumption is that it is not that important. So in posing this question one is not just seeking to discover whether conspicuous consumption really is a dominant feature of contemporary society, one is also seeking to discover who is right, the general public or sociologists.

Sociology and Conspicuous Consumption

There can be no doubt about the fact that sociologists consider Veblen's theory of conspicuous consumption to have little contemporary relevance. David Riesman, writing as long ago as the 1950s, suggested that the theory, although to a large degree applicable to the United States in the decades between the 1890s and 1920s, was "now obsolete" (Riesman 1954, 225). C. Wright Mills, writing in 1970, also suggested that Veblen's theory had only limited applicability, being restricted both in terms of the historical period to which it applied and the section of society who were inclined to indulge in this form of conduct (Mills 1970). This largely negative judgment on the contemporary relevance of the theory has since been endorsed by other writers, with Giddens (1973), Douglas and Isherwood (1978),

McCracken (1988) and Urry (1990) all expressing the opinion that, as Trigg puts it, "Veblen's approach is ... irrelevant and out of date in relation to the new cultural makeup of contemporary consumer society" (2001, 104). In the light of this marked consensus it is hardly surprising that Juliet B. Schor (2006) should conclude, in her general review of the sociology of conspicuous consumption, that "The Dominant view [within the discipline of sociology] continues to be that this is an outmoded theory of limited usefulness in explaining consumer behavior" (Ritzer 2007, 681).[1]

However what is also clear is that this negative judgment is not shared by those outside the discipline as there exists a flourishing tradition of published work, some of it serious scholarship, some more akin to popular journalism, that takes it for granted that Veblen's theory is not merely valid but offers significant insights into the nature of contemporary life. This tradition can be traced from Veblen himself through books like Vance Packard's *The Status Seekers* (1959), John Kenneth Galbraith's *The Affluent Society* (1962), John Brooks' *Showing Off In America* (1979), Juliet B. Schor's *The Overspent American* (1998), Robert Frank's *Luxury Fever: Weighing the Cost of Excess* (1999), Susan Matt's *Keeping Up with the Joneses: Envy in American Consumer Society, 1890–1930* (2002), and John Naish's *Enough: Breaking Free from the World of More* (2008), down to such recent publications as Oliver James' *Britain on the Couch: How Keeping Up with the Joneses Has Depressed Us Since 1950* (2010) and Geoffrey Miller's *Spent: Sex, Evolution and the Secrets of Consumerism* (2010). What is significant about these works is that even though not all these authors show themselves to be fully acquainted with Veblen's work, they nonetheless take the reality of conspicuous consumption for granted. But then one can see the same presumption that this form of behavior is real and prevalent in the steady flow of articles that make reference to it in the press. Examples taken from recent years alone include an article on buying organic vegetables (Burkeman 2009), the purchase of a hybrid car (Vaughan 2010), a discussion of the WAGs who accompany their partners to the football World Cup (Frankel 2010), and a review of the film *Sex and the City 2* (Quinn 2010). It is clear from this that none of the authors of these articles, or indeed of the books listed above, believe that conspicuous consumption is "an outmoded theory of limited usefulness in explaining consumer behavior."

It is also important to note that while in general sociologists are merely prepared to admit that Veblen's theory of conspicuous consumption might have applied to a particular society at one point in time, other academics, especially historians and archaeologists, seem to have little hesitation in treating it as universally applicable.

---

1   A contrary opinion is expressed by Stephen Edgell who claims that Veblen's theory has "proved its usefulness" (1996, 7) and cites the Lynds' studies of Middletown (1929 and 1937) as well as Warner and Lunt's study of Yankee City (1941) in support of this claim. However the data gathered in these studies is at best merely consistent with individuals acting in the manner described by Veblen. It does not contain proof that their consumption conduct was motivated by a desire to enhance their status in the eyes of a target audience.

Thus one finds it used to help explain patterns of consumer activity in such varied historical periods, places and civilizations as England in the sixteenth and seventeenth centuries (Fisher 1948; Stone 1965), as well as the eighteenth century (Vichert 1971; McKendrick, Brewer and Plumb 1982; Weatherill 1988), and during the Victorian and Edwardian period (Johnson 1988), seventeenth-century Italy (Burke 1987), Middle Bronze Age Crete (Schoep 2004) and the terminal period of the Central American Mayan civilization (Neiman 2008). This rather suggests that some academics, far from judging conspicuous consumption to be a form of conduct of very limited significance, appear to assume that it is a universal or near-universal phenomenon—a position that gains some credence from the widely acknowledged fact that Veblen obtained much of the inspiration for his theory from the potlatch, an institution distinctive of a non-literate tribal people, the Kwakiutl of the Pacific North-West coast of North America (Codere 1956; Boas [1897] 1966). But then historians and archaeologists are of course not the only academics to dispute the sociologists' judgment that Veblen's theory has limited contemporary applicability, as there is no shortage of articles on this topic in economic journals, as well as in such related disciplines as marketing and consumer behavior. Indeed the vast majority of articles that include this term in their title (as revealed by a survey of *Google Scholar*) are to be found in such publications.[2] Economists and sociologists do of course have rather different interests in the phenomenon of consumption, with the former being more concerned with the matter of who buys which products and at what price, while the latter tend to focus on questions relating to the more general behavior of consumers and especially the role that consumption occupies in everyday life—a contrast that leads the two disciplines to employ Veblen's name to refer to somewhat differing phenomena. Even so, not all economists or academics working in the general field of marketing eschew the more sociological usage and in this context it is interesting to note that in recent publications some have argued that conspicuous consumption, far from being rooted in the past, is a phenomenon that has intensified over recent decades (Schor 1998), and may well become worse in the future (Eaton and Eswaran 2009).

----

2   For examples of economic treatment of conspicuous consumption see Bagwell and Bernheim 1996, and Trigg 2001. It is important to note that the meaning economists give to this term does not correspond that closely to Veblen's original usage. What economists refer to as the "Veblen effect," in which an increase in the price of a good leads to an increase in demand is not necessarily evidence of conspicuous consumption; nor for that matter does the term "Veblen effects" in the plural, which refers to consumption in which consumers either attempt to copy others (bandwagon effect), or distinguish themselves from others (snob effect) necessarily refer to such conduct. The reason for this is that in the first case there is evidence that consumers are willing to pay a higher price for a functionally equivalent good because they are under the impression that a higher price is actually indicative of greater utility (see Erickson and Johansson 1995; Lichtenstein, Bloch, and Black 1988, and Tellis and Gaeth 1990), while in the second the behavior in question does not necessarily include any intention to use consumption as a means of impressing others.

The Meaning of Conspicuous Consumption

What then are we to make of this sharp difference of opinion? Why is it that sociologists consider the theory of conspicuous consumption to have very little relevance to an understanding of contemporary society when so many authors and commentators on modern life take its significance for granted? Should sociologists be taking a far greater interest in this phenomenon? Or is it that academics in other disciplines, together with journalists and popular commentators on contemporary society, are misguided in believing that conspicuous consumption is a significant feature of contemporary life? Clearly both positions cannot be correct, unless, that is, these differences arise from starkly contrasting interpretations, or understandings, of Veblen's theory, and more especially of the precise nature of the phenomenon to which he gave the label "conspicuous consumption." Unfortunately it is no easy matter to determine the exact meaning of this critical term, given that the man who coined it, Thorstein Veblen, was something of a unconventional thinker, as well as a bohemian, with the result that the book in which he first outlined this concept, *The Theory of the Leisure Class* (1899), is more of a polemic than a standard academic text. What this means is that a detailed analysis of this work reveals a number of significant ambiguities and difficulties of interpretation that have to be confronted in making sense of its central argument (Campbell 1995), difficulties that suggest the theory itself might never have been valid. What is more, as Mason notes, none of Veblen's claims, "was (sic) supported by original research" (1981, viii) (see also Mason 1984). This might not have mattered over-much had Veblen based his argument on data carefully compiled from other sources; however his attitude toward such scholarly conventions as referencing was cavalier in the extreme, while the prose style he adopted has been described as "vague and obfuscating" (Brooks 1979, 278). Indeed it is pertinent to observe that, from the time of its publication in 1899, Veblen's *Theory of the Leisure Class* has been criticized for presenting a theory that is both obscure and contradictory in nature. Indeed there has long been a school of thought which has suggested that Veblen's theory is little more than an elaborate polemic, and so essentially confused in content and lacking in supporting evidence that it should not be taken seriously. As Edgell observes, the earliest reviewers of Veblen's work were quick to criticize him for failing to use terms consistently and unambiguously, one going as far as to assert that "If this is Sociology, it is the kind that brings the subject into disrepute among careful and scientific thinkers" (1996, 4). Adorno has also criticized Veblen for a lack of consistency, suggesting that it arose from the fact that his entire work was "permeated by the motif of spleen," with the result that conspicuous consumption became "an *idée fixe*" (1967, 89); while C. Wright Mills has gone so far as to assert that his work should not be read as "serious sociology" but rather as "art" (Gilder 2010, 1).

Despite these obvious drawbacks it would seem that a general consensus concerning the meaning of the term "conspicuous consumption" does exist, one subscribed to by sociologists and non-sociologists alike, one that focuses on the idea that this is a pattern of conduct undertaken with the specific intention of realizing the goal of maintaining or enhancing an individual's social status through a display of wealth. Thus on *Wikipedia* it is defined as "a term used to describe the lavish spending on goods and services acquired mainly for the purpose of displaying income or wealth. In the mind of the conspicuous consumer such display serves as a means of attaining or maintaining social status" (Wikipedia 2010); or more pithily at *YourDictionary*, as "Showy extravagance in using goods and services, meant to impress others with one's wealth, status, etc." (YourDictionary 2010) Similarly *The Blackwell Dictionary of Sociology* defines conspicuous consumption as "the practice of buying and displaying material possessions in order to indicate or enhance one's prestige in the eyes of others" (Johnson 2000, 59); while the entry in the *Blackwell Encyclopedia of Sociology* refers to the fact that those engaged in conspicuous consumption "are deeply intentional in their spending decisions, making choices for the purpose of maximizing their social status" (Ritzer 2007, 683). Such an understanding of the term seems broadly consistent with Veblen's original statement, although—as will be noted—it does disguise a significant disagreement among sociologists. There are some differences between popular and sociological usages nonetheless, as one might expect. Thus popular accounts of the term sometimes fail to make it clear that conspicuous consumption requires consumers to try and impress others with their spending power or wealth, rather than any distinct personal quality such as fashion sense or aesthetic sensibility (Edgell 1996).[3] At the same time, popular accounts are also inclined to omit the fact that impressing others is not a goal in itself so much as the means to the end of maintaining or enhancing status in the eyes of a target audience. However the real difference between the popular and sociological treatment of this phenomenon is not so much in the way in which it is defined as in the ease with which it is identified, especially when coupled with the nature of the examples provided. For while sociologists tend to be shy about providing contemporary examples of conspicuous consumption and resort— if indeed they provide any examples at all—to using ones taken from the society that Veblen himself described, the general public not only seem to have no difficulty in thinking of examples, but routinely choose their illustrations from closer to the present day. But then the populist approach does characteristically involve a markedly literalist interpretation of the phenomenon such that any consumption activity that strikes the observer as conspicuous in the sense of being excessively

---

3 However Veblen, as one might expect, attempted to assimilate the two by arguing that the high regard people have for beautiful objects is merely, in reality, a high regard for costly items, and hence that a beautiful object which is not expensive is not accounted beautiful ([1925] 1970, 155). Not only is this a far from convincing claim (if it were then scenery and sunsets would not be accounted beautiful) but, in modern pluralist societies, there tends to be a variety of fashionable styles in favor among different social groups at the same time rather than the single monolithic, wealth-based, structure that Veblen assumed to be the case.

extravagant, wasteful or ostentatious, is judged to warrant the application of the term. Thus when members of the public are asked to give examples of conspicuous consumption they routinely mention either the purchase of expensive products (such as cars, jewelry or items of clothing) or consumer activities that appear particularly wasteful or ostentatious (Answerbag 2010; Everyday Sociology Blog 2008). At the same time, when asked to identify conspicuous consumers they typically cite such categories as yuppies or the *nouveaux riches* (WiseGEEK 2010). In other words among the population at large it is widely assumed that this is a form of conduct that can easily be identified because it is manifestly visible. Dick Meyer of CBS News provides a specific example of this. He comments on why "a Judith Leiber handbag or a pair of Manolo Blahnik shoes" might be important to consumers, continuing by saying that "they may not be prettier or longer lasting than less costly alternatives, but they are instantly recognizable to strangers as expensive and wasteful; conspicuous consumption" (2006).

What is interesting about examples of this kind is that in the absence of any information relating to either intention or consequence the simple fact that consumers possess particular identifiable branded goods is considered to constitute sufficient evidence to prove that they are engaged in conspicuous consumption, the justification for this assumption deriving from the judgment that these items are "expensive and wasteful." And one can in fact find examples of this kind throughout the media, while even sociologists sometimes assume that conspicuous consumption is easily identifiable through observation alone. Thus Bradley Wright, in his *Everyday Sociology Blog* gives as a "classic example of conspicuous consumption" the

> using of silver utensils and fine china for meals, especially when guests are over. Bringing out the good stuff does show that you've attained a certain level of material comfort, but it is also not very practical [...] Their (sic) main purpose, then, is one of status display. (2008)

There are some rather obvious problems with this popular method of identifying conspicuous consumption. In the first place whether particular acts of consumption are considered to be expensive, wasteful or ostentatious is clearly a subjective judgment, one that is likely to reveal as much about the values and assumptions of the observer as the consumer or consumers in question. Then there is the little matter of the taken-for-granted binary mode of thinking that tends to underpin many of these statements, as in Bradley Wright's assumption that if a product or practice is deemed not to be practical then it must be undertaken for status purposes. This tendency to think in terms of just these two possibilities derives from Veblen himself and is an especially marked feature of the approach to consumption that predominates in the discipline of economics. It is however unjustifiable as there are many reasons why individuals might engage in acts of consumption other than simply to obtain utility or to maintain or enhance status. Then there is the related matter of deducing the purpose or intention underlying an action from an observation of its presumed consequence, as Wright does in assuming that the hosts in his example brought out their best cutlery and crockery with the express intention of impressing their guests through "status display." The obvious difficulty here, given that as noted above conspicuous consumption is "deeply intentional," is that it is no easy matter to deduce intentions (and more especially motives) from observations of behavior. Or rather it is all too easy to do so, that is, to impute motives and intentions to actors solely on the basis of an observation of their actions, as indeed Dick Meyer also does in the example quoted above, as opposed, that is, to establishing the actual motives and intentions guiding their behavior. For, in order to be certain that any particular item of consumer behavior is indeed indicative of conspicuous consumption it is first necessary to demonstrate that it could not possibly have been prompted by any other intention than that of maintaining or enhancing status in the eyes of others. Unfortunately this process of excluding possible alternative explanations is rarely undertaken.

Sociological Understandings of Conspicuous Consumption

In view of these considerable difficulties it would seem that sociologists are entirely sensible in their cautious approach to the provision of examples of acts of conspicuous consumption, preferring, as we have seen, to choose ones from the society that Veblen himself described. But then in contrast to the populist understanding (and misunderstanding) of the phenomenon, the sociological approach to conspicuous consumption does typically start with Veblen's own account. Whilst this has the merit of meaning that sociologists generally have the benefit of understanding how Veblen's theory of consumer behavior is but part of a wider theory of societal evolution and the role of the leisure class, it can also be counted a mixed blessing. This is because the "vague," "obscure" and even "contradictory" character of Veblen's work noted earlier means that more than one version of his theory can be extracted from his writings. On the face of it he appears to present conspicuous consumption as a particular form of rational purposive conduct, one in which status considerations predominate. For he states that individuals "seek to excel in pecuniary standing" and so "gain the esteem and envy of [their] fellow-men" ([1925] 1970, 32), while also referring repeatedly to individuals as either struggling "to outdo one another" ([1925] 1970, 88), "desiring to excel everyone in the accumulation of goods" ([1925] 1970, 32), or engaging in "a restless straining to place a wider and ever-widening pecuniary interval between (themselves) and (the) average standard" ([1925] 1970, 31). Hence, understood as a form of conduct in which individuals seek to excel in their manifestation of pecuniary strength in order to impress others and thereby gain their envy or esteem, the theory of conspicuous consumption appears to be one that can be reduced to a series of clearly-linked propositions. The first is that consuming is an activity that is significant for what it says rather than what it does (or to be accurate what it does by means of what it says), that is, as a signal or message to others rather than as a means of providing direct satisfaction or utility to the consumer. Second, that this message is conveyed by means of the price of the product, which is taken to be indicative of the spending power or "pecuniary strength" of the consumer (and hence indirectly of wealth). Third, that the act of consuming is engaged in with the specific intention of conveying this information to a given target audience. Fourth, that the expectation is that the message will persuade the members of this audience to accord the consumer enhanced esteem or prestige. Fifth, that the consumer's principal satisfaction derives from this response. Sixth, that consumers are engaged in an on-going program of actions of this kind as a consequence of comparing their own standing in a prestige or status ranking with those of their peers, a comparison that inevitably leads to dissatisfaction, and consequently new acts of consumption aimed at maintaining or enhancing their position in this hierarchy.

Now it is necessary to recognize that the third of these assertions is especially controversial within sociology, given that some commentators have claimed that the enhancement of the consumer's social status as a consequence of sending messages about pecuniary strength is an accidental or unintended consequence of the act of consumption (Ramsted 1998; Trigg 2001). Robert K. Merton most famously expresses this view in his discussion of the manifest and latent functions of action where he chooses Veblen's concept of conspicuous consumption as one of the principal examples that serve to illustrate the difference between the two. For, having stated that manifest functions are "those objective consequences contributing to the adjustment or adaptation of the system which are intended and recognized by participants in the system," while latent functions are consequences "which are neither intended nor recognized" (1957, 51), he then specifically identifies conspicuous consumption as an instance of the latter. In other words enhancing one's status in the eyes of others as a consequence of displaying pecuniary strength through one's extravagant purchases is an outcome that Merton declares to be neither intended nor recognized by the consumer. Other commentators have endorsed this position, with Arthur K. Davis for one referring to Veblen's treatise in *The Theory of the Leisure Class* as "essentially an analysis of the latent functions of consumption" (1944, 306), while others have apparently concurred with this judgment in expressing the view that conspicuous consumption should be seen as a non-deliberative or at least an unconscious act. Thus Trigg declares that Veblen's theory was one in which conspicuous consumption "was not postulated to be a conscious act" (2001, 113). Those who espouse this interpretation can point to the fact that Veblen does imply that consumers may not be aware of the extent to which their activity is driven by the need to display wealth (in order to gain or protect status) because such conduct has in effect become "habitual" (1970, 100) or a matter of unthinking routine (1970, 115). In fact what Veblen actually suggests has become a matter of habit is the acceptance of the scheme of life in vogue in the next higher stratum as an embodiment of the ideal of decency, with the result that individuals "bend their efforts to live up to that ideal" (1970, 168). This, as Veblen himself admits, implies that the law of conspicuous consumption guides behavior "chiefly at the second remove, by shaping the canons of taste and decency" (1970, 168). Such an interpretation would of course fit with Merton's claim that conspicuous consumption is a "latent," which is to say "unrecognized and unintended" function of the consumer's conduct, although it is pertinent to note that Veblen's version of the relevant manifest function (to live up to an ideal of decency) is somewhat different from Merton's (to obtain utility from the products purchased). What this brief summary reveals is that "conspicuous consumption" is something of a contested term within sociology, with the main bone of contention being whether conduct that serves to maintain or enhance status through pecuniary display should be seen as a conscious and deliberate act, as routine, non-deliberated habit, as conduct that occurs under the guise of striving to realize a specified ideal of decency, or as the accidental byproduct of the straightforward purchase of goods for the utility they provide. Significantly all parties to this dispute have no difficulty finding quotes from Veblen to support their interpretation of his theory.

Clarifying the Sociological Meaning of Conspicuous Consumption

The crucial point that would appear to be at issue in this debate is the long-standing problem in sociological theory of the status of functionalist explanations, specifically under what circumstances, if any, a consequence can serve as a cause (Hempel 1965; Nagel 1979). What this means in this case is that if conspicuous consumption is to be employed as a name for a theory of consumption, rather than merely a term for a distinctive outcome of consumer behavior, then it has to offer an explanation of why consumers do what they do, and hence make reference to their intentions, if not also their motives. Simply to emphasize that certain forms of consumption appear to serve the function of maintaining or enhancing social status does not count as a theory in this sense unless the analyst can show some plausible feedback mechanism by which such consequences can also act as a cause of the behavior in question. In this case the only possible means would seem to be via a conscious awareness on the part of the consumer of the status-modifying effect of the action, an awareness that leads directly to the repetition of similar acts that are undertaken with this specific aim in mind. To suggest that such a feedback loop can work unconsciously, that is, without a conscious intention being present in the mind of the actor, would seem implausible in a society in which there is a widespread awareness of the status-signifying nature of consumption; implausible because either it would require consumers to be unaware of the satisfaction they gained from the audience's response in awarding them enhanced esteem or prestige, or of the connection between this reaction and the act of consumption itself, both of which would seem unrealistic.[4] For "keeping up" with someone, as in the phrase

---

4   It is also difficult to reconcile the suggestion that consumers engage in conspicuous consumption unconsciously with the often repeated assertion that this is an activity that

"keeping up with the Joneses," is clearly a deliberate act; it requires both an assessment of the conduct of another person (or persons) followed by the selection of an appropriate response. It is thus highly unlikely to be something performed by accident, or as a byproduct of an action undertaken for other reasons. There would also seem to be little justification for asserting that conspicuous consumption is an unconscious act because it operates "at one remove," via conduct aimed at embodying a given "ideal of decency." For if the term "conspicuous consumption" is to be used to refer to conduct in which actors consciously seek to maintain or enhance their status then for the sake of logical consistency the same term should not be used to refer to conduct in which they believe themselves to be engaged in doing something quite different, and "living up to an ideal" is a different action from "endeavoring to maintain or enhance one's status." Hence, even if it could be shown that the one form of action is somehow connected to the other, it would still be necessary to use different names to distinguish the two forms of conduct.

As far as the issue of habit is concerned (see Dwyer 2009) it is of course quite possible that an act undertaken initially in order to maintain or enhance status may continue to be performed even though it has achieved its purpose, either out of simple inertia, or because it has now come to fulfil some other function. It is also the case that engaging in conspicuous consumption, in the sense of being highly competitive in status matters, could itself become a habit. What is exceedingly unlikely is that individual acts of conspicuous consumption could be performed habitually in the sense of being undertaken without premeditation, or that such acts could be repeated habitually and still continue to warrant the label of conspicuous consumption. The reason for this is that it is the purchase and subsequent initial display of a product to a target audience which, taken as a whole, constitutes a single act of conspicuous consumption. Obviously the purchase alone would not count as such an act unless the product is subsequently displayed, but it is also the case that displaying an old and previously seen purchase could also not count as such an act; only new purchases when displayed for the first time to the target audience would warrant this label. Subsequent displays cannot really be referred to as acts of conspicuous consumption if the initial display achieved its intended effect, as they cannot be expected to cause the audience to increase their estimation of the consumer's purchasing power any further.[5] Consequently these acts will not be marked by the presence in the mind of the consumer of an intention to achieve a change in status. Only the decision to embark on a new purchase, of what is a more expensive item, could constitute a new act of conspicuous consumption. In this respect consuming conspicuously involves undertaking actions that, like the consumption of novelty (Campbell 1987), are—if successful—necessarily self-extinguishing. It is the failure to appreciate that the act of conspicuous

---

consumers will not, or are reluctant to, admit to doing, while the idea that consumers act intentionally but unconsciously would seem to take us into Freudian territory.

5   Where repetitions of the act might serve to indicate greater purchasing power of course is where wealth is spent on services rather than products.

consumption consists of the purchase and initial display of a new product and not any subsequent displays that has led to widespread confusion between what are genuine acts of this kind and those that merely serve to indicate rather than change a consumer's status; a confusion that is exacerbated by the fact that the genuine acts necessarily decay into the latter once the product or service has been purchased and displayed, that is to say, once its purpose has been fulfilled.

This tendency to apply the term "conspicuous consumption" to conduct that lacks conscious purposeful intent on the grounds that it serves to indicate something to those who witness it is the principal reason why some commentators have made the mistake of thinking of this phenomenon as a latent function of consumption. Yet conspicuous consumption is not a mere act of indication, or the simple unconscious sending of a message; it is an act that is intended to achieve change in status or prestige by means of the message, which cannot therefore be regarded as an end in itself. It is also important to recognize that the message is aimed at those who are in a position to affect the consumer's standing in a ranking system, and not simply at anyone who may be in a position to observe it. Correspondingly the fact that individuals can "read" a person's consumption behavior, that is, deduce something about their social position from observing it, or at least believe that they can, has no necessary connection with conspicuous consumption.

The Evidence for Conspicuous Consumption: The Problem of Personal Testimony

Having decided that the crucial defining feature of conspicuous consumption is the presence of a conscious intention to maintain or enhance status by impressing one's target audience with one's extravagance, it is now necessary to return to the controversial issue of determining whether this phenomenon is or is not widespread in contemporary society, that is to say, to the difficult question of evidence. Now in one respect the obvious tactic here—thinking back to the discussion of the "I Am Rich" app mentioned in the introduction—would be to ask consumers about their intentions. That this strategy has rarely been adopted would seem to be because it is widely believed that, as Mason puts it, "Conspicuous consumption is a form of economic behavior to which individuals will not admit" (1981, x). He then elaborates by stating that, "the principal reason why specific studies into conspicuous consumption have been particularly difficult to design and carry out has been the entirely rational and understandable reluctance of consumers to admit that any purchases are motivated by personal status considerations" (1981, 125). Now it is unclear where the evidence is to be found that supports this assertion; one that is often made in connection with the problem of establishing evidence of conspicuous consumption. For not only do those who make it usually cite no sources, but it is unclear what kind of evidence could be produced that would justify such a claim. Clearly the fact that consumers say that they are not engaged in this form of conduct wouldn't in itself warrant such a conclusion. Indeed under normal circumstances the fact that respondents deny engaging in a particular form of conduct would be accepted at face value unless there was substantial and reliable independently-sourced evidence to suggest the contrary. But it is unclear where the counter-evidence is to be found which has to be set against the personal testimony of consumers; evidence considered so powerful that it warrants declaring their denials to be false. And would such evidence support the claim that consumers won't admit to such behavior, or simply that they are reluctant to do so? There is a significant difference between these two positions, although Mason does not seem to be aware of it. For in the latter case the consumers' eventual confession supplies the necessary proof to show that this is indeed what they are doing while in the former some other source of evidence is required. Of course if Merton is right in judging this form of behavior to be a latent function of consumption, no consumer would be in a position to admit to engaging in it anyway, given that it is something they "neither intend nor recognize," in which case Mason's claim would be untrue. But then it is also necessary to wonder why there should be reluctance to admit engaging in this form of behavior. Mason suggests that this is entirely understandable claiming that "by acknowledging that a particular purchase decision is undertaken primarily for status or other 'social' purposes the conspicuous consumer loses any advantage such consumption might otherwise afford him [sic]" (ibid.). Yet this argument would only seem to apply if this "acknowledgment" is made to those people who constitute the target audience, since it is their response—in terms of the award of esteem—that might be put in jeopardy by such an admission (this, one might suggest, could explain the failure of the "I Am Rich" app). However, it is hard to see how admitting that this was the underlying reason for engaging in this particular form of conduct to a third party such as a market researcher or sociologist should mean that the consumer would lose "any advantage such consumption might otherwise afford him [sic]." It is also important to distinguish between intention and consequence, for while it is possible to see why consumers might be reluctant to admit that it was their intention to engage in conspicuous consumption, it is much less easy to understand why there should be any such reluctance to admit that they gained satisfaction from the target audience's response to it. But then it is also difficult to understand why there should be any reluctance to admit to engaging in defensive conspicuous consumption, that is to say, consumption aimed at maintaining, as opposed to enhancing, one's social standing in a given status group or community. After all, this involves little more than being seen to make use of products or services that are widely regarded as appropriate to that position in an overall ranking system which the consumer currently occupies. Finally what also makes the suggestion that consumers might be coaxed into admitting engaging in this activity plausible is the fact—noted earlier—that there is a widespread acceptance in contemporary society of its ubiquitous nature. This means that those who deny engaging in it look like falling victim to what could be called the "everyone but me" syndrome, something that one would have imagined could hardly have escaped their notice.

A more sophisticated take on the issue of consumers' reluctance to admit to others that they are engaged in conspicuous consumption would be that it is principally a byproduct of a more basic reluctance to admit to themselves that this is what they are doing. In other words they understand that a desire to impress others with their wealth in order to gain their esteem is at least part of the motivation for undertaking the conduct in question, but fear that allowing themselves to be too aware of this intention might interfere with the successful accomplishment of the action. This concern is reasonable enough, given that one is far more likely to be successful in impressing others if impressing others is not the focus of one's attention (Shaw 1988). However, once again this would only really seem to be a critical consideration either prior to or during the consumption process. Once completed—with whatever result—there would no longer seem to be the same necessity to engage in such self-distraction let alone self-deception. Hence, here too there would seem to be scope for a researcher to elicit a frank and honest response from the consumer. However despite the absence of any convincing evidence to show that consumers are unwilling to admit to engaging in conspicuous consumption, in addition to the apparent existence of opportunities for obtaining evidence of such behavior in the form of actor self-admissions, it does seem to be a taken-for-granted assumption that it is difficult to get actors to confess to engaging in this form of conduct, which is presumably why the tactic of asking them is rarely employed. What this is then popularly taken to mean is that, as Juliet B. Schor puts it, "Evidence of status seeking is largely behavioral" (2007, 685).

Evidence for Conspicuous Consumption: The Problem of Observable Behavior

Essentially the problem with any attempt to establish the existence of conspicuous consumption on the basis of observation alone is that it requires the investigator to prove that the conduct in question could not have been prompted by anything other than an intention to maintain or enhance status in the eyes of a target audience, a process that requires the successive elimination of all other explanations for the action in question. Unfortunately there are more alternatives than the one—that of the need for the intrinsic satisfactions offered by the material characteristics of the product—that is commonly mentioned. For, in addition to demonstrating that the action in question is not prompted by such a need, it is also necessary to show that it is not the symbolic significance that attracts the consumer, even when not employed as a message intended for others to read. Then there is the much neglected issue of action that is undertaken with no other intent than that of meeting what are considered to be the requirements or obligations of the role the consumer is currently occupying, a consideration that might be encompassed by the term convention. This is relevant to those suggestions, like that of Chao and Schor for example (1996), which claim that conspicuous consumption can be identified simply by noting the different ways that consumers behave when in private as opposed to in public. Yet one does not have to invoke conspicuous consumption in order to account for the fact that contrasting behaviors—including differential patterns of expenditure—occur when actors are subject to the scrutiny of others as opposed to when they are alone, for it is a truism of social life that different standards of conduct apply in different contexts. Indeed the power of convention is quite sufficient in itself to account for many of those examples repeatedly cited as illustrating conspicuous consumption, such as the use of best cutlery and crockery when entertaining, the over-catering for parties, or the over-spending on special events such as betrothals, wedding receptions or bar mitzvahs (Spero 1988). Indeed convention, or at least the expectations typically associated with certain occupations or social positions, may be quite sufficient in itself to explain why some individuals engage in lavish or ostentatious consumption. It is, for example, how people expect royalty to behave, as it is too for film stars, rock and pop idols and highly paid professional sportsmen and women, where lavish expenditure (on houses, cars, and clothes for example) is tantamount to being part of the role definition. Consequently individuals who occupy these roles could feel obliged to behave in this manner even if they have no particular interest in employing expenditure as a means of maintaining or enhancing their status. The question that now naturally arises, in view of the obvious difficulties confronting anyone seeking to determine the existence of conspicuous consumption by means of observation alone, is why it is popularly believed to be widespread throughout contemporary society.

Signaling One's Intentions?

Among the several reasons for this belief is the fact that examples of conspicuous consumption are routinely treated as if they constituted evidence of conspicuous consumption, that is to say, while it is easy enough to imagine the kind of behavior individuals might engage in if they decided to conspicuously consume it does not follow that people who do behave in this manner are so engaged. For example, if individuals wanted to impress others with their wealth, then buying a top of the range Ferrari sports car and driving around in it might be one way of doing it. On the other hand buying a top of the range Ferrari and driving around in it does not prove that you are seeking to impress others. One of the reasons people are inclined take it for granted that, in such instances as this, it is possible to deduce actors' intentions simply from observing their behavior, is because they know that actors are unlikely to be unaware of the impact of their actions on those who witness them. Hence, in this instance, observers assume that the Ferrari owners are unlikely to be unaware of the effect their cars are having on passers-by as well as other road users, and since they are aware of this it is assumed that it is intended. However, just because actors are aware of the consequences of their actions it does not imply that they intend them.[6] The simple truth is that many actions

---

6   That recognition and intention are very different and that Merton made a mistake in combining them in his concept of the latent function is a point made by Helm (1971).

have consequences actors are aware of, do not desire, and yet cannot avoid. The comments of the international tennis player Andrew Murray illustrate this point in relation to just this very Ferrari-driving example. For although he confesses to loving his Ferrari, "it's great" he says, "an unbelievable car … I really, really enjoy it," he then goes on to say,

> I just don't like getting out of it [in public]. I guess you would say that it's a poser's car and I don't like drawing attention to myself. I love driving the car, I just don't like what goes with it. So I don't really drive it … as much as I would like to. (Mitchell 2010)[7]

What Murray is complaining about here is the widespread assumption that consumers intend the effect that their consuming has on those that witness it, an assumption that is a specific instance of the more general error (made by sociologists as much as the general public) of assuming that the actions of individuals can routinely be treated as if they were signals, or messages of some sort, ones intended to be read by others (Campbell 1997).

But then there is a similar widespread assumption that, in so far as actions could justifiably be treated as if they were signals, the messages they contain necessarily relate to issues of status. For although it is not unreasonable to assume that a person's mode of consumption may serve to indicate something about his or her identity, this does not necessarily mean that what is most manifest to an observer is his or her social position let alone their social status. The products that individuals choose to purchase and use may be better suited to indicate their gender, age, ethnicity, sexual orientation or religious affiliation than their position in any putative system of social ranking. Indeed "the message" that the product is perceived to send may be more to do with character or personality than with either social identity or status. It may also be more to do with fashion and here it is important to stress that expenditure on fashionable items has no direct relationship with conspicuous consumption (contrary to the claim Dick Meyer makes in the example given above), a confusion that also frequently conflates imitation with emulation. The purchasing and displaying of an object because one wishes to be thought fashionable is not the same as purchasing and displaying an object because one wishes to impress other people with one's wealth; indeed these would be different acts even in a society in which the degree of fashionability of a product coincided perfectly with its price, as the specific intention in each case would still differ.

---

7   This could be described as the connoisseur's dilemma: the problem confronting those people who love and appreciate expensive, luxurious objects for their own sake yet do not want to be thought of as owning and using them in order to flaunt their wealth. Unfortunately for them, many of these products cannot be consumed inconspicuously, hence the dilemma.

But then, even when there is good reason to treat an act of consumption as principally indicative of an individual's social standing, there is a common failure to distinguish between the different meanings of the term "social status" (Bullock et al. 1977). One of these refers to a specific position within a given social group or collectivity. It is in this sense that one refers to the "status" of father when discussing the institution of the family, or "citizen" in relation to the state. The key point about this meaning of the term is that it is purely descriptive and is in no way evaluative. The other usage refers to the different social evaluations, in terms of prestige or esteem, of that position within a given social system. It is because of this dual meaning that one can talk sensibly of the status of a status, as in the observation that the status (of the status) of father within the social group of the nuclear family has declined during the course of the twentieth century. The problem here is that because observers find it relatively easy to make assessments of the first kind—that is to say, judgments concerning an individual's approximate status in its meaning as a social position—they also assume that they can make judgments of the second kind, to wit, assessments of an individual's social standing in a ranking system. Indeed they frequently conflate the two assessments. However the second requires knowledge of the consumer's social circle, specifically the identity of those people who constitute the consumer's comparative reference group.

This latter mistake often stems from the tendency to confuse conspicuous consumption with upward social mobility, whereas in reality these are two rather different processes depending on whether or not the reference group that consumers take as the target audience for the display of wealth is also their membership group. If it is the case, then effectively the consumer's aim is to enhance prestige, which can be defined as the personal status of the individual within the group. If on the other hand the reference group is not equivalent to the consumer's current membership group but is rather a whole section or rank of society (effectively a social class in modern industrial societies) which the consumer hopes to join, then the aim is to be upwardly socially mobile—a process that involves the enhancement of social position rather than personal prestige. However it is also a process that would appear to be only tangentially connected with conspicuous consumption, and only then in a plutocracy. The reason for this is that individuals who seek to be upwardly socially mobile must necessarily reject the values and norms of their peers as they engage in anticipatory socialization, a process which involves taking on the values and norms of the social group they aspire to join (see Merton 1964, 262ff.). It follows from this that they can no longer be in status competition with those whom they had formerly been accustomed to compare themselves. At the same time they cannot yet be said to be enhancing their status in the eyes of those in the group they hope to join, as these people are probably not even aware of their existence. Effectively what such ambitious social climbers are engaged in doing is attempting to adopt a new lifestyle and success constitutes being seen to do so to the extent necessary to be accepted into the target group, which is essentially a process of acknowledgement, or acceptance as "one of us." A higher level of wealth may be necessary in order to gain entry into the target class although an ostentatious display of such wealth may not be sufficient in itself to qualify for entry and may indeed even act as a barrier to acceptance. It is true that, as a result of this process, those who have succeeded will be identified by strangers as now belonging to a different social class but it is questionable whether this recognition (which crucially will have little or no effect on their status) is a more important aim than that of being acknowledged as equals by members of the target class.

Is the Theory of Conspicuous Consumption Plausible?

The above discussion leads to two clear conclusions. The first is that, in the absence of confessional data from consumers themselves, it is exceptionally difficult to prove that conspicuous consumption is a real and widespread phenomenon. The second is that the popular view that it is indeed both of these is largely based on confused thinking and dubious assumptions. This is not so say, however, that the sociologists' judgment of conspicuous consumption as "an outmoded theory of limited usefulness in explaining consumer behavior" is therefore correct. For such a conclusion would only be warranted if research had been undertaken which actually showed that consumers did not behave in the manner predicted by the theory, something that has not only yet to be attempted, but would appear to be just as difficult as demonstrating that they do. One is therefore forced to conclude that there is insufficient evidence to settle the issue either way. If therefore a judgment of some sort is to be made it can only be on the basis of an attempt to estimate the plausibility of the assumptions upon which the thesis is based.

The central premise upon which Veblen's theory rests is not only that consumers are preoccupied with their status in a ranking system based on wealth, but that as a consequence of continually comparing themselves with their peers, are sufficiently dissatisfied with their position in this system to engage in a continuing program of acts of consumption in an effort to enhance it (or at the least prevent its decline). It follows that the key questions to be considered are: (a) Is it likely that consumers are preoccupied with status? (b) Are they continually engaged in comparing themselves with their peers in this respect? (c) If so, do they feel dissatisfied as a result (d) Do they, as a consequence, repeatedly act to enhance their status? When it comes to looking for evidence that people in contemporary society are preoccupied with their social status there is no shortage of commentators who are prepared to assert this as if it were indeed a well-established fact. Unfortunately these tend to be the very same commentators who confidently assert that conspicuous consumption is a real and widespread phenomenon. Indeed, the argument commonly encountered is that the principal evidence that people in modern societies experience a good deal of status anxiety is to be found in the very fact that they engage in conspicuous consumption (de Botton 2004; James 2007, 2010; Frank 1999; Wilkinson and Pickett 2010), and even that this kind of consuming actually helps to create such anxiety. Clearly, one can hardly turn to these authors for supporting evidence that favors Veblen's theory.

When it comes to assessing the plausibility of the claim that individuals are continually comparing themselves (mainly unfavorably) with their peers, a comparison that drives them to strive to enhance their status, one encounters the difficulty represented by the tendency to collapse the crucial distinction between normative and comparative reference groups, that is to say, between those people whom individuals regard as their equals and those whose values and attitudes they aspire to adopt. What can be said with some confidence is that in a society in which fewer and fewer people actually know who their neighbors are (Smithers 2010), it seems increasingly unlikely that "the Joneses" will feature at all prominently in either category. Indeed the evidence suggests that celebrities are more likely than either neighbors or peers to be taken as comparators (Schor 1998). But then, such well-known figures are typically not used, as peers might be, for the purpose of comparison but rather as models to be imitated, imitated in the full knowledge that one is unlikely actually to equal the ideal person who is being copied. In that respect, such comparisons are unlikely to lead to any sense of relative deprivation, even if the individuals concerned do redouble their efforts to live up to the ideal. However, such conduct would seem to be more consistent with the claim that restless consumption stems from the desire of individuals to embody a given ideal lifestyle rather than any desire to outdo, in status terms, those with whom, as Veblen puts it, they are in the habit of comparing themselves. But then, a comparative indifference toward the judgment of one's peers in comparison with one's own self-assessment of the extent to which one's pattern of consumption embodies an ideal is what one would expect to be the case in a media-dominated and increasingly individualized society. Yet one of the strangest features of Veblen's theory has always been the assumption that people obtain greater satisfaction from the esteem accorded to them by others as a consequence of being considered wealthy than they might obtain simply from being wealthy. In other words, in Veblen's opinion, being held in high esteem by others is, from the perspective of the individual, the highest good, in comparison with which all other desirable goods, including wealth itself, is of lesser significance. It is difficult to believe that most modern consumers would share this opinion.

Conclusion

The story of the "I Am Rich" app with which I began this chapter suggests that some of the commercial advisors at Apple, unlike sociologists of consumption, actually shared the popular opinion that conspicuous consumption is a significant and widespread feature of modern societies, and believing this, sought to cash in on it. That this initiative failed so spectacularly could be interpreted as suggesting that the sociologists of consumption are right in their judgment and that public opinion is wrong. But then this leaves several unanswered questions. One, quite obviously, relates to the issue of what is it that accounts for the restless and apparently endless striving to acquire ever-more goods that lies at the heart of modern consumerism if it is not anxiety arising from concerns over status. But then there is also the question of the contrast between popular opinion and sociological judgment. Surely this suggests that not only should sociologists take more interest in the phenomenon of conspicuous consumption, but they should also engage with public opinion on this topic, setting out the reasons for their skepticism concerning its significance. Of course any such exercise would be more convincing if the research needed to support this position had actually been undertaken. However the truth is that, at present, almost none of the key questions have even been posed, let alone answered. For example it is not known who does engage in conspicuous consumption, under what circumstances, or with what degree of success. Is it just the exceptionally wealthy, or possibly just the *nouveaux riches*, as some commentators on Veblen seem to imply, or is this a form of behavior that anyone can engage in? Do those who consume in this way do so regularly or merely occasionally, and when they do so is it the defensive or the aggressive form that they attempt? Are there perhaps particular products that typically feature in this form of consumption, or indeed particular occasions or events when individuals are more likely to engage in it? And does conspicuous consumption exist in its pure form, which is to say as an activity undertaken solely for status purposes quite un-mixed with any utilitarian concerns. Finally, and perhaps most crucially, is this form of behavior becoming more or less prevalent? Here current opinion would seem to be sharply divided. Thus while some think that conspicuous consumption will diminish in significance as "inconspicuous consumption" becomes more prevalent (Sullivan and Gershuny 2004; Shove and Warde 2002), others believe that, as productivity increases "the search for status," will come to dominate the economy (Eaton and Eswaran 2009). It is hard to imagine a more important question in need of a definitive answer if we really are to understand the role of consumption in a humane and therefore sustainable society.

References

Adorno, T.W. [1941] 1967. *Prisms*. London: Neville Spearman.

Answerbag. 2010. Accessed June 7. http://www.answerbag.com/q_view/17210194 07/06/2010.

Bagwell, L.S. and B.D. Bernheim. 1996. "Veblen Effects in a Theory of Conspicuous Consumption." *The American Economic Review* 86, 3: 349–54.

Boas, F. [1897] 1966. *Kwakiutl Ethnography*. Chicago: University of Chicago Press.

de Botton, A. 2004. *Status Anxiety*. London: Hamish Hamilton.

Brooks, J. 1979. *Showing Off in America: From Conspicuous Consumption to Parody Display*. Boston, MA: Little Brown.

Bullock, A., O. Stallybrass and S. Trombley. 1977. Sv. "status" in *The Fontana Dictionary of Modern Thought*. London: Fontana Press.

Burke, P. 1987. "Conspicuous Consumption in Seventeenth-century Italy." In *The Historical Anthropology of Early Modern Italy: Essays on Perception and Communication*, edited by P. Burke, 132–49. Cambridge: Cambridge University Press.

Burkeman, O. 2009. "This Column Will Change Your Life: Conspicuous Consumption." In *The Guardian*, August 22. Accessed September 30, 2014.http://www.theguardian.com/lifeandstyle/2009/aug/22/change-your-life-conspicuous-consumption.

Campbell, C. 1987. *The Romantic Ethic and the Spirit of Modern Consumerism.* Oxford: Basil Blackwell.

Campbell, C. 1995. "Conspicuous Confusion? A Critique of Veblen's Theory of Conspicuous Consumption." *Sociological Theory* 13: 137–47.

Campbell, C. 1997. "When the Meaning is Not a Message: A Critique of the Consumption as Communication Thesis." In *Buy this Book: Studies in Advertising and Consumption*, edited by M. Nava et al., 340–51. London: Routledge.

Chao, A. and J.B. Schor. 1996. "Empirical Tests of Status Consumption: Evidence from Women's Cosmetics." *Journal of Economic Psychology* 19: 107–31.

Codere, H. 1956. "The Amiable Side of Kwakuitl Life: The Potlatch and the Play Potlatch." *American Anthropologist* 28: 334–51.

Davis, A.K. 1944. "Veblen on the Decline of the Protestant Ethic." *Social Forces* 44: 282–6.

Douglas, M. and B. Isherwood. 1978. *The World of Goods.* Harmondsworth, Middlesex: Penguin Books.

Dwyer, Rachel E. 2009. "Making a Habit of It: Positional Consumption, Conventional Action and the Standard of Living." *Journal of Consumer Culture* 9: 328–47.

Eaton, B.C. and M. Eswaran. 2009. "Well-Being and Affluence in the Presence of a Veblen Good." *Economic Journal* 119, 539: 1088–104.

Edgell, S. 1996. "A Centennial Reassessment of Veblen's Theory of Conspicuous Consumption." Delivered to the International Thorstein Veblen Association, Carleton College (Northfield Minnesota, USA), 30 May–1 June 1996.[8]

Erickson, G.M. and K. Johansson. 1985. "The Role of Price in Multi-Attribute Product Evaluations." *Journal of Consumer Research* 12: 195–9.

Fisher, F.J. 1948. "The Development of London as a Centre of Conspicuous Consumption in the Sixteenth and Seventeenth Centuries." *Transactions of the Royal Historical Society* Fourth Series 30: 37–50.

Fox News. 2008. "'I Am Rich' iPhone App Removed After 8 Bought it." Accessed April 29, 2014. http://www.foxnews.com/story/0,2933,399461,00.html.

Frank, R.H. 1999. *Luxury Fever: Weighing the Cost of Excess*. Princeton: Princeton University Press.

---

8   The writer wishes to point out that, while the source cited is a confidential "draft" version of Edgell's work, he nonetheless assumes that it is appropriate to quote herein given that it is "published" on the website.

Frankel, S. 2010. "Ready to Wear: Perhaps the WAGS Will Have to Sharpen Up Their Acts." In *The Independent*, May 3. Accessed September 30, 2014. http://www.independent.co.uk/life-style/fashion/frankel/ready-to-wear-perhaps-the-wags-will-have-to-sharpen-up-their-acts-1960708.html.

Galbraith, J.K. [1958] 1962. *The Affluent Society*. Harmondsworth: Penguin.

Giddens, A. and J.H. Turner. 1973. *Social Theory Today*. Cambridge: Polity Press.

Gilder, E. 2008. Book Review, Thorstein Veblen. The Theory of the Leisure Class, with an introduction by C. Wright Mills. New Brunswick NJ, USA and London UK: Transaction Publishers, 1992 [1899]. *American, British and Canadian Studies* (A Volume Edited by the Anglophone Society of Romania) Volume 11 (2008). Accessed May 2014. http://abcjournal.ulbsibiu.ro/volume_11_2008.html.

Helm, P. 1971. "Manifest and Latent Functions." *Philosophical Quarterly* 21: 51–60.

Hempel, C. 1965. *Aspects of Scientific Explanation*. New York: Free Press.

James, O. 2007. *Affluenza*. London: Vermilion.

James, O. 2010. *Britain on the Couch: How Keeping Up with the Joneses Has Depressed Us Since 1950*. London: Vermilion.

Johnson, A.G. 2000. *The Blackwell Dictionary of Sociology: A User's Guide to Sociological Language*. Malden, Mass: Wiley-Blackwell.

Johnson, P. 1988. "Conspicuous Consumption and Working-Class Culture in Late-Victorian and Edwardian Britain." *Transactions of the Royal Historical Society* 38: 27–42.

Lichtenstein, D.R., P.H. Bloch and W.C. Black. 1988. "Correlates of Price Acceptability." *Journal of Consumer Research* 15: 243–52.

Lynd, R.S. and H.M. Lynd. 1929. *Middletown*. New York: Harcourt, Brace and Company.

Lynd, R.S. and H.M. Lynd. 1937. *Middletown in Transition: A Study in Cultural Conflicts*. New York: Harcourt, Brace and Company.

Mason, R.S. 1981. *Conspicuous Consumption: A Study in Exceptional Consumer Behavior*. London: Gower.

Mason, R.S. 1984. "Conspicuous Consumption: A Literature Review." *European Journal of Marketing* 18, 3: 26–39.

Matt, S.J. 2002. *Keeping Up with the Joneses: Envy in American Consumer Society, 1890–1930*. Philadelphia: University of Pennsylvania Press.

McCracken, G. 1988. *Culture and Consumption: New Approaches to the Symbolic Character of Consumer Goods and Activities*. Bloomington, Ill.: Indiana University Press.

McKendrick, N., J. Brewer, and J.H. Plumb. 1982. *The Birth of a Consumer Society: The Commercialization of Eighteenth-Century England*. London: Europa Publications.

Merton, R.K. 1964 [1949]. *Social Theory and Social Structure*. New York: Free Press.

Meyer, D. 2006. "Aggressive Ostentation." Accessed April 29, 2014. http://www.cbsnews.com/news/aggressive-ostentation/

Miller, G. 2010. *Spent: Sex, Evolution and the Secrets of Consumerism.* Harmondsworth, Middlesex: Penguin Books.

Mills, C.W. 1970. "Introduction." In *The Theory of the Leisure Class*, by T. Veblen. London: Unwin Books.

Mitchell, K. 2010. "Murray Seeks Top Gear for his Two-week Title Race." *The Guardian* June 21.

Nagel, E. 1979. *The Structure of Science.* Indianapolis: Hackett.

Naish, J. 2008. *Enough: Breaking Free from the World of More.* London: Hodder and Stoughton.

Neiman, F.D. 2008. "Conspicuous Consumption as Wasteful Advertising: a Darwinian Perspective on Spatial Patterns in Classic Maya Terminal Monument Dates." *Archeological Papers of the American Anthropological Association* 7, 1: 267–90.

Packard, V. [1959] 1965. *The Status Seekers: An Exploration of Class Behavior in America.* Harmondsworth, Middlesex: Penguin.

Quinn, A. 2010. "Sex And The City 2." *The Independent*, May 28. Accessed September 30, 2014. http://www.independent.co.uk/arts-entertainment/films/reviews/sex-and-the-city-2-15-1984792.html.

Ramsted, Y. 1998. "Veblen's Propensity for Emulation: Is It Passe?" In *Thorstein Veblen in the Twentieth-First Century*, edited by D. Brown, 3–27. Aldershot: Edward Elgar.

Riesman, D. 1954. *Individualism Reconsidered.* Glencoe, IL.: Free Press.

Ritzer, G. 2007. *The Blackwell Encyclopedia of Sociology.* Oxford: Blackwell.

Schoep, I. 2004. "Assessing the Role of Architecture in Conspicuous Consumption in the Middle Minoan I-II periods." *Oxford Journal of Archaeology* 23, 3: 243–69.

Schor, J.B. 1998. *The Overspent American: Why We Want What We Don't Need.* New York: HarperCollins.

Schor, J.B. 2007. "Conspicuous Consumption." In *The Blackwell Encyclopedia of Sociology*, edited by George Ritzer, 681–6. Oxford: Blackwell.

Shaw, M.C. 1988. *The Paradox of Intention: Reaching the Goal by Giving UP the Intention of Reaching It.* New York: An American Academy of Religion Book.

Shove, E. and Warde, A. 2002. "Inconspicuous Consumption: The Sociology of Consumption, Lifestyles, and the Environment." In *Sociological Theory and the Environment*, edited by R.E. Dunlay, 230–50. Lanham MD: Rowan and Littlefield.

Smithers, R. 2010. "Neighbours, No One Really 'Knows' their Neighbours—Survey." *The Guardian*, August 16. Accessed September 30, 2014. http://www.theguardian.com/society/2010/aug/16/neighbours-community-survey-legal-general.

Spero, A. 1988. "Conspicuous Consumption at Jewish Functions." *Judaism* 37: 103–10.

Stone, L. 1965. *The Crisis of the Aristocracy 1558–1641.* Oxford: The Clarendon Press.

Sullivan O. and J. Gershuny. 2004. "Inconspicuous Consumption: Work-rich, Time-poor in the Liberal Market Economy." *Journal of Consumer Culture* 4, 1: 79–100.

Tellis, G.J. and G.J. Gaeth. 1990. "Best Value, Price-Seeking, and Price Aversion: The Impact of Information and Learning on Consumer Choices." *Journal of Marketing* 54: 34–45.

Trigg, A.B. 2001. "Veblen, Bourdieu, and Conspicuous Consumption." *Journal of Economic Issues* 35, 1: 99–115.

Urry, J. 1990. "The Consumption of Tourism." *Sociology* 24: 23–35.

Vaughan, A. 2010. "Shoppers Choose Green Products to Improve Social Status, Says Study." In *The Guardian*, March 29. Accessed September 30, 2014. http://www.theguardian.com/environment/2010/mar/29/green-products-social-status.

Veblen, T. [1925] 1970. *The Theory of the Leisure Class: An Economic Study of Institutions*. London: Unwin.

Vichert, G. 1971. "The Theory of Conspicuous Consumption in the 18th Century." In *The Varied Pattern: Studies in the 18th Century*, edited by P. Hughes and D. Williams, 253–8. Toronto: A.M. Hakkert.

Warner, W.L. and P.S. Lunt. 1941. *The Social Life of a Modern Community*. New Haven, CN: Yale University Press.

Weatherill, L. 1988. *Consumer Behavior and Material Culture in Britain 1660–1760*. London: Routledge.

Wells. D.C. 1899. "Review of The Theory of the Leisure Class." *Yale Review* 8: 213–18.

Wikipedia. 2010. "Conspicuous Consumption." Accessed June 7. http://en.wikipedia.org/wiki/Conspicuous consumption.

Wilkinson, R. and K. Pickett. 2010. *The Spirit Level: Why Equality is Better for Everyone*. London: Penguin Books.

WiseGEEK. 2010. "What is Conspicuous Consumption?" Accessed June 7. http://www.wisegeek.com/what-is-conspicuous-consumption.htm.

Wright, B. 2008. "Conspicuous consumption and your iPhone." *Everyday Sociology Blog*. Accessed April 29, 2014. http://nortonbooks.typepad.com/everydaysociology/2008/09/conspicuous-con.html.

YourDictionary. 2010. Accessed June 7. http://www.yourdictionary.com/conspicuous-consumption.

PART II
Consumer Culture as Mediation in Human Relationships

Chapter 4

The Two Faces of Consumerism: When Things Make Us (In)Human

Pablo García-Ruiz

Introduction

The identification of "consumerism" as one of the major evils of contemporary society has become a popular trend in the media and the academy (Bauman 2007; Röcklinsberg and Sandin 2013). In general, we accept that we often buy, use, keep, and eventually dispose of more things than we actually need (Humphery 2010). Such overspending can have devastating effects, including damage to the natural environment and can contribute to increased social inequality. It also seems to harm our own body and soul, since it fosters materialism, selfishness and even new forms of addiction.

However, it is not so easy to abandon the so-called consumerist way of life. Indeed, it is not so simple to draw a line between what is enough and what is too much. Colin Campbell (2010) and Daniel Miller (2008a), have both dealt with "the problem of consumerism." Their work provides a set of interesting insights that I would like to comment on and build upon in the following pages. Campbell's article, entitled "What's Wrong with Consumerism?" shows how criticisms of consumerism are usually built on taken-for-granted assumptions that are highly questionable and frequently contradictory. Daniel Miller's text has a similar title, "What's Wrong with Consumption?" which also points to some basic confusion about the use and abuse of material things. The extent of this confusion is not at all surprising. As a starting point, capturing the precise notion of need for consumers is a difficult task. Moreover, the meanings assigned to commodities by consumers, as well as the motives that go along with their acquisition, use and dismissal vary widely from place to place and person to person. Commodities may express gratitude and care as well as greed and envy.

The "discourse of consumerism" places us all in a troublesome situation. Miller suggests that the rhetoric behind the present-day condemnation of consumerism has become hopelessly muddled, submerged in a much older and wider critique of consumption as something intrinsically bad. On the one hand, one must of course agree with the impulse to protect and preserve the natural environment as well as the desire to avoid the pursuit of morally repugnant courses of action that appear to be supported by a culture of consumerism. At the same time, however, consumption activities are very important in our personal and social lives.

We cannot obviate consumption, because we use the world of "stuff" as a language to express our feelings and our projects. We use it to build, maintain or dissociate our many social relationships. The material side of our existence is definitely part of any normal human and social life. We may ask, alongside Lee (2010, 570): "Is consumerism always bad? Do consumers always consider this to be so?"

This chapter aims to explore the distinction between consumption as a creative human practice and consumerism as a contemporary disease. Therefore, the question I would like to examine in the following pages is this: *what (if anything) is right about consumption?*

Consumerism and its Critics

Contemporary consumption and its consequences have become increasingly important facets of contemporary life. Consumption decisions have become a common channel through which to achieve a wide range of diverse ends including: the day-to-day management of one's household (for example, by use of particular appliances, cooking products, and foodstuffs), emulation of persons we admire and respect, developing a personal public image, expressing the sentiments and aspirations of one's lifestyle, maintaining certain social relations and status, and, more simply, procuring a little bit of entertainment or excitement. The versatility of contemporary consumption has no clear alternative or, to put it in slightly more technical terms, contemporary consumption has no "functional equivalent." We might presume that the unique functional status of consumption accounts for the increasing amount of time, energy and attention we give to our consumptive habits.

It should be noted, however, that our current practices of consumption have some troubling consequences, some of an aggregate form and others of a still emerging character. Of these, I will name just a few. The increase in the level of consumption threatens to disrupt the global ecological balance and the renewal of natural resources. Inequalities in access to goods and services multiply the distance between the privileged and disadvantaged globally. Some authors (Humphery 2010, Schor 1999) have shown how consumerism erodes the collective ability to build lasting forms of communal life. Maintenance of the current level of expenditure requires longer working hours for persons to achieve the necessary income for consumption. The increasing phenomena of *overwork*, needed to maintain current levels of *over*consumption, tends to erode people's capacity to engage in (unpaid) social activities.

Tourism is a good example of consumerism (Higgins 2010). It is clearly one of those "induced wants," widespread in our current culture of consumption, and which results in the privileged being able to fulfill their consumption "rights" (to travel, to experience other places and cultures, to have fun and improve their knowledge), while the less privileged work as "hosts" or "servers" to the privileged holidaymakers. To an extent, the consumerist society transforms everything—objects, experiences, time, and other people's lives—into commodities (Featherstone 1991).

Gradually, the spirit of consumption has managed to infiltrate the sphere of the family, religion, politics, unions, culture, and leisure. As Roberta Sassatelli (2007, 10) explains, consumer society is coterminous with the process of commoditization, so that more and more objects and services are exchanged on the market and are conceived of as commodities. Consumer society develops along with globalization of commodities and cultural exchanges; with the increasing role of shopping as entertainment and spectacle; with the democratization of fashion; with the growth of sophisticated advertising; with the spread of credit to consumers; with the proliferation of pathologies like kleptomania, obesity or compulsive buying, among other emergent consequences of present overspending.

*Over*consumption is harmful not only to the global environment and ecological balance, but also to the human person herself. Indeed, our method of consumption seems to deserve the classification "inhuman." The negative evaluation and consequences of consumer spending are not unknown to the contemporary consumer. It is widely agreed that our current levels of consumption are excessive and harmful, but this fact alone does not seem to be enough to curtail the consumption of individual consumers.

Why don't we reduce our consumption? Among the many responses offered to this question, I want to focus only on two.

It may be that, although we (as citizens) accept the criticism of consumerism, we (as individual consumers) are not entirely convinced it is true. As a result, we neglect to follow its dictates. Perhaps the criticism holds water on a macro level, that is, for society, but it does not necessarily apply specifically to me. I have good reason to justify my level of personal expenditure.

It may be that, in reality, our consumption decisions are not so much the result of our true desires, but rather that they result from various forms of persuasion found in advertisements and the media. These forces take advantage of our "weak wills" in order to promote the commercial interests of manufacturers and distributors. If this is so, contemporary consumption is indeed "inhuman," but this time in the sense of being "non-human," that is, as more responsive to the functional criteria of some system than it is to the true interests of particular human individuals.[1]

---

1 Here I utilize the distinction proposed by Pierpalo Donati between the human and non-human relation to social formation. In the words of the author himself (2010, xvi): "a social formation is human insofar as the social relations constituting it are produced by subjects who orient themselves reciprocally towards one another on the basis of a meaning that surpasses functional requirements." As a consequence, a social formation may be regarded as "non-human" when it is reduced to a mere functional logic and could be produced by mere technological or mechanical means without a chance for (right or wrong) human intervention. In this sense, "the relations between the human and the social are no longer immediate as they were in the past. To a greater extent than in other periods, our society produces social forms which, although originating from people, are perceived, lived and represented as in-human or de-humanizing" (2010, 24).

It is worth pausing to consider the merits of each of these arguments. To begin with, we might consider whether the criticism of consumerism is really convincing. Campbell has set out his views on this point in the article mentioned above. For him, the assumptions of what can be called the "ideology of consumerism" are not merely highly questionable but frequently contradictory. Let us examine this discussion.

Needs, Wants, and Desires

One of the most common criticisms directed against modern consumerism is that it leads to people consuming more than they need. If only individuals could restrict themselves to buying, using, and keeping only what they really "need," many dangers and risks would be avoided. Campbell (2010, 281) considers this a very seductive and apparently self-evident argument but inconclusive for a number of reasons.

Firstly, it demonstrates that those spare items we keep at home are no longer needed, but not that they never were, particularly when we bought them.

Secondly, and more importantly, it does not take into account the conditional (or relational) aspect of our necessities. It makes no sense to ask whether we need something or not, without a (explicit or implicit) reference to its goal or purpose. As the author explains, what we need to eat in order to be fit and healthy may be rather different to what we might need to eat to make us feel happy and content, let alone what we would need to eat if we were to entertain friends and relatives in our homes, believe ourselves to be successful, or indeed attain our life-long ambition of being a gourmet chef. Something analogous can be said about those involved in different social networks and who therefore face different social situations. The "needs" of an unattached, single person are quite different from a similarly unattached person who, without compromise, must care for their ailing father. A young scholar who aspires to launch a scientific research group has very different needs from an older scholar nearing retirement. Similarly, the Abbott of a monastery and the religious "ascetic" face different challenges and have different needs. It seems obvious that it is not possible to assert what individuals or groups do or do not really need in the absence of a full understanding of their values, goals, and life circumstances, not to mention their specific conception of the good life.

It could be argued that those *caveats* justify an unlimited number of wants and desires on the part of consumers, and open the door to the approval of any subjective gratification. Campbell argues back that it is not clear on what grounds certain needs may be considered legitimate while other desires and wants are to be considered illegitimate. Even if it were possible to set them apart, there is no clear reason to allow needs while forbidding or limiting our wants and desires. Indeed, many people are ready to go without things they need in order to have what they desire.[2]

---

2   As Margaret S. Archer (2000, 240) puts it: "The prioritisation of concerns fall in the practical order, and has its own sacrificial iconography: from artists starving in garrets ...

If this is what people want, who is going to criticize them for it? As Campbell stresses, among the things human beings desperately need to lead a worthy life is the fulfillment of some of their wants and desires. Imagine how miserable life would be if those aspirations and dreams were never fulfilled.

Dehumanizing Materialism

Another criticism of present consumer behavior is that people attach an undue importance to material objects. Materialism is the idea that consumption itself somehow diminishes our humanity, as if the attachment to material items prevented the authentic development of ethical, spiritual or religious life, as if the attachment to material items separates us from the respect and consideration we owe to our fellow man or even God (Lasch 1980). From this perspective, consumption is suspected of leading individuals to form vicious habits, preventing them from living a fully "human" life, and promoting egoism, individualism, and social isolation.

However, the claims and accusations made against materialism often fail to be fully substantiated. To begin with, people often spend their money on intangible services and experiences rather than (mere) physical objects. In addition, our motivation to purchase particular "products" is often driven by their beauty, design, or other (non-material) features that go beyond their mere chemical composition and/or mechanical functionality. All the people waiting to enter into a museum surely cannot be called "materialistic." Can we say that the dynamics of fashion are pure materialism? Many have argued to the contrary. According to Lipovetsky (2002, 107), contemporary society has psychologized fashion, creating models of fashion that concretize emotions, personality traits, and character. Accordingly, a man or woman's dress may manifest various "personalities" or "moods" like melancholy, carefreeness, sophistication, sobriety, brashness, naivety, imaginativeness, romance, happiness, youth, fun, or athleticism. In other words, each fashion season, consumers look for something more than mere clothes; they are looking for psychological renewal. Is this a victory of capitalist materialism, as argued some time ago by Herbert Marcuse (1964), or is it, on the contrary, a kind of "spiritualization" of material objects?

The relationship between the materiality of objects and their ability to incorporate or manifest the immateriality of people's emotions, desires and hopes is often summarized by the word "fetish." According to a well-known argument coming from Karl Marx, commodities can be converted into fetishes, whereby one forms an intense attachment to their "use," all the while concealing their

---

to the archetypical ascetic monk. This category also includes all those intriguing sub-groups who organise their lives around canal restoration, ballroom dancing, vintage motors, etc., and who 'make' their social life around this practical passion."

true substance.[3] According to Miller (1987, 203ff), the common reading of this "fetishization of commodities" includes, on the one hand, a general discontent with consumer culture and, on the other, a vilification of those people that, instead of engaging in social interaction, become obsessively concerned with material goods. However, for this author, such fetishism is not a necessary outcome of mass consumption. As a matter of fact, mass consumption may also be seen as "a key instrument in exactly the opposite tendency; that is, the creation of an inalienable world in which objects are so firmly integrated in the development of particular social relationships and group identity as to be clearly generative of society" (Miller 1987, 204).

How much does involvement with the world of material objects separate us from the world of people? For Miller (2008a, 44), there is no such confrontation; in fact, precisely the opposite occurs. In his research it becomes clear that the people who develop strong and multiple relationships with things are the same people who develop strong and multiple relationships with other people. While those who find it difficult to maintain their relationships with commodities are the people who have problems maintaining their relationships with other persons. In one of his books, titled *The Comfort of Things*, Miller (2008b) provides some convincing examples of this parallel. Each one of its 20 chapters tells a life story of families and individuals who manage their houses, home furnishing, dressing, body decoration and so on, in very different ways.

Hedonism and Other Vices

The failed accusation of materialism may be transformed into the condemnation of some negative attitudes such as hedonism, greed, lust, envy and many other vices, regarded as direct consequences of immoderate mass consumption. The claim that consumer behavior goes hand in hand with hedonism has been explored largely in the literature and this is not the place to engage in this discussion (Campbell 1987; Sassatelli 2007). I would instead like to focus on the following related question: is contemporary consumption a harmful, "vice promoting" practice?

According to Miller (2008a, 44–6), behind this current rhetoric of consumerism as a destructive practice (not only for the planet but also for society and for consumers themselves) there is an older and wider critique of consumption as something intrinsically bad. This critique is rooted in originally religious and moral concerns with materialism as a dehumanizing attitude. Today, this negative judgment of consumption is alive and well under a more secularized ideology. This ideology of consumerism claims that contemporary society's preoccupation

---

3   "It is nothing but the definite social relation between men themselves which assumes here, for them, the fantastic form of a relation between things […] I call this the fetishism which attaches itself to the products of labour as soon as they are produced as commodities" (Marx [1867] 1967, 165).

with its current welfare has displaced other noble aspirations and commitments. Gilles Lipovetsky (2005, 7) notes that, in the course of a few decades, the growing affluence of contemporary society has altered lifestyles and customs as well as launched a new hierarchy of human ends, and a new way of relating to oneself and others, to material items and time. "Living in the moment" has replaced expectations associated with the future; the fever of comfort has replaced nationalistic passions and the amusement of political revolutions. There is no importance given to social change or revolution since, with consumer capitalism, people are instead carried away by the endless pursuit of commercial rewards and hedonism promoted by consumer societies.[4]

Campbell analyzes three distinct aspects of this general criticism of consumer society. First, he makes note that there is not much force to the argument that the practices of consumption are oriented to the *satisfaction* of the subject. After all, what else could they do? In Campbell's opinion, the real objection against consumerism is rather that it has been allowed "to invade areas of life were it has no right to be, specifically that consumerism has increasingly come to replace the ideals of professionalism, public service and citizenship" (2010, 292).

Second, there is the idea that consumption is often harmful and dangerous to the consumer him or herself. The emergence of various forms of addiction reinforces this perception. But, as Campbell notes, seriously addicted people constitute only a small minority of all consumers. If there is a sense in which the majority could also be said to be addicted then it would be related to the phenomenon of novelty, which is experienced every time we go on shopping. Campbell (2010, 293) argues that the love of novelty is, of course, present in, say, the purchase of fashionable garments and in frequent changes in home decor. However, the love of novelty is also present when anyone searches for new novels, films, or music. It is not so clear why we accept these latter purchases as normal and (sometimes) even enlightened, but consider the former as suspect, containing silliness and vacuity.

Finally, Campbell addresses the topic of happiness. According to critics, consumers seems to be fooled by the world of goods and its promise of acquiring happiness through the acquisition of new, better or more sophisticated things. Campbell suggests that this statement is misleading: usually, consumers are not so stupid. They look for more modest goals, such as obtaining some pleasure or excitement, or improving their health, security or peace of mind. Consumers have their own motives for going after some particular object, experience or service.

Nevertheless, Campbell (2010, 295) concludes by noting that the current level of consumption is worrisome and deserves careful and nuanced criticism. His suggestion for this renewed criticism is "to shift from the supposed motives that impel individuals to consume, as well as the values it is assumed guide such behavior, to the consequences of the behavior itself," particularly, the uneven distribution of opportunities to consume. We should forget about consumer

---

4 Of course, apart from other considerations, present history speaks against this: in particular in Syria, Egypt, Libya, Ukraine, Thailand, among other countries.

motives and values and focus on fighting poverty and ecological damage and climate change. In order to get clear results in these fights, "it becomes acceptable to ask people to re-examine their consumption habits and see if they can adjust their practices to help address these collective problems."

The current level of consumption generates collective problems that cannot be ignored. But I am not sure the solution to such problems (ecological and social) can prescind from the motives and values of persons while, at the same time, we ask them to change their habits in order to avoid the dangerous and harmful effects of their cumulative consumption. Miller points out two reasons for this that strike me as interesting. He argues, in the first place, that if it is true that certain behaviors are harmful to the natural or social environment, then it should not be hard to get people to change their behavior. If it is true that there are gas pollutants or blood diamonds, then "what we surely need is something much more effective and authoritative. We need government working internationally, to take responsibility for making sure that we cannot choose that which is demonstrably harmful" (Miller 2008a, 47). To address this problem, it makes little sense to accept an ideological use of anti-consumerist discourse, which presents climate change or Fairtrade as a new form of consumer choice. Nor does it seem sufficient to request a general reduction in the consumptive habits of the inhabitants of richer countries. Indeed, existing inequalities require redistribution policies. For how will a decrease in consumer demand from Europe and North America help factory employees in Africa?

On the other hand, people's motives, values, and concerns do matter for our understanding and evaluation of their consumption practices and choices. We often look suspiciously on those who work longer hours in order to make more money, but our opinion probably changes when we know that the worker is an immigrant trying to make more money to send back to his family in his home country so that they may one day join him in his new country of residence. On the other hand, does increased workload and saving so that one's children might have the same new cell phones, mp3 players and fashionable clothes as their classmates count as a dangerous and harmful consumerism?

The Strength of the System

Perhaps now is the time to address the second of the previously proposed responses to the problem of consumerism. According to it, our consumption is not indexed to our individual desires, but rather to outside forces that are imposed on us, forces that re-shape the motives and aspirations (that is, the "hierarchy of ends") guiding our day-to-day lives. As a result, we become a people unable to reduce our level of consumption.

For some authors (see Humphery 2010, 132ff.), there is a dire need to re-emphasize within current debates the degree to which consumers are systematically impelled to live, earn, spend, and overspend in certain ways.

Their options as decision makers are limited, and differ significantly across the categories of class, gender, race, age, and mental and physical ability. People are to varying degrees compelled to live in certain areas, in certain types of housing and use particular types of transport, to consume or overconsume various kinds of products and services, to shop in various places, as they are also compelled to map out their lives in structured ways. To opt out of those ways of consumption can be both logistically difficult and economically risky. This is especially the case given the fact that an ability to consume or not consume now constitutes, as Zygmunt Bauman (2003, 53–5) has argued, a marker of social marginality in our developed societies.

According to Jean Baudrillard's discourse on the system of signs, advertising has become the main source of public meanings in consumer societies. However, this ideological function of advertising, as Sassatelli (2007, 117) explains, is growing ambivalent: it promotes "visions of identity, the family, gender, race, etc., which serve to reproduce cultural hierarchies and consolidate social differences." In this sense advertising is often singled out as acclaiming acquisition and celebrating consumption at the expense of other (and better) values, and has been labeled as the most value-destroying activity of Western civilization (Lee 2010, 567). Yet, on the other hand, especially with the development of increasingly diverse niche markets, advertising also provides a space for minority, marginal, and even subversive images to circulate widely. Commercial images and messages are frequently used for different purposes from those managers intended, as Dick Hebdige's (1981) study on British motorcycles argued convincingly.

This multifaceted function of advertising introduces a fracture within the structural deterministic viewpoint prevalent in consumption studies. The "social hydraulics" that (post)structuralism implies ignores important aspects of contemporary consumer behavior.[5] Its neglect of human sociability and authenticity dismisses the power of real people to interpret social meanings and use them to shape their lives around their general commitments and the things they care about. Of course, we do not make our decisions under circumstances of our own choosing, since our being embedded in society is part of what it means to be human. But, the personal powers and abilities of the consumer (among which there is the ability to be an active agent) cannot be ignored. This is not to discount the possibility that many consumers act as "dupes" or "puppets" in the hands of marketing managers and advertisers. George Ritzer (1999) has shown numerous ways in which this actually occurs in our everyday lives. But it is crucial to interpret this possibility as precisely that: a possibility—a contingent outcome of the relation between consumers and their socio-cultural context (Campbell 2005).

---

5   As Archer (2007, 6) asserts, "social hydraulics" are "the generic process assumed by those who hold that no recourse need be made to any aspect of human subjectivity in order to explain social action. All necessary components making up the 'explanans' refer directly or indirectly to social powers, thus rendering any reference to personal powers irrelevant or redundant."

One of the personal powers I refer to above is "reflexivity." It is defined by Archer (2007, 4) as the regular exercise of mental ability, shared by most persons, to consider themselves in relation to their social contexts and vice versa. Such deliberations are important since they form the basis upon which people determine their future courses of action—although always fallibly and under their own descriptions.

This "reflexive turn" of the consumer implies that we must keep in mind a basic fact: most people have some kind of internal conversation about their "consumption projects," that is, about what, when and how they are going to shop for, organize, and utilize their various goods. Most of these activities are "forgettable," but some consumption decisions lead to the achievement of important goals for the agent. Therefore, those decisions require specific processes of discernment, deliberation and dedication.[6] Unless we pay attention to this active process of setting up meaningful courses of action through the selection of objects, services and experiences, there is little chance that we will fully grasp the complex activity in which contemporary consumers engage.

Miller (2008b) mentions how something as simple as choosing the furniture for our houses is more than just a merely decorative exercise: the material culture of the home can express an order equivalent to what we might call a social cosmology, a way in which various material objects, values, and relationships are ordered within a given society. Accordingly, we can have smaller and larger personal cosmologies, ranging from that of a single person to a single family. Of course, the majority of people could not articulate the particularities of this symbolic order and are probably unaware that their consumer choices play an important role in establishing the kind of life they are really living.

In this sense, I think one can affirm the following: "consumption projects" are a tangible expression of the commitments and concerns that define the social identity of human persons. If this is true (and I think it is) consumption is one of the most important practices in the personal and social life of human beings. Human beings are not just mind and spirit; we are corporeal beings with all the consequences of said corporeality. The inner language of material objects helps us to better understand ourselves and others. As such, the language of material objects—"signs"—proves to be a highly significant way of communicating with others on important issues.

---

6 Discernment means making forward- and backward-looking comparisons: it is a moment of review, so as to clarify our relationships to our main concerns, in the light of our satisfaction or dissatisfaction with our present situation. Deliberation implies organizing, even if provisionally, our concerns, rehearsing the *modus vivendi* that each of them would entail, as well as listening to the emotional reactions that they prompt in us. Dedication consists in deciding not only whether a particular course of action is worth the candle or seems attractive to us, but also whether or not we are capable of living such a life. I explained elsewhere (García-Ruiz and Lluesma 2010) how these processes give shape to consumption projects.

Life Projects, Consumption Projects

In the preceding pages I have mentioned at least two different senses in which we might use the term "human" in relation to consumption. On the one hand, consumption is human insofar as it is pursued in a courteous or respectful manner, and consumption is inhuman insofar as it does damage to the natural environment, to other persons or even to oneself. On the other hand, consumptive practices are less human to the extent that they are the result of "thoughtlessness," that is to say, when they are more responsive to structural forces than they are to genuine human aspirations. Therefore, authentic "human" consumption would, in the first place, stem from a sufficient discussion about its proposed ends as well as a discernment of what would count as adequate and reasonable means to their provision and implementation in practice. But this formal approach is insufficient: an authentically "human" consumption must also pay respect and consideration to one's natural and social environment. Can our consumptive practices meet all these expectations?

Certainly, as a social practice, consumption is subject to numerous conditions, motives and expectations. Some are of a systemic character, driven by advertising, no doubt. Roberta Sassatelli (2007, 54) notes how, in the face of a growing advertising system which undoubtedly traffics in meanings and lifestyles, consumption practices can configure themselves in various ways: as actions which express and consolidate social bonds and personal relationships; or as actions oriented towards values, towards whatever is considered to be in keeping with good taste; or as ways of presenting oneself in interaction and obtaining deference; or yet again, as aimed at the construction of a world of pleasure. Consumption decisions may also express other political or cultural values including, for example, purchasing local products, boycotting companies unfriendly to the environment, or supporting publically funded services and education. In fact, as a social practice, consumption is not subject to a fixed set of functions and is always open to new and unpredictable directions of meaning.

Consumption decisions are thus a way of relating between oneself and the environment, which is subject to different forms of underlying logic, that is, subject to different sets of motives, conditions and expectations that await attention from the consuming subject. The way we usually deal with these underlying "logics" is by way of organizing, that is, by setting an order according to which we might prioritize, sequence, and set limits to our day-to-day decisions and needs. The way in which humans construct such a sense is by way of narrative. As Alasdair MacIntyre (1981) affirms, the human being, in her actions and practices, is essentially a storytelling animal. Constructing a narrative sense of our lives allows us to construct a significant network of relationships among things and events. To make something understandable in the context of a narrative is to give it historicity and relationality, because within a story "events" become "episodes" (Somers 1994, 616). It is the placing of such "events" within a larger narrative that gives significance to independent instances more than their being part of some chronological or categorical order. Social practices, then, may only be intelligible through the enactment or appropriation of narratives. Of course, this does not mean that social actors are free to fabricate narratives at will. Which kinds of narratives will socially predominate is contested and will depend on the distribution of power and the diffusion of ideas and beliefs.

According to Mary Douglas (1996, 65), the most general objective of consumers can only be to construct an intelligible universe with the goods they choose. Food, housing, clothing, transport and sanitation are means for discriminating their own personal values. Ethnographic descriptions of consumer practices show how consumers develop and imagine those social relationships they most care about through the medium of selecting goods (Miller 1998). This selection often confronts difficult situations. Sometimes it is necessary to redefine in acceptable terms the object of our desire to make it compatible with our values and beliefs. This is what apparently happens when people in places so distant as Romania, Turkey, Western Europe, or the United States, try to reconcile their belief that materialism is bad with their increasing level of consumption. Materialism, then, is either re-coded as something else ("connoisseurship," "instrumentalism," or even "altruism"), or excused as "compensation" for prior depravation, external pressure, or just the way things are in the "modern world" (Sassatelli 2007, 150). However, there is not always a "rational" solution to the conflict. Sometimes people just confront contradictions with a mere shrug of their shoulders. In any case, all these contradictions need, from the part of the subject, what Charles Taylor (1995) describes as an "articulation of the good."

Indeed, providing us with some idea of the "good" is a central task of moral philosophy. Usually, moral philosophers seek to explain what generates valid obligations for moral agents. A satisfactory moral theory is one that outlines some criteria by which we might deduce the obligations to which we are necessarily bound. A problem arises, however, when some set of obligations appears to be incompatible with another. So, *qua* moral agents, human beings need more than a single criterion for distinguishing between normative and relative obligations. We need, in short, a way to prioritize our obligations.

Taylor argues that what enables us to so order and prioritize our obligations is the notion of the "good," not because the "good" offers us a more basic reason for acting, but because the concept of the "good" gives meaning to the rules that guide our decision-making and so enables us to prioritize and organize their implementation within our daily life. Miller (1998, 3) suggests an example, which I quote here at length, that is particularly illuminating:

> Maybe you are a single mother living on a student grant, who was in the supermarket looking at baby bath products. You had a choice of a well-known brand and the supermarket's own brand. The latter was a good deal cheaper and you are in more debt than you care to admit to yourself. But nothing is more important than that child, the mere thought of her sends waves of emotion through you. But then, who is to say the brand name is better? Someone once

told you it's simply more expensive because they spend money on advertising, and the money saved will help towards the baby carrier you really need, the one that lets you carry her on your front, which would be so much better than having her behind where you can't see her gazing up at you. In the back of your head is a darker thought: a resentment that starts from knowing what else this money could be spent on, like so much else that your daughter has in some sense taken from you. There is that totally unwarranted but much desired expensive pair of shoes that your sister the lawyer was wearing and that hovers guiltily somewhere in your head, but remains well suppressed by your sense of love.

Effectively, making decisions in complex situations requires one to distinguish between diverse goods, by identifying what is most important and urgent given the circumstances at hand. Doing so, however, implies giving a certain priority to a higher good, which gives order and meaning to the rest of one's intermediate goods. Higher goods—"hypergoods," says Taylor (1995, 63ff.)—are those goods that are not only incomparably more important than other goods, but also provide the standpoint from which one can weigh, judge, and decide between other intermediate or lower goods.

Consumption decisions typically retain a relation with some higher good. As proposed by Campbell (2010), they follow a conditional logic based on one's hierarchy of needs. It is impossible to establish beforehand the general boundary between those items that qualify as "necessities" and items that are only "extras." Instead, we can only ask what good (or evil) a consumption decision has on the environment, other persons, and ourselves.

According to MacIntyre (2001, 83–6), there are three distinct ways of assigning goodness to a thing: 1) as a means to another end (for example, a harpoon for fishing); 2) as a good in itself (the enjoyment of fishing); 3) if the practice (like fishing) is good for one person or for the life of that community at that particular time. The human being always acts, explicitly or implicitly, as a practical reasoner in regards to her ordering of the different kinds of good mentioned above. As practical reasoners, human beings routinely make this classification whenever we deliberate about what ought to be done in this or that situation according to the kind of life we see as the most fit for us personally. Returning to the example of the young mother, she has to decide if the cheap baby bath product is good enough for her child, her budget, and also her self-esteem. She must also organize her daily expenses such that she can afford to buy the new baby carriage as well as (when possible) the expensive pair of shoes. In addition to the objects themselves, there is another type of goods involved in the field of consumption. As in other practices, the consumer suffers consequences from his consumption decisions. If the young mother adequately saves the money needed to buy the new baby carriage, she not only receives the benefit of seeing her daughter's lovely face but also the added willpower acquired from her sticking to a difficult plan. If, on the other hand, she decides to buy the shoes, she will have something to wear at dinner parties, but will have to feel occasional pangs of guilt.

Every practice (whether fishing, chess, or homemaking) requires certain dispositions, knowledge and technical skills. Those who take the time to acquire and develop these elements of a particular practice will become, in time, an expert of sorts in the practice. But, as MacIntyre is apt to suggest, while advances in one's mastery of a practice yield certain tangible results (large fish, for example) it also increases one's sense of the point and purpose of the virtues necessary to sustain particular practices and human social life generally. Taking into account the three-fold definition of good offered by MacIntyre, we can distinguish between a "good catch," a "good fisherman" and a "good person" who fishes. In the sphere of consumption we might make a similar classification: that between a "good buy," a "good consumer" and a "good mother" who consumes. These three things are not necessarily synonymous nor are they always instantiated at the same time in the life of particular persons.

A practice that requires and, at times, generates virtues, is the practice of "gift giving." Since the groundbreaking work of Marcel Mauss, it has been frequently noted how the gift creates reciprocal obligations and reinforces social ties. It also has been noted how gift exchange can easily lead to arrogance, envy and destructive competition. Less has been said, however, about the extent to which the virtues make gift giving and receiving a constructive activity. MacIntyre (2001, 148–9) refers to these virtues as the "virtues of acknowledged dependence" and describes them as follows: industriousness in acquisition, thrift in saving, discrimination in giving; knowing how to exhibit gratitude without allowing that gratitude to be a burden, courtesy towards the graceless giver, forbearance towards the inadequate giver. While the recognition of dependence can lead one to resentment, it can also help form networks of mutual aid.

In a similar vein, we should explore other activities, exchanges, and experiences related to consumption practices in search of specific goods and virtues stemming from them. For instance, many authors have pointed at the risks and dangers derived from fashion and its capricious and volatile trends (Campbell 1994). However, can anyone imagine how a fashionless society would be? No doubt, fashion must produce some kind of goods for people and for our society as a whole. Therefore, it is a vital challenge to identify and protect these goods while being aware and putting aside those evils and dangers. This same reasoning could be applied to diverse aspects and modes of consumption such as entertainment, leisure, tourism, and the like. From this perspective we could approach the distinction between consumption and consumerism in a more positive way.

In this sense, I would like to offer a brief reflection on the role religion plays in our evaluation of consumption. Many religions understand that offering sacrifices is both pleasing to God and required of God's subjects. Those living in the domain of the mundane—"in the world"—appear to be separated from God with nothing to offer. As it is often said, the sacred connects us with God while the mundane takes us further away from the glory and majesty of the One. This particular form of the sacred-mundane distinction contains a negative evaluation of the material world, seeing it as oblivious, ambivalent, or even hostile to a life with God.

Such a view has deep roots within various religions, but particularly from within the Christian faith. Nevertheless, I might recall a point made by Josemaría Escrivá (1975, 9), a Catholic priest venerated as a saint by the Roman Catholic Church: "It is in the midst of the most material things of the earth that we must sanctify ourselves." There, a Christian should "discover the invisible God in the most visible and material things (…) We can therefore rightfully speak of a Christian materialism (which is boldly opposed to that materialism which is blind to the spirit)." This is not the forum to develop the implications of such an idea, but it does seem clear that, even from a religious point of view, our relationship to the material world needn't be construed negatively. Consumption, like other common practices, can demonstrate and develop our relationships not only with our fellow man, but also with God.

Conclusion

We would do best to refocus the issue of consumerism. At the beginning of this chapter we asked, on the one hand, whether we can distinguish between consumption and consumerism; and on the other hand, we raised a general question about the moral significance of consumption: what (if anything) is good about consumption? As a conclusion I would offer the following responses:

I don't think one can set an acceptable overall level of consumption which, when transgressed, leads to crass consumerism. Who will be responsible for establishing said consumption level? For how long will it be in force before review? And to what standards of measurement will the threshold answer? Even where the consequences of crossing said threshold are not binding, it is difficult to see how to articulate a feasible standard.

I agree that there are many worrying consequences of the current rapid pace of consumption. With Miller, I think that when certain consumptive habits are causing definitive harms to people's health or the environment, governments ought to take the necessary steps to prevent and control the risks associated with consumption.

When studying the practice of consumption through the prism of morality, there is a tendency to overemphasize the evils associated with the practice and overlook the various goods made possible by responsible consumption. As a result, I do not think it wise to set quantitative restrictions on consumption, but rather to focus things in a more qualitative direction; that is to say, the extent to which habits of consumption lead persons to develop virtues (or vices) and to the instantiation of greater goods (or evils). In this sense, we may make a distinction between "consumption" and "consumerism," that is, that between social practices that help us to be more fully human and practices that may make us "expert consumers" but worse people.

So, then, what's right with consumption? My view is that consumption gives us a chance to produce goods and to develop virtues. We should consider whether and what kind of goods and virtues we are bringing about, and to what extent they are helping us to build a more humane world.

References

Archer, Margaret S. 2000. *Being Human: The Problem of Agency*. Cambridge: Cambridge University Press.

Archer, Margaret S. 2007. *Making our Way through the World: Human Reflexivity and Social Mobility*. Cambridge: Cambridge University Press.

Bauman, Zygmunt. 2003. *Work, Consumerism and the New Poor*. Maidenhead: Open University Press.

Bauman, Zygmunt. 2007. *Consuming Life*. Cambridge: Polity Press.

Campbell, Colin. 1987. *The Romantic Ethic and the Spirit of Modern Consumerism*. Oxford: Basil Blackwell

Campbell, Colin. 1994. "The Desire for the New: Its Nature and Social Location as Presented in Theories of Fashion and Modern Consumerism." In *Consuming Technologies: Media and Information in Domestic Spaces*, edited by Roger Silverstone and Eric Hirsch, 48–66. London: Routledge.

Campbell, Colin. 2005. "The Craft Consumer." *Journal of Consumer Culture* 5, 1: 23–42.

Campbell, Colin. 2010. "What's Wrong with Consumerism?" *Anuario Filosófico* 43, 2: 279–96.

Donati, Pierpaolo. 2010. *Relational Sociology*. London: Routledge.

Douglas, Mary. 1996. *Thought Styles: Critical Essays on Good Taste*. London: Sage.

Escrivá, Josemaria. 1975. *Passionately Loving the World*. New York: Scepter.

Featherstone, Mike. 1991. *Consumer Culture and Postmodernism*. London: Sage.

García-Ruiz, Pablo and Carlos R. Lluesma. 2010. "Reflexive Consumers. A Relational Approach to Consumptions as a Social Practice." In *Conversations about Reflexivity*, edited by Margaret S. Archer, 223–242. London: Routledge.

Hebdige, Dick. 1981. "Object as Image: The Italian Scooter Cycle." *Block* 5: 44–64.

Higgins-Desbiolles, Freya. 2010. "The Elusiveness of Sustainability in Tourism: The Culture-ideology of Consumerism and its Implications." *Tourism and Hospitality Research* April: 116–29.

Humphery, Kim. 2010. *Excess: Anti-Consumerism in the West*. London: Polity.

Lasch, Christopher. 1980. *The Culture of Narcissism: American Life in an Age of Diminishing Expectations*. London: Abacus Press.

Lee, Monle, Anurag Pant and Abbas Ali. 2010. "Does the Individualist Consume More? The Interplay of Ethics and Beliefs that Governs Consumerism Across Cultures." *Journal of Business Ethics* 93, 4: 567–81.

Lipovetsky, Gilles. 2002. *The Empire of Fashion: Dressing Modern Democracy*. Princeton: Princeton University Press.

Lipovetsky, Gilles. 2005. *Hypermodern Times*. Cambridge: Polity Press.

MacIntyre, Alasdair. 1981. *After Virtue: A Study in Moral Theory*. Notre Dame, IN: University of Notre Dame Press.

MacIntyre, Alasdair. 2001. *Dependent Rational Animals: Why Human Beings Need the Virtues*. Chicago: Open Court.

Marcuse, Herbert. 1964. *One-Dimensional Man: Studies in the Ideology of Advanced Industrial Society*. London: Routledge.

Marx, Karl. [1867] 1967. *Capital*. Vol. 1. New York: Internacional Publishers.

Miller, Daniel. 1987. *Material Culture and Mass Consumption*. Oxford: Blackwell.

Miller, Daniel. 1998. *A Theory of Shopping*. Ithaca, NY: Cornell University Press.

Miller, Daniel. 2008a. "What's Wrong with Consumption?" *RSA Journal* (Journal of the Royal Society for the Arts). Summer: 44–7.

Miller, Daniel. 2008b. *The Comfort of Things*. Oxford: Polity Press.

Ritzer, George. 1999. *Enchanting a Disenchanted World: Revolutionizing the Means of Consumption*. Thousand Oaks: Pine Forge Press.

Röcklinsberg, Helena and Per Sandin. 2013. *The Ethics of Consumption: The Citizen, the Market, and the Law*. Wageningen: Academic Publishers.

Sassatelli, Roberta. 2007. *Consumer Culture*. London: Sage.

Schor, Juliet B. 1999. *The Overspent American: Why We Want What We Don't Need*. New York: Harper Collins.

Somers, Margaret R. 1994. "The Narrative Constitution of Identity: A Relational and Network Approach." *Theory and Society* 23, 5: 605–49.

Taylor, Charles. 1995. *Sources of the Self*. Cambridge, MA: Harvard University Press.

Chapter 5

Accepting and Resisting Insecurity: Using Consumer Culture to Have it Both Ways?

Allison J. Pugh

Introduction

How does consumer culture shape the way we respond to increasing insecurity? Trends in many developed countries point to increasing insecurity at work and at home, and thus increasing opportunities for other people to fail us in our close relationships (Beck and Beck-Gernsheim 1995). In this chapter, I explore the ways in which adults manage uncertainty through consumer culture, based on in-depth interviews with 80 parents who are part of a larger research project on commitment and flexibility in postindustrial society (Pugh 2015).[1]

I found that people who are insecurely employed—both highly advantaged people who consider insecurity more like flexibility, or the less advantaged who experience insecurity as unmediated precariousness—use a consumerist ideology when they talk about relationships at work, in the community and at home. This ideology is rife with references to choice and authenticity, and renders invisible the histories and places from which people come, serving as a sort of commodity fetishism of other people. They adopt this consumerist approach—which often seems to dislodge people from their relationships—despite the fact that many use consumer spending to convey care and relationship.

At the root of this chapter is my own assumption about what it means to be human—which is fundamentally about establishing and enriching connection to others. This relational, interactive approach emphasizes the embeddedness of the person, the notion that the self is only a self-in-relation. I am particularly interested in dependence as a relationship that is emblematic of humanity because of its very universality, dependence not just over the life course, for example, of children, sick, elderly, disabled, but also over the day, in the routine needs and care of even the most autonomous individual, itself a consumerist construct (Kittay 2011). I focus on uncertainty and flexibility as particularly challenging for the

---

1   Many terms have been coined to capture these trends—neoliberal, postfordist, postmodern, and so on. Following Bernstein (2007), I use the imperfect term "postindustrial" to emphasize their ties to a particular set of economic practices.

interpretation and experience of dependence, for our capacity to think about it usefully as well as to handle it well.

I also use my work to expand our notion of consumption. In my first book (Pugh 2009), I looked at not only the material culture of childhood—electronic games and sneakers—but also something I termed pathway consumption, meaning the spending on the contexts of childhood—the private school, the particular neighborhood, and so on—to get at how consumption intersects with structural inequality. In this project, I urge us to think about consumption as including not just material goods, but also a consumerist discourse, involving particular tenets that undergird market exchange, and I ask us to think about this discourse specifically with regard to how it affects human connections.

Background: Consumer Culture, Ambivalence and Insecurity

Americans are concerned about insecurity at work and at home. Even before the Great Recession, books like *The Disposable American* (Uchitelle 2007) or *The Big Squeeze: Tough Times for the American Worker* (Greenhouse 2008) documented the perils of rampant layoffs. At the same time, in a different aisle in the bookstore, works like *Coming Apart* (Murray 2012) and *Unhitched* (Stacey 2011) debate what to think about pervasive divorce and unstable unions. Films like *Up In the Air*, *Outsourced* or *The Company Men* portray new work relationships that are fluid, insecure and abbreviated, while terms like "friends with benefits" and the ill-defined "hooking up" capture the ambiguity of modern intimacy. These themes reflect a sense of tumult about new and different connections to each other at work and at home—looser ties, negotiable rights and responsibilities, new relationship forms that carry meanings, and obligations we can no longer take for granted.

While there is some debate, scholars have generally reached a consensus that work has indeed become increasingly precarious, especially for white men, who were the primary beneficiaries of the long-term career in the middle 50 years of the twentieth century (Kalleberg 2009; Farber 2009). Thanks to management practices widely adopted without hard evidence of their impact on the bottom line—such as outsourcing, downsizing, and the widespread use of temporary or contract labor—employers no longer appear to be subject to what used to be called the "social contract," in which they owed job security and a wage in return for the workers' unremitting effort and dedication (McCall 2004; Baumol, Blinder, and Wolff 2003). In the United States, these changes swept over manufacturing labor in the 1970s and 80s, hitting white-collar workers in the 1980s and 1990s, although their impact is international in scope (Farber 2007).

In developed countries, corresponding trends have taken place in families, where the predominance of married couples with children has given way to a more fluid and diverse array of family forms; we might consider these "postindustrial families." The deinstitutionalization of the dominance of one form of family, such as the male breadwinner/female caregiver family, has led to its replacement not by another dominant model but rather by multiple forms, from two-income families to step-families, gay and lesbian families, single-parent families, grandparent families, and other iterations (Stacey 1997; Cherlin 2009).

There are undoubtedly parallels between these changes in families and in jobs, in both their contemporaneous development in time, and in their characteristics: networked, modular, flexible, recombinant, and transient (Streek 2008). Nonetheless this chapter does not attempt to argue that these developments in work and family lead to each other in some simplistic vision of causality. A number of scholars have begun to identify the ways in which these trends affect each other, however, rejecting the notion that they might be occurring in entirely autonomous systems.

Scholars have grappled with these global economic and cultural changes, and their impact on the self (Giddens 1991; Sennett 1998, 2006; Gabriel 2004), work (Castells 2000a, 2000b, 2010; Beck 1992, 2000), family (Hochschild 1997; Giddens 1992; Bauman 2003; Beck and Beck-Gernsheim 1995; Stacey 1997) and other domains (Carnoy 2002; Streeck 2008; Bernstein 2007). Most of these efforts are on the level of grand theory, and a number are internationally prominent scholars who have launched extensive research programs, including Ulrich Beck's "risk society," Zygmunt Bauman's "liquid modernity," Manuel Castells' "networked society," and Anthony Giddens' "late modernity." While space prohibits a detailed critique of these works, overall these scholars contribute a broader view of many linked and simultaneous changes—the decline of authority, the increase in personal risk, newly customized lifestyles and reflexive choice. These explanations attempt to decipher the causes and consequences of the collapse of mutual expectation and commitment, such as the rise of "individualization" (Beck 1992), the rise of the "pure relationship" (Giddens 1991), and the corrosion of "character" (Sennett 1998). Their work points to a rise in endemic uncertainty about ourselves and other people.

Elizabeth Bernstein's work is particularly germane to those who want to excavate the links between these uncertainties. In an impressive ten-year comparative ethnography of prostitution (2007), she argues that in contrast to the "relational model of sexuality," which refers to the idea of sexual intimacy taking place within a long-term love relationship, "bounded authenticity" is characteristic of more contemporary relations. "Bounded authenticity lends itself less to engrossing time commitments or unwieldy rafts of dependents and more to the intimate relations that are cost-efficient and well-suited to the structure of the modern corporation—temporary, detachable and flexible," she contends (175). A neoliberal culture shapes both the dominant modes of production and reproduction, then, which interact with the cultural narratives that prevail and are expressed through consumer products and cultural practices.

Given links between work and intimate life, how do people on the cusp of postindustrial insecurity talk about contemporary relationships? What do we owe each other, at work and at home, when employer commitment is perceived to have attenuated dramatically? How do people seek to steer their children through the visions of commitment and obligations that they maintain?

Methodology

Qualitative data does not attempt to ask or answer how widespread a trend is, in other words the statistical generalizability of a particular correlation. Instead, the qualitative researcher strives for logical generalizability, in which she uses theoretical sampling to develop a case that explores and illustrates the larger, abstract principles at work (Luker 2008). This research allows us to explore the ways in which women and men of various social locations, and with different commitment histories, experience and interpret postindustrial culture, constructing different roadmaps for traversing the challenges of contemporary cultural trends.

The material for this chapter is based on in-depth interview data collected for a larger project, in which a graduate student researcher and I talked to 80 women and men who varied in their experience of job insecurity. The interviewees formed three groups, including two employed in insecure work: more advantaged people who had been relocated by their employers, many of whom with graduate degrees and six-figure incomes, and laid-off people, who were less advantaged, most of whom with some college and five-figure incomes. The third group was composed of the stably employed, in occupations such as firefighting, police, and public school teaching, most of whom had a college degree or less of schooling, and mid-five figure earnings.

Thus I use this purposive sampling to vary the experience my informants have had in the labor market—whether as people with firsthand knowledge of the newly precarious position of many workers, either because they could benefit from it like the more advantaged workers, or because they were subject to it like the less advantaged laid-off. Two of the three groups were of more modest means, with most of the interviewees being white women with some college attendance (the social location of the majority of employed women [US Census 2004]). I also included other informants who varied from this profile by race and gender, to be able to generate some theoretical ideas about how the processes and meanings of commitment and flexibility differed depending on social category and circumstances. All interviewees were parents of teenagers, in an effort to capture the moment at which people might try to explain their vision of the world for which they are preparing their children to meet, as another window upon how they perceive the ambient culture.

Interviews involved the taking of what we might call a "commitment history," a narrative of work and intimate life that hinged on moments of change and stasis. Interviews took place in people's homes, offices, cafés, and other locales. Interviewees received a nominal sum for their participation.

Coding involved the listening and re-listening to tapes, the reading and re-reading of transcribed text, until the data were almost memorized. I maintained logs of themes that sprung up across the interviews, of telling phrases and jokes, of different iterations of commitment, of meanings of obligation and sacrifice. I developed memos about themes and returned to the texts to ascertain their aptness and accuracy, elaborated upon different themes that emerged, and revised others when it became clear they were less salient (Emerson et al. 1995). More detail about methods can be found in Pugh 2015.

Consumer Culture and Ambivalence in Relationships

Consumer culture figures in the relationships of those who are insecurely employed in two ways: in the exchange of commercialized goods and services in which people take part to cement or establish or define their relationships, but also in the way they talk about those relationships, at work, among friends, and in their intimate lives—a kind of talk I have termed "consumerist discourse." Elsewhere (Pugh 2013) I have outlined three tenets of a consumerist discourse in greater detail. In sum, this discourse includes three components: 1) *choice*, or the notion that there are plenty of options (jobs, friends, partners) from which to choose; 2) *authenticity*, or the concept that it is important that one's choice reflect and express some core principle of the self; and 3) *the replaceability of people*, in which—in line with Marx's notion of commodity fetishism—we pay more attention to a particular object (say, a certain job, or principle, or ambition) than the relationships that surround, support or produce that object. In what follows, I explore how people at once deploy and contest the consumerist discourse at work and at home, specifically with regard to their teenaged children.

The Consumerist Discourse at Work

Even as people invoke the consumerist discourse to explain and justify behavior at work, they also resist it simultaneously with counter-framings. Because these resistant framings rely on nostalgia, however, their wistfulness helps to cloak precarious work with a certain inevitability.

Some, particularly those itinerant workers who were more advantaged as well as some of the laid-off, were what I came to term "low-loyalty, high-performance workers" (Pugh 2015). They attested to an impressive work ethic, but they assumed that they would jump for better opportunities when they arose. In general, more advantaged insecure workers viewed the marketplace of jobs through the lens of the market ideology, weighing the best offers they had at any one time, considering when to make the jump from one employer to another, thinking about their own needs and desires and the best way to satisfy them in a fairly limited temporal landscape.

Lucy, for example, left a job she loved for a better one, only to get laid off the following year. But at the time, leaving the first position seemed like an obvious choice.

> And I meant every word of this when I left Synergy I said, "I didn't think I would be leaving here. I thought I would be retiring from here. As long as you had me but this opportunity has come about, and I really want to explore it. I think it's a good opportunity for me." And what can you say to that?
>
> And it was the absolute truth. And we actually worked together on some things. So that was a good parting.

Lucy clearly believes the answer to her rhetorical question—"and what can you say to that?"—is "nothing," that the appeal of the better opportunity is undeniable, and that to leave to take advantage of one such opportunity is "a good parting."

These workers were not typical in the consistency with which they adopted a consumerist approach to work. Most insecure workers, particularly among the less advantaged, laid claim to an intense work ethic as the sign of an honorable person, even as they absolved their employer of any loyalty or dedication, suggesting that the loss of employer commitment was merely the symptom of a social problem. In *The Tumbleweed Society* (Pugh 2015), I explore the paradoxical unevenness of the expectations insecure workers tend to hold for themselves and for their employers, which I term the "one-way honor system." These workers seemed to apply the consumerist discourse to their employers, who might shop around for better workers with impunity, but not to themselves, who were beholden to their own sense of honor.

Some people noticed the discrepancy, however, and it disturbed them. Said James, who worked in a high school:

> And then what you find is you're actually giving more to your director who, as nice as the person may be, if you said you had problems and you needed a leave of absence, would replace you in a heartbeat. You know, that's not what it's supposed to be all about.

James found himself perturbed by the extent to which he was in his employer's thrall, a connection that violated the "way it was supposed to be," especially since the employer could "replace you in a heartbeat."

Even as they invoked a consumerist discourse to explain their employer's actions, some workers like James also lamented this state of affairs, blending critique with a sort of nostalgic resignation. Thus counter-framings persisted, to be found in the way people talked about how it was in "my dad's time," or how it is in countries other than the United States. In these framings, another vision of employer–employee relations prevailed, one of steady, long-term employment bolstered by cultural norms about what we owe each other at work—a trope that existed mostly in the memories of informants recalling their father's stable lifetime jobs.

"In my dad's time, where you worked with a company and you kind of did your time and then they owed you because it was a relationship, [that] doesn't seem to be there anymore. I would say we kind of feel like it doesn't exist at all," said Mary, a massage therapist whose husband's occupation means he finds his career mobility by hopping from job to job. "With Peter and his work issues, and I think [information technology], I mean all his friends are in computers. The average is three to five years and then ... it's really [fast] and you never plan on just staying."

A certain nostalgia could even be found among those advantaged workers who embraced job insecurity as a form of flexibility, as a freeing development rather than a fearsome one. Tara recalled when her husband worked for a company that had since been bought by a larger firm.

> Well, before it was corporate, they had a … that huge sense of family and community. And they had a passion for their product and so there was a brotherhood and an extended family. And he was always seen in a very gleaming light, because he was very good from the very beginning of what he did. And they were very verbal about [that].

It was a wonderful company to work for, she said, precisely for its reliability, its constancy. "It was a feeling of great security until this move, because it was a different company," Tara said. "And now it's been purchased by [a huge multinational corporation], so it's become very, very the norm corporate."

Tara's words "very, very the norm corporate" demonstrate her sense that the change is unavoidable, even inevitable, and make clear her resignation to the new insecurity as part of the conventional workplace. They might have loved working at the familistic company where you were a known entity and mutual obligation reigned, but that way of life is essentially gone, not worth fighting for but rather to be remembered nostalgically. "So I mean the dynamics of it was so unique. And we've all kind of mourned that like it was a death," Tara said. "You know, because that's not what you find here."

James, who was a teacher but who nonetheless approached his job as an insecure worker, had spent time in Central Europe, and considered the American peripatetic approach to career a cultural anomaly, rather than a historical one. "And there is definitely something to say about loyalty to your job. I mean, America is very—switch jobs—what do I want to say—a very mobile society as far as career is concerned," he said.

> Austria's much more like Japan in this respect where you get a job, you stay with it until retirement. And that's probably seen as a cultural loyalty. You know, you fight in your job, you know, the administration treats you horribly and then you decide not to teach a few classes in rebellion. But then you kind of make up.

Finally, a few insecure workers seemed to resist the consumerist discourse completely, to reject that it had infiltrated the workplace, to cling to the notion of mutual obligation between employer and employee, even when their own experience had proven them wrong. Claudia, who worked in sales in a small firm, had declared bankruptcy some years before after a layoff, and her husband earned very little in their church ministry. Yet even though losing her current job would threaten her family's livelihood, she said she and her employer owed each other their commitment.

> If my boss tells me that they're going to stay in business through this economic downturn, I'm not going to look for a job. And so I'm counting on the company being there, you know, because they've told me they're going to keep us all there. So honesty from that angle and, in return, honesty from me that when, you know, I say I'm going to be selling and I think my billing this month is going to be $40,000, I need to do everything I can to make that $40,000, because they're counting on me for expenses to come in with that much money.

It was common for informants to profess high standards for themselves as workers just as Claudia did, but she was unusual in restricting her own freedom to move based on her sense of felt obligation.

Clark, who found himself to be on his fifth job and his second wife, also resisted the consumerist approach to relations at work, but distinguished between what his "head" told him and what his "heart" said:

> Clark: "Again, because of my upbringing when I take a job, I assume I'm going to have that job for the rest of my life. I realize that that's not going to happen anymore. I mean, intellectually, I can make that realization. Okay. But in terms of what my heart says, because of my upbringing, I still expect things to be like they were in the 50s and 60s, where you get a job and that's the same job you have for the rest of my life. I hate looking for jobs. I really hate the whole procedure. You know. Some people like job-hopping, I don't. I like the stability. Just like I like the stability of having a steady relationship with somebody."

> Int: "Uh-huh. And how does it make you feel when you don't have this kind of stability?"

> Clark: "Lost."

Despite their resistance, most people employed in insecure work accepted the advent of precarious work, and management practices that adopted a consumerist approach to relationships on the job, as inevitable. Willfully rejecting what his head told him was happening at work, Clark could not escape the sense that he was being left behind.

The Consumerist Discourse in Intimate Life

The consumerist discourse did not stop at the workplace door, however. Instead, people also seemed to deploy it in their approach to intimate life (Pugh 2013). Informants' use of metaphors and images particularly communicated the prevalence and appeal of the consumerist discourse. Furthermore, they did not just use it to govern their own relationships (Pugh 2013), but they also invoked a consumerist discourse when they talked about their children's friendships. As parents discussed the ways their children handled conflict with friends of troubled peers, the language of choice, authenticity and the replaceability of people came through.

Language Use

People used particular images and metaphors to characterize their relationships, language that communicated the consumerist discourse. Said Holly, a relocator whose son had a difficult adjustment to his new home:

> This boy that lived on our cul-de-sac actually, they spent summers together. This is the first summer they haven't been together since he moved in fourth grade, because they're both in college now. *I know it's a little cheesy*, but he kept a relationship with this one little boy. They'd just spend hours playing whatever.

Holly uses the word "cheesy," slang for overly sentimental or falsely sweet, to describe a relationship of almost a decade, one that anchored her son when he had trouble adjusting to the new location. Similarly, when Vanessa discussed a group of friends from law school, she noted how unusual it was that they had gotten together for annual vacations for 30 years. "Most of us have stayed very close and that was almost 30 years ago, so that is *kind of weird*," she said, designating their behavior as outside the mainstream with the slight pejorative. This sort of discourse frames these relationships culturally, so that even as informants actually treat them as important enough to maintain for years, they denigrate them as odd or offbeat, in keeping with, I argue, a market ideology of friendship that venerates choice, authenticity and the replaceability of people.

Who are the people who stay in one place? To relocators, they are at risk of becoming rigid, narrow-minded, ossified in old social contexts that did not reflect the broad horizon of choice and self-growth. Alexis's family came back after ten years and "it was like coming home. Sometimes it is nice. It is like an old shoe, but then," she added, with a laugh, "it's an old shoe."

> Alexis: "Yeah, and nothing has changed. The first Sunday we went back to church I turned to Bill and I said, 'Those people have been sitting in that same pew … '"

> Int: "For ten years."

> Alexis: "For longer than that, since we started going to church there. I said, 'I just want to scream, you guys on the left move to the right, guys on the right move to the left.' They are just in the zone. You do the same things at the same time, same seasons. It is not a positive for me but I think for what it is it is just comfortable. 'I don't have to think, I'm on autopilot. I don't know anything different so I'm very happy doing what I'm doing.'"

Alexis's perception of those who stayed behind was that they did not change, did not grow, did not stretch themselves in ways that moving had stretched her family. Her comments reflected an assumption about time, that it somehow stopped while her family was in another location, that also made it easier for the relocators to leave. Metaphors like "the old shoe" denigrated a more sedentary lifestyle, capturing the ascendancy of a flexible approach to intimate life.

The Consumerist Discourse and Raising Teenagers

Parents of teenagers struggled with how to handle their children's relationships with troubled peers, fearful that the friends were going in the wrong direction or that their behavior was contagious and would portend trouble for their own youth. In light of this, they were sometimes fierce in their adoption of consumerist language with its disembedding implications.

Choice

In recounting conversations they had had with their teenagers, parents often emphasized just how much choice their children had for friendships, hoping this would get them to be pickier in whom they chose. Felicia, divorced with two children, whose primary goal was to be a more active nurturing parent than her own unstable mother, said she often counseled her daughter away from bad friend choices:

> If I see someone [a friend] as going in the wrong direction and I can't do anything to help it, go the other way, then I tell her [her daughter] or I suggest, well, I suggest it first—"that person, I have a bad feeling, that person is not good to— I have a feeling it's just going to go the wrong way and you might want to distance yourself because you could fall into whatever trouble she's getting into."

Felicia acted to steer her daughter away, even from those with whom she had been friends for many years. "A friend that she's been friends with for years now, yeah, she's gotten into a lot of trouble," Felicia recounted. "Well, my daughter, she wants to still be friends ... . Well, I'm the boss," she laughed, without apology.

> So, I told her when she's 18, she can be friends with whoever she wants to and I also tell her "you have so many good friends, who are not horrifying. [Laughs.] And I know you have fun but you also, you know, if you limit yourself in this one regard, then maybe I'll lighten up on something else." [Laughs.] Yeah, make a compromise, because some people are just horrifying.

Felicia guided her daughter away from "horrifying" others, even those who had been longtime friends, partly through bargaining, and partly through reminding her about choice, since she had "so many good friends, who are not horrifying."

Authenticity

The pursuit of a "true self" identity also found its way into how the insecurely employed talk about their children's friendships. Some commended their children for staying true to themselves, even if that meant abandoning old relationships. Claudia was proud of her daughter for distancing herself from friends who had broken her chastity pledge, which she saw as stemming from a powerful commitment to her faith.

> Claudia: "As of right now, she said that she is going to stay a virgin until she gets married. And, you know, I've told her that's a great goal. And, you know, 'I admire you for that. I wish I could have done that.' She said she's lost a lot of good friends as they've become sexually active."
>
> Int: "You mean girlfriends who have felt constrained by her pledge?"
>
> Claudia: "Just that they, not that her girlfriends would leave her, but she doesn't accept it. She's, she's—"
>
> Int: "So when they do it, she leaves them? Wow."
>
> Claudia: "Yeah. She's amazing. She's real strong in her faith."

Rather than prioritizing commitment to people, Claudia's daughter prioritized a commitment to principle, in the pursuit of authenticity that would brook no challenge.

Similarly, Sarah was also proud of her daughter for not dwelling on lost commitments, on being able to move on.

> I think as grown ups we tend to hold onto things ... It's like oh, we fret and we carry on and we feel bad and we lose sleep over it. And as we move into opportunities it's kind of like you take responsibility for something and then you move on. And, I've noticed with Sonya in particular—and maybe it's because I realize she's leaving—but she does a great job with that. I wish I could encourage as she gets older to continue with that. It's like she doesn't dwell on things. She doesn't go back over it. She's doesn't beat herself up. She doesn't beat somebody else up. And I don't remember necessarily having that feature at her age. Maybe I did ...

Sarah was not sure where her daughter got this ability to leave behind situations and people, and she was working with a theory that it involves her youth—although Sarah did not think she herself was ever like this. But she used language to portray "holding onto things" as a negative, as "fretting" and "beating yourself up."

The replaceability of people

Many parents also maintained a sense of their children's friends as interchangeable on some level. For Bruce, sticking with a high school sweetheart was perplexing, when there was a whole universe of others out there.

> I'm not saying they should bounce around or be promiscuous or any of that, but I don't want them to marry their high school sweetheart. I don't want to see that happen. Well, God, there's got to be something else out there in the world. I mean I just think that is just so limiting. That is my point of view. You think you're going to be with this person fine. Then go to Ireland for three years and come back or something. Go do something, but don't just stay here and settle down. That doesn't mean you can't have a really good long-term relationship either.

The love interests they found in high school were replaceable, since to settle down with them would be so "limiting."

Even those parents who thought their children might want to keep relationships they began in their early lives seemed to talk about them in the abstract, without reference to particular qualities or benefits. Barbie counseled her son not to worry about leaving elementary school friends behind when he went to middle school.

> "When you walk away from this and when you get done with high school and you get done with college, if you still have five friends that you can count on one hand, then that's all you need." I'm like, "if you pick up the phone you can call any of those five friends, and they are there for you for whatever," I was like, "Then that's all you need, because most people don't have that."

Her dictum focuses on the number and not their particulars: five friends—whoever they were—are plenty.

Parents thus deploy the consumerist discourse when they try to disembed their children from their friends, whom they sometimes seem to perceive as potential snags that could menace their childrearing projects. They emphasized that their teenagers had plenty of choice, that they should maintain their commitments to authentic principles rather than troubled peers, and they spoke of their friendships in abstract terms, as largely replaceable.

Conclusion

The tripartite dimensions of the consumerist discourse can be found everywhere. In insecure work, advantaged people invoke it to describe what they and their employers owe each other, and the less advantaged use it to describe their employers' behavior, even as they lay claim to a different yardstick—one that emphasizes their work ethic and loyalty—by which they themselves are judged. In intimate life, people adopt a consumerist approach to spouses and partners, friends and community members. In this chapter, we have seen how the consumerist discourse also informs how insecure workers raise their teenaged children, how they justify and frame their approach to their children's friends.

Where insecure workers invoked a consumerist ideology, it was generally found to attenuate commitment, at work, in the community or at home. Yet elsewhere (2015) I have documented how they used the material culture of stuff to communicate care and relationships, to forge the very commitments that the market discourse served to erode. This paradox is rooted in the ambivalence of consumer culture: the ambivalence that consumption is supposed to resolve materially, even as it fosters it discursively.

Of course, endurance is only a worthwhile goal when the relationships are satisfying, respectful, even joyful. On the one hand, I am agnostic about the goals here: recognizing, for example, that an intense but short relationship at work and at home can be as important in preserving and attaining humanity as a long but deadening one. The personal costs of commitment, particularly for women, whose gendered role in maintaining and caregiving has often entailed a subjugation of self, root any study of loyalty in ambivalence itself. Nonetheless, my sense that commitment is worth studying stems from a focus on the centrality of care and dependence, specifically the impossibility of dependence under a system of perpetual choice and authenticity. I argue that how we handle this dependence— and the consumerist discourse that threatens it—is at once the challenge and the measure of our humanity.

References

Bauman, Zygmunt. 2003. *Liquid Love: On the Frailty of Human Bonds.* Cambridge: Polity.

Baumol, William J., Alan Blinder, and Edward N. Wolff. 2003. *Downsizing in America: Reality, Causes, and Consequences.* New York: Russell Sage Foundation.

Beck, Ulrich. 1992. *Risk Society: Towards a New Modernity.* London: Sage.

Beck, Ulrich. 2000. *The Brave New World of Work.* Cambridge: Cambridge University Press.

Beck, Ulrich and Beck-Gernsheim, Elizabeth. 1995. *The Normal Chaos of Love.* Trans. Mark Ritter and Jane Wiebel. Cambridge, MA: Blackwell.

Bernstein, Elizabeth. 2007. *Temporarily Yours: Intimacy, Authenticity, and the Commerce of Sex.* Chicago: University of Chicago Press.

Carnoy, Martin, 2002. *Sustaining the New Economy: Work, Family, and Community in the Information Age.* Cambridge, MA: Harvard University Press.

Castells, Manuel. 2000a. *The Rise of the Network Society, The Information Age: Economy, Society and Culture*, vol. I. Second edition. Cambridge, MA; Oxford, UK: Blackwell.

Castells, Manuel. 2000b. *End of the Millenium, The Information Age: Economy, Society and Culture*, vol. III. Second edition. Oxford: Blackwell.

Castells, Manuel. 2010. *The Power of Identity, The Information Age: Economy, Society and Culture*, vol. I. Second edition. Oxford: Wiley-Blackwell.

Cherlin, Andrew. 2009. *The Marriage-Go-Round*. New York: Knopf.

Emerson, Robert, Rachel I. Fretz, and Linda L. Shaw. 1995. *Writing Ethnographic Fieldnotes*. Chicago: University of Chicago Press.

Farber, Henry. 2007 "Is the Company Man an Anachronism? Trends in Long-Term Employment in the U.S., 1973–2006." In *The Price of Independence*, edited by Sheldon Danziger and Cecilia E. Rouse, 56–83. New York: Russell Sage.

Farber, Henry. 2009. "Job Loss and the Decline in Job Security in the United States." Working paper #520. Princeton University Industrial Relations Section. Accessed September 5, 2012. http://dataspace.princeton.edu/jspui/bitstream/88435/dsp01xk81jk38d/1/520revision2.pdf.

Gabriel, Yiannis. 2004. "The Glass Cage: Flexible Work, Fragmented Consumption, Fragile Selves." In *Self, Social Structure and Beliefs: Explorations in Sociology*, edited by Jeffrey Alexander, Gary T. Marx and Christine Williams, 57–76. Berkeley: University of California Press.

Giddens, Anthony. 1991. M*odernity and Self-Identity. Self and Society in the Late Modern Age*. Cambridge: Polity.

Giddens, Anthony. 1992. *The Transformation of Intimacy*. Cambridge: Polity.

Greenhouse, Stephen. 2008. *The Big Squeeze: Tough Times for the American Worker*. New York: Alfred A. Knopf.

Hochschild, Arlie. 1997. *The Time Bind: When Work Becomes Home and Home Becomes Work*. New York: Metropolitan/Holt.

Kalleberg, Arne L. 2009. "Precarious Work, Insecure Workers: Employment Relations in Transition." *American Sociological Review* 74, 1: 1–22.

Kittay, Eve F. 2011. "The Ethics of Care, Dependence, and Disability." *Ratio Juris* 24: 49–58.

Luker, Kristen. 2008. *Salsa Dancing into the Social Sciences*. Cambridge, MA: Harvard University Press.

McCall, Leslie. 2004. "The Inequality Economy: How New Corporate Practices Redistribute Income to the Top." Working Paper. Demos. P. 32. Accessed September 7, 2012. http://www.demos.org/sites/default/files/publications/the_inequality_economy_final.pdf.

Murray, Charles. 2012. *Coming Apart: The State of White America 1960–2010*. New York: Crown Forum.

Pugh, Allison J. 2009. *Longing and Belonging: Parents, Children and Consumer Culture*. Berkeley, CA: University of California Press.

Pugh, Allison J. 2013. "The Planned Obsolescence of Other People: Consumer Culture and Connections in a Precarious Age." *Culture and Organization* 19, 4: 297–313.

Pugh, Allison J. 2015. *The Tumbleweed Society: Working and Caring in an Age of Insecurity*. New York: Oxford University Press.

Sennett, Richard. 1998. *The Corrosion of Character: The Personal Consequences of Work in the New Capitalism.* New York: Norton.

Sennett, Richard. 2006. *The Culture of the New Capitalism.* New Haven: Yale University Press.

Stacey, Judith. 1997. *In the Name of the Family: Rethinking Family Values in the Postmodern Age.* Boston: Beacon Press.

Stacey, Judith. 2011. *Unhitched: Love, Marriage, and Family Values from West Hollywood to Western China.* New York: NYU Press; Crown Forum.

Streeck, Wolfgang. 2008. "Flexible markets, Stable Societies?" MPIfG Working paper 08/6. Max Planck Institute for the Study of Societies. Accessed May 21, 2009. http://www.mpifg.de/pu/workpap/wp08-6.pdf.

Uchitelle, Louis. 2007. *The Disposable American: Layoffs and Their Consequences.* New York: Random House.

US Census. 2004. "Educational Attainment in the United States: 2003." Current Population Reports. Document P20–550. Accessed November 3, 2010. http://www.census.gov/prod/2004pubs/p20–550.pdf.

Chapter 6

Conformity and Distinction in Scandinavia's Largest Department Store[1]

Karin M. Ekström

Introduction

The progression of consumption in society makes it interesting to reflect upon the development of consumer culture over time (see Featherstone 1991; Sassatelli 2007). Featherstone (1991, 84) describes consumer culture as follows:

> To use the term "consumer culture" is to emphasize that the world of goods and their principles of structuration are central to the understanding of contemporary society. This involves a dual focus: firstly, on the cultural dimension of the economy, the symbolization and use of material goods as "communicators" not just utilities; and secondly, on the economy of cultural goods, the market principles of supply, demand, capital accumulation, competition, and monopolization which operate within the sphere of lifestyles, cultural goods and commodities.

In the Western world, the development of consumer culture has been particularly noticeable during recent decades. Slater (1997) argues, however, that consumer culture arose in a recognizable form in the eighteenth century, not as a consequence of industrial modernization and cultural modernity, but as part of the making of the modern world. Since the 1950s, the progression of consumer culture has occurred parallel to the development of welfare with an increasing number of goods in larger and still-full wardrobes, houses and garages. Also, a stronger emphasis has been put on symbolic consumption reflected both in consumption for social comparison as well as distinction (see Bourdieu 1984; Ekström and Hjort 2009). Social comparison has probably always existed, but becomes more prevalent in a consumer culture where consumption is highly manifested. Consumption has become an increasingly important social marker. Some researchers (for example, Bauman 1998) even claim that consumption has taken over the role that work previously had in reflecting social success.

---

1   The author thanks Gekås Ullared for permission to use photographs of the supermarket in this chapter.

Consumer culture developed extensively also in Sweden after the Second World War and in particular during the 1950s and onwards (Ekström 2010a). As welfare increased, consumption came to play a major role in people's lives and shopping represents today an important leisure activity. Increased leisure time has led to more time for consumption activities such as shopping. In 1951, a Swedish law stating that all citizens had the right to three weeks of holiday was introduced, and in 1957 the number of working hours was reduced to 48 hours per week (Eriksson 1999). The history of consumption in Sweden has followed the global development of larger shopping malls. This chapter focuses on the largest department store in Scandinavia, Gekås Ullared (subsequently referred to as Gekås in the chapter). The purpose of the chapter is to describe what motivates families to travel to shop at Gekås and to discuss their shopping in relation to conformity and distinction.

The study is based on three days of observing and interviewing families shopping, as well as camping on the camp site nearby in August 2009. The study is also based on interviews with employees and the Managing Director Boris Lennerhov at Gekås. In addition, information has been added from the Internet to update the statistics (www.gekas.se), and from a book published to celebrate Gekås 50th birthday (Nilsson 2013).

The interviews and observations of the families gave different insights and complemented each other. However, family consumption is difficult to study since behavior is linked to social norms and expectations (Ekström 2010b). Family members may act differently in public from in private. By focusing on practice, that is to say, families' behavioral patterns, some insight into how families behave in different social contexts can be gained (see Ekström 2010b); in this study the department store and the campground. The disposition of the chapter is as follows. First, the department store is described, followed by a presentation of families shopping at Gekås, family decision-making, and consumer socialization. The chapter ends with a discussion of conformity and distinction experienced by customers as well as created by the company.

The Largest Department Store in Scandinavia

Gekås is the largest department store in Scandinavia and Sweden's biggest tourist attraction. Its rural location in Ullared, a village of approximately 800 inhabitants situated in Halland County, differs considerably from other established commercial centers in and outside Sweden. People travel to Gekås to go shopping and some also decide to combine the shopping visit with camping. Since 2001 Gekås has owned a nearby camp site including spaces for tents (100), caravans and mobile homes (500 places) and 220 cabins for rent (900 beds). A hotel was recently built (115 rooms and conference facilities for 40 people).

Gekås was established in 1963 and sales have increased ever since. During the last three years (2011–13), sales have increased by 900 million SEK. For 2013, Gekås's sales amounted to 4.7 billion SEK, including revenue from the camp site.

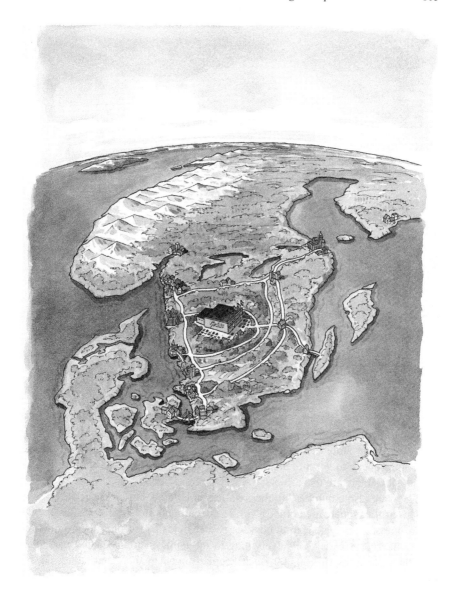

Figure 6.1   Map of the Gekås Ullared location in Sweden

Statistics from Gekås show that in 2008 the average visitor had a one-way trip of 230 km, spending 3,600 SEK on shopping and visited Gekås twice yearly. The average customer shops for more than four hours.

During 2013, 4.8 million people visited Gekås. The sales record for one day, 33 million SEK, is from October 5, 2013. The record number of visitors at Gekås

Figure 6.2   Entrance to Gekås Ullared

is 27,500 customers on July 30, 2013. People sometimes have to queue to get into the department store. The longest queue ever was 1.4 km on October 30, 2010. The department store can house 7,000 customers at once. Even though people sometimes queue to get into the department store, it often takes a shorter time to get out since there are 69 cashiers.

There are also a number of other retailers in Ullared, but Gekås is the largest, both in terms of square meters and sales. The department store encompasses 35,000 square meters, equivalent to almost six soccer fields. According to information on the Internet, Gekås "sells everything to the home that can fit in a car." The assortment consists of 100,000 stock keeping units. In their marketing, Gekås emphasizes their low prices. From the very start in 1963, the products consisted of remainder stock that was purchased, and naturally this involved a low degree of fashionable items. Today, only a small percentage of the inventory is made up of remainder stock. Gekås does not sell "seconds." Over the years, Gekås has established a significant network of companies from which to purchase stock, and these sell goods of high quality to the store at a low price. The goods increasingly consist of well-known brands, but no luxury brands since the low price is the determinant. The store has become more sensitive to trends. For example, recent interest in society in relation to equine sports, fishing, home interiors, and home lighting is represented to a greater extent in the department store's stock.

Turnover is high: the department store is emptied of goods three times per week. The rapid turnover makes it necessary for employees to manually watch the stock in the store in order to fill the shelves continuously rather than rely on the information from the cash registers. There is a stockroom in the building (29,000 square meters) and a warehouse a couple of kilometers away (44,000 square meters).

Gekås has a restaurant (3,000 square meters with room for 550 guests), a cafeteria, a sports bar and a salad bar. There are also smaller cafeterias in the department store. There is a hairdresser in the department store and a dog care center nearby with room for 30 dogs. The restaurant, the hotel, the cafeteria, and the camp site are called "the restaurant," "the hotel," "the cafeteria," and "the camp site" respectively; simplicity is emphasized.

Gekås has 8,000 trolleys and 5,000 customer baskets. There is parking for shopping trolleys in some places in the department store, the largest of which can take 700 trolleys. Some examples of sales figures are: 700,000 pairs of jeans per year, 13 million pairs of socks, 1.7 million bottles of shampoo, and 4.6 million toys per year. According to information from Gekås, the average customer is a 43-year-old woman living in a household of three. The majority (63 percent) of customers are women. Besides driving by car (there are 3,500 parking spaces), there are also bus trips to Gekås from different parts of Sweden. The record number of buses is from October 30, 2010 when 81 buses arrived. About 3,200 long-distance buses come to Gekås every year. The passengers are mainly retired women, and each bus customer spends about 1,000 SEK.

Gekås does not spend money on advertisements in Sweden. However, a reality TV series filmed in the department store and at the camp site started in 2009 including customers, employees, the Managing Director and camping guests. It had about a million viewers per episode when it was broadcast for the first time and has led to a significant increase in customers in recent years. It is estimated that it led to an increase of approximately 15 percent in the number of visitors during 2009 (Dagens Industri 2009). The company also has a blog that has about 18,000–25,000 visitors per day during peak season. Gekås is of course also on Facebook.

During peak season 1,400 people work in the department store; at other times there are approximately 520 full-time employees. The store has quite a number of staff who fill the shelves when empty, assist customers, and also keep an eye on the inventory. The management emphasizes the importance of the employees enjoying their work and feeling proud of working at Gekås. Management is not isolated from the store employees. The Managing Director actually walks around the store every day. It appears as if there is team spirit in the company; the management and the employees build the brand together. The department store is privately owned by two people who work as purchasers. According to the store, it has no debt and profits are invested back into the business.

Families Shopping at Gekås

Interaction within families in today's society is to a high degree related to consumption. For example, children's birthday parties are commonly celebrated at McDonald's (Brembeck 2007). Shopping has become a leisure activity and a way for family members to be together. Gekås is a good example of this, and illustrates shopping as a social activity for families. Some families travel to Gekås solely to shop, while other families choose to combine the visit with a holiday, staying at the camp site. Facilities at the camp site include saunas, hot tubs, jacuzzis, barbecues, and miniature golf. Gekås, originally just about shopping, is nowadays emphasizing more experiences related to the shopping visit.

Several of the families I met during the three-day visit had travelled a long way. For example, the family at the front of the queue on Saturday morning waiting for the store to open had travelled 500 km during the night in order to be there when the department store opened at 7 am. The family at the end of the queue had also travelled 500 km during the night.

The shopping experience at Gekås differs depending on the amount of time spent there. An employee pointed out that the customers organize their buying at Gekås in a different way if they have more time to spend when staying at the camp site for a few days compared to if they are only on a one-day visit. The employee expressed it like this:

> You can see to some extent from the style of dress whether they are from the camp site: holiday wear, sandals, shorts with pockets, something like that. It feels as though people who are here for longer target one department at a time, clothes first, then they go to the pharmacy and toiletries department and buy all they need from there: they are a little more strategic.

Many of those visiting Gekås for the day only are well organized with shopping lists (on paper, recorded on mobile phones, or mentally stored), placing two baskets inside and two underneath their shopping trolley to keep items from different departments separate from each other. Limited time requires better organization of the shopping. Organization skills are acquired over time, that is to say, consumers learn how to shop more efficiently the more they visit.

One employee pointed out that it is not trendsetters who come to shop at Gekås, but rather people who follow trends. She said that it is more "the man on the street" who comes to Ullared. Families who shop at Gekås represent a variety of socio-economic backgrounds. One employee described who the visitors might be:

> I think it's like this, a bit of the thrill of the chase. I don't think you have to be poor exactly to come here, but there are lots of families with children, middle class as well as people who need to find slightly lower prices. And then there seem to be people who are slightly a cut above: "I see, so you shop here too?"

Figure 6.3   Queue to the store one Saturday morning in August 2009

Figure 6.4   Baskets in a shopping trolley

You wonder if they talk about it at home. I think people want to find a bargain no matter how much money they have ... you can't be really destitute ... If you come here once a year you must have some capital at the time. So perhaps it's not people who need to make their salary stretch, but the ones who can plan ahead a little ... then you notice that more people come when child benefits have been paid. There are slightly more people then.

The employee stressed bargains, and said also that people regardless of income want to find a bargain. However, you need to have some money to spend when going to Gekås. You also need a car, or you can take the bus if you live somewhere where bus tours to Gekås are organized. In another study focusing on how grocery stores meet the needs of foreign-born consumers (Ekström and Norén 2011), I travelled with an association of immigrants to Gekås by bus. They talked about the bargains and showed high price awareness, possibly as a result of having modest incomes. On the way back, the bus was packed full of shopping bags, and I remember one woman telling me that she was looking forward to the day when she could return and spend several thousand SEK at Gekås.

In today's society when consumption has developed as a social marker (see Ekström and Glans 2011), it has become more important to be able to consume. Consumption is about inclusion, but can also mean exclusion if you lack the means to consume. A lack of resources in the form of money can mean that individuals or families are excluded from consumption and group cohesion (Ekström and Hjort 2009). This can involve social and psychological risks and can be stigmatizing (Ekström and Hjort 2009). Low price stores allow everybody to consume regardless of income. Low price products are sometimes sold in large packages, thereby limiting purchases by someone who has little money. At Gekås, there are very few large-pack items. Instead, the items are sold individually, allowing people to buy only one package at a low price. The customers, however, often buy several packages because of the low price. Then the choice is made by the customer rather than by the company selling the product.

Although low prices make shopping possible, it is also likely that low prices can contribute to overconsumption. Sometimes at Gekås customers purchase more than is needed. A customer stated:

You have to admit that you come here and buy loads of things that you wouldn't have bought otherwise. You think that that sweater is so cheap, I'll take that too: you buy more than you really need.

The role of low price stores in social sustainability, making shopping a democratic practice regardless of income, needs to be recognized in future research. This needs also to be discussed in relation to ecological sustainability, and the consequences of overconsumption on the environment.

Family Decision-making

As mentioned earlier, shopping has become a leisure activity and a way for family members to be together. One employee put it this way:

> They think it is genuinely enjoyable to shop. Nowadays it is something of a popular pastime. They see it as a fun holiday, with things for the children to do. Gekås really invests in this all-in experience. There's bathing, there's mini-golf and you can rent canoes at the campground. You can make the most of your holiday even though you are here. People don't need to feel like tragic figures because they travel to Gekås on their holidays: you can still get an experience. I think they increasingly feel that.

Family members negotiate identities, relations, and lifestyles through consumption (Ekström 2011). They inform and influence each other in different ways. Direct influence is when someone explicitly asks for some item or gives advice about a purchase (Ekström 1995). Indirect influence takes place when consideration is shown to a family member's wishes without the person saying anything (Ekström 1995). The interviews indicated that both types of influence occurred in the families shopping at Gekås.

Family decisions are sometimes made jointly, especially important decisions. In particular, couples at the beginning of a relationship often seem to strive to make joint decisions, but their roles over time gradually become more specialized (Ekström 2010b). By dividing the buying roles, time can be saved, for example: "You buy this and I will buy the other item." This role specialization was noticeable among the couples I met at Gekås. Some couples had begun their shopping tour together, but then decided to shop separately and meet later at a given time and place or kept in touch via mobile phone. Role specialization was noticeable regarding women's clothing, where mainly women were prevalent, as well as among tools and electronics where men dominated. However, both men and women could be found in the men's clothing department. One explanation is that women are often highly involved in purchases of their husband's clothes. Apart from role specialization, it was also noticeable that some couples did all their shopping in the department store together. This was particularly the case among elderly couples. Retired couples seem often to return to joint decision-making after previously having more specialized buying roles (Ekström 2010b). One reason could be that they now have time to spend together and to make joint decisions.

There are 76 fitting rooms in the women's clothing department and 19 in the men's. During the visit, I gained the impression that some men who accompanied their wives to Gekås seemed somewhat bored. In particular, I recall bored men hanging around in the women's clothes department. This is something Gekås is well aware of, and they have therefore tried to make the visit more comfortable for bored or tired visitors by introducing snack bars,

Figure 6.5   **A couple of men waiting among the shopping trolleys outside the women's fitting room**

a restaurant, cafeteria, and a sports bar. Food is vital for gaining energy to shop, particularly at a department store such as Gekås where customers often spend several hours. The sports bar, which was established in 2012, is intentionally located close to the women's clothing department so that the women can bring clothes to show to their possibly bored spouses.

Families with children often travel to Gekås with the intention of buying low-price children's clothes. Children's all-in-one winter suits in particular were mentioned during our visit. The reason may be that the study was carried out in August, when people were buying winter clothes. It was common that both parents visited the children's clothing department together even though their degree of involvement varied.

I got the impression that families with children planned their shopping trip, for example by writing down what children's clothes they wished to buy. Also, grandparents had shopping lists that included their grandchildren's clothing sizes. Shopping lists seemed common among the visitors in general, not just among families with children. However, interviews and observations also indicated that impulse buying was common. One employee put it like this: "I don't think anyone arrives with a shopping list and sticks to it. I don't think there are many. They must be very, very, very, few."

It is possible that customers with shopping lists at Gekås spend more than customers without such lists, since in addition they also make impulse purchases. This would be an interesting research question in the future.

Consumer Socialization

For some families, the visit to Gekås has become a tradition. Children who travelled to Gekås with parents during their childhood (family of orientation) have now in their adulthood begun to travel there on their own initiative, sometimes with their own established families (family of procreation). In other words, they have been influenced to follow their parents' consumption patterns. This can be called "keeping up with the parents," similar to "keeping up with Joneses."[2]

The process whereby consumers learn to become consumers is studied as "consumer socialization." Ward (1974, 2) defines consumer socialization as "the process by which young people acquire skills, knowledge, and attitudes relevant to their functioning as consumers in the market place." Much of the research into consumer socialization has focused on families, and in particular on how children learn to be consumers (see Ekström 2006; John 1999 for an overview). One example of consumer socialization related to Gekås is the fact that some children have learned consumption patterns (to shop at Gekås) from their parents. Consumer socialization can be seen as a stronger form of influence than simply accompanying one's parents to shop, since the children have continued to shop at Gekås as adults. I also gained the impression that some families seemed to be loyal customers for life.

Shops also play a role in consumer socialization (see Hollander and Omura 1989). Consumers often learn how to navigate in shops over time, and stores play a role in making the shopping trips as convenient as possible. For example, at Gekås, the shopping trolleys are conveniently placed in the car park and customers have learned to take a trolley when they go into the shop and drop it off before leaving for home.

The fact that Gekås customers learnt to place baskets in and under the shopping trolleys to be able to separate items from different departments is another example of consumer socialization in the department store. Skills that are acquired over time to shop more efficiently illustrate a consumer socialization process at the department store. In order to facilitate tidiness when returning the tested garments, the company has installed a rotating stand outside the fitting rooms on which to hang garments that are returned to the inventory. There are also spaces to leave shopping trolleys outside the fitting rooms, which creates order. Furthermore, the shopping trolleys are nowadays visibly numbered in case they get lost.

---

2   In another study, I identified parents being influenced to follow their children's consumption patterns: "keeping up with the children" (see Ekström 1995, 2007a).

Figure 6.6   Consumers learn to take a shopping trolley before entering the department store

Figure 6.7   Shopping trolley parking outside the fitting rooms

Conformity

When trying to understand what motivates families to travel to shop at Gekås, it might be helpful to think of different driving forces behind consumption. One driving force is material necessity, for example for food and clothing (Hjort 2004). Another is social emulation, that is to say, we consume to be part of society, which Duesenberry (1949) among others has discussed. Hjort (2004) calls this socially necessary consumption, that is, being like others and not deviating. As mentioned above, consumption has become increasingly important as a social marker. Everyone participates in the "catwalk of consumption" (Ekström 2007b; Hjort and Ekström 2006); even people who choose a more restrictive approach show through their consumption who they are or want to be.

Different theories have been developed over the years to describe how consumers influence each other's consumption. Early on, Simmel (1904) developed the trickle-down theory for understanding fashion, implying that fashion is diffused from higher to lower social classes. Over time, trickle-up from lower to higher social classes (for example, jeans), and trickle across different social classes could also be recognized, in particular as social media have come to play an important role for diffusion of goods. Frank (2007) discusses how consumption among the wealthy is continually upgraded in order to be perceived as unique from the middle class who follow and copy upper class consumption behavior.

Gekås relies largely on "word of mouth," that is, people telling each other about the shopping experience. As mentioned above, the department store does not advertise. The reality TV show about Gekås has, as mentioned above, led to people who earlier had not visited Gekås being encouraged to do so.

The trip to Gekås in itself can be seen as a kind of conformity, visiting the department store like many other people. As mentioned above, the lower prices at Gekås make it possible for lower-income families to shop and participate in consumer culture as mainstream consumers do. Some items are big sellers as mentioned earlier. During my visit, I noted also that baking paper, plastic film, and aluminum foil were common in shopping trolleys. These items are big sellers and found at the department store's entrance. The way in which these items are displayed means that customers see others buying them, which certainly contributes to new customers also buying them. This too is an example of conformity. Another observation was that black-and-white posters, featuring for example images of Marilyn Monroe, and Hula Hoops seemed popular in shopping trolleys. Again, this buying pattern among many customers reflects conformity.

Consumers Experiencing Distinction

A third driving force behind consumption is distinction (see Bourdieu 1984; Hjort 2004). Distinction is about differentiation and appearing unique, but within certain prevailing norms. Social boundaries decide how unique one is "permitted"

Figure 6.8   Shopping trolley with plastic film and aluminum foil

Figure 6.9   Shopping trolley with Hula Hoop and poster

to be (see Ekström 2007b). Distinction is about being seen and conspicuous in the crowd, but is still related to a social context, conformity. Gekås claims to differentiate itself through "good quality at unbeatable prices." Low prices and bargains are forms of distinction. By getting a bargain, customers can feel like smart or rational shoppers.

Gekås cannot be compared with high quality/high price department stores, but neither does it present itself like other low-price department stores. One reason is that brand names can be found at Gekås too, as mentioned above. Other reasons are good order and emphasis on good customer relations.

Another form of distinction is the customer's unique experience. One employee said that the queuing in itself provides a unique experience:

> It's a little funny that they quite enjoy queuing. That they think it's enjoyable to have been standing queuing into the store. Then they have a little story to tell when they get home; fun: we stood there for a whole hour and it was hard work, they think it's great fun ...

The queues can grow long, and this builds up expectations before visitors get into the store. A further distinction is that the trip to Gekås can be perceived as "free" through the savings made by shopping. Bargains can mean that they have more money left over for other purposes. Perhaps they can feel that the camping holiday is partly or fully financed by the bargains? Or as one customer expressed: "If you add it all up, there may not be any economic gain, but you have an excursion at the same time."

As mentioned above, the visit can involve a personal experience as well as doing what many others do. Conformity and distinction can accompany one another. Another example is the Shakti mat that was a popular buy during my visit and was selected as the Christmas Present of the Year 2009 by the Swedish Trade Federation. The Shakti mat is an example of conformity since people influenced each other to buy this product. At the same time, the Shakti mat can reflect distinction in the form of a bargain and because the purchase in relation to the visit to Gekås can be perceived as unique for the visitor.

The Company Creating Distinction

Gekås creates distinction in different ways: by offering low prices, understanding and making it possible for consumers to experience bargains, creating good order, and emphasizing customer relations. The Managing Director Boris Lennerhov expressed in his interview: "[...] if the prices were not so low, then half the visitors would not come." He also emphasized the customer's experience of finding a bargain: "The way to the purchase is at least as much fun as possessing the item bought. The satisfaction lies in finding the bargain."

Figure 6.10   The Shakti mat—conformity and/or distinction

Figure 6.11   Loss leaders at the entrance

As mentioned earlier, shopping at Gekås involves a lot of impulse purchases. Visitors are surrounded by loss leaders right from the entrance to the exit.

Another distinction is the good order created by Gekås. When moving around in the store, the visitor is struck by the good order that prevails despite all the products and the fast stock turnover. Every ten minutes a truck arrives at Gekås to deliver goods. One customer put it this way: "What fascinates me about Ullared is the fantastically good order here. Such an incredible number of people and yet such good order. Things aren't higgledy-piggledy—everything is tidy. Pleasant and helpful personnel, it's fascinating." The order in the store is, however, not predictable. Sometimes customers who eventually decide not to buy items they have placed in their shopping trolley leave the items in the wrong place. Staff take care of such things and make sure that order is restored.

Another distinction that also affects the customer's experience is customer relations. The Managing Director Boris Lennerhov expressed during our visit:

> I personally have only one criterion: how I myself want to be treated.
>
> [...] That smile (the employees' smile) costs absolutely nothing. That treatment is what decides the verdict on (our business). So there is a good deal of belief in, focus on, that it is them (the customers) and it does not matter what they look like, who or what they are, their money is worth just as much.
>
> At all information meetings, a lot of focus is placed on telling who is paying our salary. It is emphasized. It is such messages that I send, a smile and what it means ...

He emphasized that customer relations are central to operations and that all customers are to be treated the same way. Gekås builds the brand name Gekås Ullared, but the customer can also be seen as a co-producer. Both producers and consumers are involved in brand building (see Ekström and Norén 2008; Salzer-Mörling and Strannegård 2004). Customers give meaning to the Gekås Ullared brand and also contribute to creating distinction.

Conclusion

This chapter has illustrated that going to Ullared is not only about conformity—visiting Gekås like other people and buying similar goods, but also about distinction in the form of finding bargains and an unique experience. It is not only about low prices, but also about the experiences during the visit. The company is well aware of the fact that it is important to make it a pleasant and memorable experience. Other companies can also sell low-price goods. It is the customers' experiences in particular at Gekås that make the visits unique, and this is something the company has understood and accentuated over the years.

In the future, I believe the experience will be emphasized even more in building the brand since it is a unique competitive advantage in relation to other low-price stores.

Both Gekås and customers contribute to creating distinction. Conformity and distinction are paradoxical in that, while they are one another's opposites, they often occur in one and the same consumption activity. For example, wearing a brand name sweater expresses distinction for some and conformity for others depending on the situation. In a similar manner, a visit to Gekås can express conformity for some, and for others distinction.

Other companies also express conformity and distinction in relation to Gekås in their marketing. A seller of kitchen towels at a market in Strängnäs in October 2009 explicitly stated that the towels were cheaper than at Ullared ("Billigare än Ullared"). This reflects conformity, that is to say, towels comparable to those at Gekås Ullared, while at the same time expressing distinction: towels cheaper than at Gekås Ullared.

Figure 6.12   Market in Strängnäs, October 2009. "Cheaper than at Ullared"

In a consumer culture with an increasing range of goods and increased competition, conformity and distinction will probably continue to be of importance in the future.

Future Research

This chapter has given merely a limited insight into family consumption at Gekås, and a more overarching reflection of consumption related to conformity and distinction. To understand why families shop at Gekås, there is a need for in-depth studies that come closer to consumers' everyday lives, where consumption takes place. We need to know more about how consumers influence each other regarding shopping and consumption.

It is also interesting to reflect over what is considered refined or coarse in relation to distinction. The Managing Director expressed: "[...] someone has decided that shopping or football are not considered sophisticated." Why is some shopping considered more refined than other? Why is it considered more refined to shop at NK Stockholm than at Gekås? Is dearer more refined than cheap? Is shopping coarse and are other cultural activities more refined or vice versa? How are perceptions of refined and coarse established in a socio-cultural context? There is a need for more research regarding these issues.

There is also a need for more research into how status is constructed in different families (Ekström 2011). How and by whom are family members socialized to learn what is and is not status shopping? It was discussed earlier how generations of families are socialized to visit Gekås. This is a concrete example of how values and preferences linked to consumption are passed on within families. It is also of interest to research the opposite, that is, how is the message that Ullared is "not a place one should visit" spread within families?

Furthermore, Gekås has successfully managed to build their brand together with their customers since the very start of the company in 1963. It would be interesting to study how the brand Gekås Ullared is culturally constructed (see Holt 2004). It is not an overstatement to say that Gekås Ullared has become an iconic brand.

Finally, today shopping for things is a central activity in people's lives. Inspired by literature on material culture (for example, Miller 1998, 2010), the interdependence between people and things deserves more attention in future research. There exist two opposing views: on the one hand, a concern over the materialism that things are said to cause (for example, Belk 2001); on the other hand, looking upon things as a capacity for enhancing humanity (Miller 2010). The importance of things for social interaction should not be overlooked (Miller 1998). A lonely person without things can indicate a lack of capacity to create relations (Miller 1998). Being human in a consumer society involves many relations to people and things, and this deserves more attention in future research. It is important to also consider the consequences of shopping and an accelerated pace of consumption on individuals, social relations, and the environment.

Figure 6.13 Father Christmases at Gekås Ullared in August—refined or coarse?

References

Bauman, Zygmunt. 1998. *Work, Consumerism and the New Poor*. Buckingham: Open University Press.

Belk, Russell W. 2001. "Materialism and You." *Journal of Research for Consumers* 1: 1–7.

Bourdieu, Pierre. 1984. *Distinction: A Social Critique of the Judgement of Taste*. Cambridge, MA: Harvard College and Routledge and Kegan Paul Ltd.

Brembeck, Helene. 2007. *Hem till McDonald's*. [Home to McDonald's]. Stockholm: Bokförlaget Carlsson.

Dagens Industri. 2009. "Guldregn Över Gekås Ägare." [A rain of gold over the owners of Gekås]. *Dagens Industri* digital edition, December 10.

Duesenberry, James S. 1949. *Income, Saving and the Theory of Consumer Behaviour*. Cambridge, MA: Harvard University Press.

Ekström, Karin M. 1995. *Children's Influence in Family Decision Making: A Study of Yielding, Consumer Learning, and Consumer Socialization*. Gothenburg: Bas.

Ekström, Karin M. 2006. "Consumer Socialization Revisited." In *Research in Consumer Behavior*, edited by Russell W. Belk, 10: 71–98. Oxford, UK: Elsevier Science Ltd.

Ekström, Karin M. 2007a. "Parental Consumer Learning or Keeping up with the Children." *Journal of Consumer Behaviour* 6, July–August: 203–17.

Ekström, Karin M. 2007b. "Participating in the Catwalk of Consumption." In *Children, Media and Consumption; On the Front Edge*. Yearbook at The International Clearinghouse on Children, Youth and Media, edited by Karin M. Ekström and Birgitte Tufte, 335–48. University of Gothenburg: Nordicom.

Ekström, Karin M. 2010a. "Design and Consumption." In *Consumer Behaviour, A Nordic Perspective*, edited by Karin M. Ekström, 515–29. Lund: Studentlitteratur.

Ekström, Karin M. 2010b. "Families and Reference Groups." In *Consumer Behaviour, A Nordic Perspective*, edited by Karin M. Ekström, 381–99. Lund: Studentlitteratur.

Ekström, Karin M. 2011. "Keeping Up with the Children: Changing Consumer Roles in Families." In *Beyond the Consumption Bubble*, edited by Karin M. Ekström and Kay Glans, 149–62. New York: Routledge.

Ekström, Karin M. and Torbjörn Hjort. 2009. "Hidden Consumers in Marketing, the Neglect of Consumers with Scarce Resources in Affluent Societies." *Journal of Marketing Management* 25, 7–8: 697–712.

Ekström, Karin M. and Kay Glans, eds. 2011. "Introduction." In *Beyond the Consumption Bubble*, edited by Karin M. Ekström and Kay Glans, 3–14. New York: Routledge.

Ekström, Karin M., and Lars Norén. 2008. "Stärk varumärket—släpp in konsumenten i fabriken." [Strengthen the brand—invite the consumer into the factory]. In *Marknadsorientering—Myter och Möjligheter*, [Market orientation—myths and possibilities], edited by Lars Gunnar Mattsson, 205–22. Stockholm: Liber.

Ekström, Karin M. and Lars Norén. 2011. *Den Mångkulturella Livsmedelsmarknaden—en Marknad med Möjligheter.* [The multicultural grocery market—a market with possibilities]. Stockholm: The Swedish Retail and Wholesale Development, report 2011. 2: 8–43.

Eriksson, Thomas. 1999. Älskade Pryl! Reklam- och Prylhistoria för Rekordårens Barn. [Beloved gadget! Advertising and history about gadgets for the children of the record years]. Stockholm: Bokförlaget Prisma.

Featherstone, Mike. 1991. *Consumer Culture and Postmodernism*. London: Sage Publications Ltd.

Frank, Robert H. 2007. *Falling Behind. How Rising Inequality Harms the Middle Class*. Berkeley: University of California Press.

John, D. Roedder. 1999. "Consumer Socialization of Children: A Retrospective Look at Twenty-five Years of Research." *Journal of Consumer Research* 26, 3: 183–213.

Hjort, Torbjörn. 2004. *Nödvändighetens Pris—om Knapphet och Konsumtion hos Barnfamiljer.* [The price of necessity—about scarcity and consumption among families with children]. Lund dissertations in Social Work 20, Lund: Lund University Press.

Hjort, Torbjörn. and Karin M. Ekström. 2006. "The Paradox of Consumption: Scarcity and Affluence in the Swedish Welfare State." In *Latin American Advances in Consumer Research*, edited by S. González and D. Luna, 148–53. Provo, Utah: Association for Consumer Research.

Holt, Douglas. 2004. *How Brands Become Icons, The Principles of Cultural Branding*. Boston, MA: Harvard Business School Press.

Hollander, Stanley C. and Glenn S. Omura. 1989. "Chain Store Developments and Their Political, Strategic and Social Interdependencies." *Journal of Retailing* 65, 3: 299–325.

Miller, Daniel. 1998. *The Theory of Shopping*. London: Polity Press.

Miller, Daniel. 2010. *Stuff*. Cambridge: Polity Press.

Nilsson, Marina. 2013. *50 år Alla tiders Ullared, 1963 Gekås 2013*. [50 years Terrific Ullared, 1963 Gekås 2013]. Stockholm: ICA Bokförlag.

Salzer-Mörling, Miriam and Lars Strannegård. 2004. "Silence of the Brands." *European Journal of Marketing* 38, 1/2: 224–38.

Sassatelli, Roberta. 2007. *Consumer Culture; History, Theory and Politics*. London: Sage.

Simmel, Georg. 1904. "Fashion." *International Quarterly* 10: 130–55.

Slater, Don. 1997. *Consumer Culture and Modernity*. Cambridge: Polity Press.

Ward, Scott. 1974. "Consumer Socialization." *Journal of Consumer Research* 1: 1–16.

www.gekas.se—information about Gekås Ullared.

PART III
Framing the Human Being in a Consumer Society

Chapter 7

Reflections on the Cultural Commons

Talbot Brewer

Introduction

If culture is the medium in which the animal *homo sapiens* takes on a properly human form of life, we might be tempted to measure a culture's health by how hard it is for its children to become adults. Such a measure would not be entirely inapt, since youths often sense more keenly than others what is cramped and alien about the social roles for which they are being fitted. Still this measure would be quite crude. There are worthy and unworthy coming-of-age ordeals, and the difference between being groomed for excellence and being broken for the yoke is not marked by some simple quantum of exertion. The crucial question is not how hard it is to grow up but how it is hard to grow up: What kinds of struggles and transfigurations are involved in becoming an adult, and what is the value of these struggles? Do they conduce to the flowering or the disfigurement of the most valuable human capacities?

If these are the telling questions, then clearly we cannot assess the health of a culture without making controversial judgments concerning human flourishing. While I will not skirt such controversies entirely, I hope to mitigate them just a bit by focusing on a special set of cases in which the demands of acculturation arise unbidden as the cumulative effect of self-interested market choices, and seem to conflict with the views of the human good that we ourselves tend to profess in our most serious moments, and that we flatter ourselves that we "hold" in some real way. That is, I will be looking at cases in which practices and considered ideals are at war with each other, leaving us to pick our way through the cultural crossfire.

Such cases have become increasingly common in recent years, as market-driven activity has come to play an increasingly pervasive role in shaping our attitudes and aspirations. We live in an era in which the market is finalizing its cooptation of a task that traditionally has been the provenance of the family and face-to-face community—the task of shaping the evaluative sensibility, the characteristic desires, and the dreams of youths, hence the task of determining whether and how prevailing cultural forms will be perpetuated in future generations. It is still widely said that "it takes a village to raise a child," but few communities remain healthy and coherent enough to rise to this task. The "village" has been displaced in part by an intrusive swarm of desire-shaping messages that compete daily for our ears and eyeballs and that succeed at least in mesmerizing if not in convincing us. That is, the "village" has been displaced by the advertising firm in its capacity as missionary of the corporation, and by the corporate personnel department in its capacity as arbiter of social success.

When market activity confers an uncompensated benefit or burden on some third party, economists refer to this as a market externality. I will be focusing on what might be called the "cultural externalities" of the marketplace. Yet there are many cultural externalities, not all of them worthy of attention. My inquiry will center on two externalities that are particularly troubling because they directly conflict with prevailing ideas of the human good. The externalities in question are the tendency towards consumerist understandings of proper life satisfactions, and the tendency towards careerist understandings of social identities and proper life activities. I will tentatively suggest that these externalities today have the form of tragedies of the cultural commons. The idea here is that in these cases, as in the better-known tragedies of the environmental commons (for example global warming, fish stock depletion), individual choices are having the cumulative effect of depleting a public good that the very individuals making the choices would prefer to maintain even at the cost of the personal benefits they secure from the choices. Such a circumstance can be condemned as socially irrational even without staking ourselves to an affirmation of the cultural resources under threat (though I will not hide my view that the threatened cultural resources are indeed of great value).

I do not believe myself capable of describing a concrete utopia, nor am I convinced that political philosophers ought to attempt such a feat. My more modest aim is to highlight obstacles to human flourishing that are presented by the economic structures and practices within which our lives unfold. Given this aim, my discussion will be considerably more concrete and historically bound than is typical of contemporary Anglo-American philosophy. I will proceed in an interdisciplinary fashion, drawing heavily upon the works of historians and sociologists. Some will say that this attention to actuality means that I must be doing something other than political philosophy—perhaps cultural criticism. While I do not wish to quibble over labels, still this chapter has emerged from a persisting frustration with the tightly constricted field of vision of contemporary Anglo-American political philosophy. Its normative assessments of political and economic structures tend to focus on abstract patterns in the distribution of work opportunities and in the distribution of income and wealth resulting from work. What drops from view is what our concrete practices of getting and spending do to our characters, our souls. This matter receives virtually no attention within Anglo-American political philosophy, and relatively little attention within popular political debate, partly because of a deep-seated and conceptually unstable commitment to "neutrality" about the nature of the good life for human beings.[1]

---

1   There are some notable exceptions to this sweeping generalization. One excellent new work in this genre that manages both to be philosophically deep and widely accessible, and that found a very large audience (it was a *New York Times* bestseller), is Matthew B. Crawford's *Shop Class as Soulcraft: An Inquiry into the Value of Work* (2009).

Ironically, this inattention has the result of leaving largely unnoticed and uncontested the decidedly non-neutral influence upon actual evaluative outlooks that is exercised by extant market forms.

The pattern is quite different in continental political philosophy, which has grappled forthrightly with the effects on the human soul of prevailing forms of getting and spending. In this chapter I draw upon a circle of Italian theorists—including Franco Berardi, Paolo Virno, and Maurizio Lazzarato—who have sought to show that "postfordist" forms of work are fundamentally hostile to human flourishing. I think they are right about this, yet it has not been easy to convince other Anglophone philosophers of the merits of their work. The problem they have identified cannot easily be captured in the normative frameworks on offer in Anglo-American political philosophy. The problem is not that rights are being violated, though they may be, or that the fair value of the political liberties is not being guaranteed, though it certainly isn't, or that there is unfairness in the distribution of opportunities for securing positions of prestige and high remuneration, though there certainly are, or that the least well do not enjoy as much income and wealth as they could, though certain they are not. The problem in question could persist even if all of these very important desiderata were met. The problem belongs not to the realm of justice but to the realm of human flourishing or *eudaimonia*—a notion that has become central to contemporary ethics but that has comparatively little presence in contemporary political philosophy.

Anglophone ethical theorists typically make heavy use of simple thought experiments (trolley problems, prisoners dilemmas, and so on) to generate and refine their normative intuitions. While I have my doubts about this practice in ethics, I feel more certain that it is out of place in political theory, where any thought experiment that is simple enough to be posited by the theorist is likely to be too far removed from the workings of any humanly possible politico-economic system to spark genuinely revealing intuitions. This is particularly true if one wishes to take up the traditional republican interest in the effects of political and economic practices on the souls of the citizenry. Here the devils (and angels) lie in the details, and it is exceedingly difficult to imagine these details with any confidence when considering merely hypothetical political and economic forms. This is why I forego thought experiments in favor of the actual "experiments in political possibility" in which we find ourselves enmeshed. These are the only political experiments that we can grasp with sufficient concreteness and vividness to inform our political theorizing. It is my interest in these experiments that explains the historicity and interdisciplinarity of my work.

Another notable exception is the hit television show *The Office*, which focuses in large part on the psychodynamics of alienated white-collar work.

Changing Patterns of Consumption

The historian William Leach (1994, xiii) writes:

> Whoever has the power to project a vision of the good life and make it prevail
> has the most decisive power of all. In its sheer quest to produce and sell goods
> cheaply in constantly growing volume and a higher profit levels, American
> business, after 1890, acquired such power and, despite a few wrenching crises
> along the way, has kept it ever since. From the 1890s on, American corporate
> business, in league with key institutions, began the transformation of American
> society into a society preoccupied with consumption, with comfort and bodily
> well-being, with luxury, spending, and acquisition, with more goods this year
> than last, more next year that this. American consumer capitalism produced a
> culture almost violently hostile to the past and to tradition, a future-oriented
> culture of desire that confused the good life with goods.

According to Leach, religious beliefs have been remolded in fundamental ways
to accommodate this ascendant conception of the good. Extant versions of
Christianity have become more worldly, more conformable to the pursuit of wealth
and the acquisition of material goods, and more tolerant of what might once have
been denounced as idolatry. Leach and others have made the further suggestion
that such an alteration in fundamental attitudes towards consumption was in fact
required in order to hasten the transition, in the United States and Western Europe,
from an industrial to a postindustrial economy. This suggestion is presented as a
sequel to the story of the rise of capitalism told by Max Weber in *The Protestant
Ethic and the Spirit of Capitalism*. Weber had argued that the rise of capitalism was
fueled by the combination, within Calvinist and Pietist sects of Christianity, of a
call to the zealous pursuit of a secular vocation, and of a strict asceticism that ruled
out the acquisition of luxury goods. This combination favors the accumulation of
capital and the reinvestment of that capital in new enterprises. Leach suggests that
around 1890 to 1900, American industry had increased its productivity to such an
extent that it was threatened with a glut-driven crisis, one that could be avoided
only by overturning entrenched habits of thrift in favor of a level of consumption
that would previously have been considered objectionably luxurious. Yet this
chapter of the story is notably anti-Weberian in its explanatory structure. This
time, economic processes caused a fundamental change in prevailing religious
outlooks, not the other way round.

Why this difference? The answer, in a nutshell, is that at this stage in the
history of capitalism, the route to increased profitability required the production
of an immaterial good that could not be grown in a field or manufactured in a
factory. It required the mass production of desire. And the social and technological
backdrop was in place, at least in the larger North American cities, to permit
this new requirement to be met with some measure of success. Leach tells the
story of the remaking of the world as a fosterer of consumer desire—a bid for

attention that begins with the introduction of urban window displays and neon signs, and that culminates in technologies capable of claiming the attention of the citizenry with great regularity, not only in public spaces of the city but also within the walls of the home. As Emily Fogg Mead explained in an influential turn of the century essay on marketing techniques, "the successful advertisement is obtrusive. It continually forces itself upon the attention. It may be on sign boards, in the street car, or on the page of a magazine. Everyone reads it involuntarily. It is a subtle, persistent, unavoidable presence that creeps into the reader's inner consciousness" (Leach 1994, 48). This intrusion into the public consciousness had been advanced sufficiently by 1930 that President Herbert Hoover was moved to praise the assembled executives of the Associated Advertising Clubs of the World for "expanding our upper levels of desire." As Hoover puts it:

> You have devised an artful ingenuity in forms and mediums of advertising. The landscape has become your vehicle as well as the press. In the past, wish, want, and desire were the motive forces in economic progress. Now you have taken over the job of creating desire. In economics the torments of desire in turn creates demand, and from demand we create production, and thence around the cycle we land with increased standards of living. (Leach 1994, 375)

This cycle—which counts as virtuous under any outlook that prioritizes increase in Gross Domestic Product—is still in place today. Yet there is a vast difference between the first and still quite primitive efforts to inculcate consumerist desires in the population, and the much more sophisticated efforts currently underway. The average six-year-old child in the United States sees 40,000 commercial messages per year and can name 200 brands. Each year in the United States, well over $100 billion is spent on advertising, and about $15 billion of that total is spent on advertising directed specifically at children (Schor 2005, 19–21). Worldwide expenditures on advertising in 2003 totaled something in the neighborhood of $650 billion, making advertising the second biggest business in the world today— after weapons, of course (Latouche 2009, 17). By comparison, the total annual budget of the Vatican for all purposes is $130 million. Even if the Vatican devoted half of its annual budget to proselytism, still its budget for reshaping the minds of the citizenry of the world would be 1/10,000th of the amount spent each year on commercial advertising.

This might seem an inapt comparison. After all, you might say, advertisers are not attempting to make converts to a religion. They are trying to sell goods and services. Further, their messages are not at all the same. Each is trying to sell a different good or service. If the message of one advertiser meets with success, this will often mean failure for the message of some other advertiser. Yet there is a common core to the exhortations that advertisers place before our attention. They tell us that consumption is a centrally important pathway to the happy life, and that a vast array of corporations have made it their purpose to help us along this pathway. That is, they provide a picture of the good life and an ideological justification of the prevailing economic order in terms of that picture of the good life. They invite us to enjoy a passive sort of reconciliation with the social order. One simply eases into the armchair, or feels the instantaneous surge of the car at the touch of the accelerator, and directly experiences the way that the world of things has been sculpted by others so as to guarantee its responsiveness to the wishes that it has itself helped to uncork. These palpable signs of what economists are wont to call (misleadingly, I think) our consumer sovereignty might well dull our taste for political sovereignty, breeding acquiescence in oligarchy or corporatocracy. If so, then corporate interests do not find their way into politics only by hiring lobbyists and by paying to amplify the speech of favored candidates. These interests are continually waging a campaign that is political in the broadest sense—a campaign to sustain the unreflective allegiance of the populace to the prevailing form of socio-economic cooperation. As Jean Baudrillard puts it (2006, 198), "Advertising is a plebiscite whereby mass consumer society wages a perpetual campaign of self-endorsement."

Aside from this possible threat to political autonomy, advertising promulgates a particular, highly dubious conception of the human good. This picture may well be too fragmentary to count as what John Rawls and other contemporary liberal theorists would call a "comprehensive conception of the good" (for example a religion or a comprehensive philosophy such as stoicism or existentialism), but it is suited to serve as an element of such conceptions. The $650 billion worth of commercial messages that make their bid each year for the eyes and ears of the world are a *de facto* form of proselytism on behalf of the class of comprehensive conceptions of the human good that give this consumerist element a central place.

This program of proselytism is the most potent that the world has ever seen. It makes a deeper and more inescapable bid for the continuous and exclusive attention of humankind than any other program of proselytism has ever made, and it does more to shape the actual evaluative outlooks, daily activities and desires of human beings than any other program of proselytism has ever done. Yet what is most distinctive about this sort of proselytism—if indeed we can call it by that name—is not its scope or success, but its automaticity. It has no need of preachers or zealots. The workers who create and disseminate its communiqués, and who shape public spaces in ways that convey its spirit, have reason to do their jobs with maximal effectiveness even if they themselves view consumerism with deep ambivalence. This proselytism works by an invisible hand of the contemporary market, though this hand is not necessarily of the beneficent kind that interested Adam Smith.

I say that this global proselytism can go forward without true believers. Whether it does so is an empirical question. I am not certain of the answer to this question, but I suspect that by and large it does. Yet even if this program of proselytism is not winning wholehearted converts, this doesn't mean that it is not moving hearts and minds. It could not be ineffective if most of its component elements were effective in bringing about their more limited aims, and the world business community is hardly foolish enough to waste $650 billion per year on adverts that don't work.

This "proselytism without true believers" must then be succeeding quite reliably in reshaping the pre-reflective evaluative outlooks encoded in our desires, and in shaping our voluntary actions, even if it is not bringing our considered beliefs into line with these desires and actions. It can meet its aims and perpetuate itself even if it succeeds only in making ambivalent consumers of us, uneasy with our own desires, internally divided in the manner of the *akratic* or *enkratic* soul.

This seems like a fair description of our actual relation to our consumerist pursuits. It makes sense of the fact that in the United States, home of the world's most avid consumers, more than 80 percent of the population think that their fellow Americans buy and consume far too much and that our youths are objectionably obsessed with the acquisition of material possessions.[2] They can't all be right and yet all be acting on the considered judgment that this poll unveils. The conjecture also helps to explain why there is hardly a single serious thinker who unapologetically champions consumerism, despite its pervasive and growing influence over actual human behavior.[3] It explains, in other words, why consumerism and a distaste for consumerism have arisen together, as two halves of a single, remarkably successful psychological form. Maybe this is the only form in which consumer tastes *can* propagate themselves among human beings—in a bad-faith union with an immanent self-critique that sates the conscience without stanching the urge to indulge in consumer expenditures. In any case, this amalgam of attitudes does seem to propagate itself with extraordinary success despite the fact that its elements are at war with each other.

There are reasons to suspect, then, that this program of proselytism does in fact go forward with relatively few true believers. That is, it might well be the case that its agents of persuasion—the cadres of advertising executives and the teams of writers and artists who create its messages, the investors who found and perpetuate advertising firms, and the legions of business executives who purchase their services in order to grip the attention and alter the tastes of the populace—would prefer a world that was in some ways less consumerist, yet realize that if they were to refuse to perform their role in this vast and decentralized effort, this would place their own financial well-being at serious risk without materially advancing their anti-consumerist preference. If this is right, then in the absence of a mechanism for coordinating restraint, advertisements will predictably remain more intrusive and the cultural environment more consumerist than anyone would prefer.

---

2   This finding is due to a survey conducted in 1995 by the Merck Family Fund and disseminated under the title "Yearning for Balance: Views on Consumption, Materialism and the Environment." The report can be found at: http://www.iisd.ca/consume/harwood.html.

3   James Twitchell (1999) rightly takes himself to be taking an extremely unusual stance when he sets out to offer even "two cheers" for materialism. "Who but fools, toadies, hacks, and occasional loopy libertarians have ever risen to its defense?" he asks. He goes on to claim that "The really interesting question may not be why we are so materialistic, but why we are so unwilling to acknowledge and explore what seems the central characteristic of modern life."

By the normative standards prevailing among economists, this would clearly count as a cumulative negative externality of rational market behavior, one made all the more likely by the fact that advertisements are often promulgated by a corporate agent whose interests are simpler and more purely pecuniary than the interest of almost any actual human being.

These ruminations suggest that the contemporary phenomenon of automatic consumerist proselytism might well have the same basic structure as the cases that environmentalists call tragedies of the commons. After all, it might well be that everyone would prefer a less consumerist cultural environment even at the cost of the personal benefits that they would have to forego to sustain such an environment. The difference from more familiar "tragedies of the commons" would lie in the fact that the public good under threat is a feature of the cultural rather than the natural environment, hence that the phenomenon in view is a tragedy of the cultural commons.

Whether or not the phenomenon under consideration has this paradoxical and troubling structure, it can hardly be denied that it threatens a cultural condition that seems valuable to many people. Since the cultural good in question here is particularly important to childrearing, its degradation tends to be noticed most frequently in discussions of the upbringing of children. A seemingly cogent protest against this form of proselytism was penned by the Institute for American Values in 2001 in a report called "Watch Out for Children: A Mothers' Statement to Advertisers." The report begins with an expression of outrage at the attitudes on display at the 12th annual "Consumer Kids" meeting, a four-day convention focused on how to advertise effectively to children. What outraged the authors of the report was that advertisers are quite self-consciously "attempting to substitute their values for the values that mothers [and, presumably, fathers] try to teach their children." Advertisers have enlisted psychological research and new media technologies with the aim of "occupying more and more of our children's psychic and physical space" (2001, 4), with advertising that "urges instant gratification, promotes self-indulgence, promotes and obsession with money and material things, and sells the idea that 'we are what we buy'" (26).

These observations seem largely apt (though I would suggest that advertisers do not amplify their own values but rather the values that it is most profitable for them to amplify). Yet they have had relatively little resonance in public debate. I believe this is due to a curious anomaly in the political alliances that currently structure political life in the United States and, to some extent, in other Western liberal democracies. The anomaly is that cultural conservatives have, by and large, made common cause with the friends of unfettered capitalist markets, despite the fact that unfettered capitalist markets pose an existential challenge to the traditional beliefs that cultural conservatives cherish. For this reason, cultural conservatives are not inclined to extend their concerns about the spread of consumerism to a broader critique of corporate capitalism. Thus, while the "Mother's Statement to Advertisers" admonishes advertisers for promulgating "selfishness, instant gratification, and materialism" by competing for "share of mind" with slogans such as "You deserve a break today," "Have it your way," "Follow your instincts, Obey your thirst," "Just do it," "No boundaries," and "Got the urge?," (2001, 6) it goes on to insist that the root of the problem is the irresponsible behavior of a few bad apples in the world of advertising, and is in no way endemic to corporate capitalism (8). What the critique fails to note is that the marketing techniques of these "bad apples" would not have proliferated if they were not effective, and that if these "bad apples" were to refrain from making use of genuinely effective techniques then they would quickly lose market share to competitors with a less restrictive conscience.

One might expect the political left to offer a more biting critique of the cultural power of corporations. Yet in the American case, at least, this expectation is in vain. This is not solely because the (so-called) American "left" is almost as unswerving in its corporatism as the right—though it is—but also because the left is gripped by the suspicion that talk of the human good portends an oppressively traditionalist agenda. This suspicion serves to thwart the traditional ambition of left-liberals to ensure social space for the flourishing of a vibrant array of conflicting conceptions of the human good, or to preserve a healthy sphere of autonomous experiments in living. It helps to position our traditions and our individual "experiments in living" in a field of symbolic communication that inclines them towards other people's pecuniary interests and gives them a superficial, self-gratifying and materialistic form. Such a decentralized mode of culture formation may be preferable to centralized statist modes, but there is no reason to suppose that these are the only two alternatives, and every reason for left-liberal theorists to probe the pathological aspects of the alternative for which we have effectively opted.

One source of liberal reluctance to pursue such questions is a basic commitment to anti-paternalism. Liberal theorists are strongly inclined to honor individual choices and to insist that political institutions or rulings must never be premised on a judgment concerning the wisdom of these choices. Yet if the choices we are making in our capacity as workers have the cumulative effect of making over the society in accordance with a distinctive, non-neutral conception of the human good—and, moreover, a conception that many of us regard on reflection as debased—this significantly weakens the liberal case for refusing any assessment of individual choices. The appeal of the liberal defense of individual choice lies in large part in the thought that this is the way to defend the social space within which idiosyncrasy is encouraged and authentic experiments in living are sculpted and pursued. In conditions where individual choices are having the cumulative effect of squeezing out the social space for such idiosyncratic experimentation, liberals must decide whether they are partisans of bare choice or partisans of some richer notion of self-direction and authenticity.

There is a well-known US Supreme Court case, much discussed by political philosophers, called *Yoder v. Wisconsin*. In this case, the Court decided that Wisconsin's mandatory schooling requirements impinged upon the religious liberty of Amish parents, because it required them to immerse their children each school day in an alien way of life—one that was deeply hostile to their religious beliefs and values. The Amish believe in working together, fostering strong communal bonds, living a simple and self-sufficient life, and refusing any technological mediation of their relationship to the earth and to the labor essential for subsistence. As is noted in the Supreme Court's majority opinion, Amish children who attend public schools remote from their own communities face "a hydraulic insistence on conformity to majoritarian standards." The Supreme Court decided that this "hydraulic" pressure imposes an undue burden on the free exercise of religion, partly because it interferes with parental efforts to pass along their religious convictions and way of life to their children.

If the picture I've offered of consumerist proselytism is roughly on target, then almost all of us bear a burden that historically has been borne only by cultural minorities such as the Amish. Almost all of us are at least mildly estranged from the best-amplified and most attention-grabbing symbolic speech through which the culture shapes its own future by sculpting the souls of its offspring. Of course, there is at least one key difference. In this more inclusive case, the "hydraulic insistence on conformity" is exerted not by another group with a different culture, but as the automatic deliverance of the market's invisible hand. The scattered individual choices that we ourselves make at work have the cumulative effect of imposing a historically unprecedented pressure upon us to conform outside of work to a set of values that strike us as quite alien. In such a circumstance, to regard individual choice as sacrosanct is to acquiesce in the self-belittlement of man by man.

Liberal interpretations of free speech rights are often elaborated in the language of neutrality. The idea is that while the time, place and manner of speech may be restricted, speech cannot be singled out for legal restriction in virtue of its content. This sort of content-neutrality is often affirmed not only by neutralitarian liberals, but also by those liberals who ground their view upon the non-neutral ideal of individual autonomy. There are powerful arguments that can be offered for this interpretative approach to free speech rights, and perhaps at the end of the day we ought to affirm it as an extremely valuable barrier to political oppression. But there is a serious, yet little noticed, cost of this approach.

Contemporary communications technology has brought it about that more attentive eyes and ears are available for commercial capture than ever before. There is a thriving market in human attention. If we ask what sorts of messages will proliferate in this technological environment, the answer is: whatever messages people are willing to pay the most money to amplify. Given that the amplification of speech with commercial content is ordinarily much more profitable than the amplification of any other kind of speech, content-neutral speech regimes can hardly be expected to have content-neutral effects on the culture. Indeed, in such circumstances, content-neutrality will largely cede to large commercial interests the field of symbolic communication through which human cultures impart or fail to impart their distinctive life-understandings and evaluative outlooks to future generations. There is a danger that this might tend over time to produce a consumerist monoculture in which idiosyncrasy becomes an increasingly superficial phenomenon—a surface variation in choice of commercial accoutrements and accessories. Content neutrality actually favors a debasing consumerism.

Political philosophies are shaped in large part by their nightmares, and communitarianism differs starkly from liberalism in its animating nightmare. The liberal nightmare is that it will not be possible for different religious communities to live together without resorting to oppression or violence. The communitarian nightmare is that the liberal devotion to state neutrality about the human good, when enacted against the backdrop of contemporary market conditions and technologies of communication, will have the effect of producing a frenetic but uninspiring consumerist monoculture. This nightmare is left entirely untouched by the elaborate attempts of liberal theorists to respond to communitarian critiques by showing that their views do not imply a covert conception of the human good. Communitarianism is not fueled by the thought that liberalism is inconsistent or conceptually unstable, though it may be. That would be a purely academic dispute. Communitarianism is fueled by the thought that liberalism threatens to crowd out the space within which any genuinely deep and meaningful cultural tradition can be sustained, and that it therefore portends a decline of human life into self-gratification and superficiality.

If we frame the temptations of communitarianism in this way, we can see more clearly why its critique ought to trouble liberal theorists of various stripes. It certainly ought to trouble those autonomist and Millian liberals who seek to sustain optimal conditions for original and idiosyncratic experiments in living. But it ought also to trouble the neutralitarian liberal. After all, the reason to insist that laws must have a neutral justification is presumably to preserve social space within which individuals and groups are able to sculpt their lives around a plural and conflicting set of religious and philosophical convictions. If the insistence upon neutral justification tended over time to reduce vibrantly pluralistic societies to consumerist monocultures, this insistence would begin to look like a formalistic fetish.

Liberal political theorists tend to favor norms of justice in the distribution of income and wealth that produce higher rather than lower levels of productivity. To take one example, John Rawls' well-known difference principle calls for the arrangement of basic laws and economic institutions that maximizes the income and wealth of the least well off (Rawls 1971, 60–75). This standard cannot be put to use unless we have a way of comparing income and wealth across hypothetical socio-economic arrangements. Since there are no currency exchange rates for merely hypothetical economies, it is hard to see how to do this except in terms of the power to purchase bundles of commodities. Given this, it is hard to see how Rawls' standard can be put to use without favoring those economic structures that maximize the production of purchasable commodities. As Hoover points out in the speech from which I have quoted, this is arguably best done by taking on "the job of creating desire," thereby fueling a self-augmenting cycle of increased thirst for consumption and redoubled labor in production. It seems plausible, then, that Rawlsian standards of distributive justice will tend in practice to favor those socio-economic orders that efficiently augment and sate consumerist desires.

The same can be said of those theories that seek to promote individual well-being but that limit their attention to the distributions of income and wealth that are called for by this desideratum. Depending upon just how well-being is specified, these theories might perhaps have the resources to approach the problems at hand. But insofar as theorists who wield this measure focus on the contribution to well-being made by differential levels of income, while ignoring the effects on well-being that owe to the activities through which this income is secured, their approach shares the blindness under consideration. It is precisely this sort of possibility that inclines me to think that in political philosophy, abstract reflection can yield perverse results, and that these perversities can sometimes be identified and mitigated by attention to concrete experiments in politico-economic organization.

Even if Rawlsian liberalism can be emended so as to resolve this concern, still we have here a potent critique of the norms that govern the public sphere today. It is very nearly a fixed point in contemporary political debate, both in the developing and the developed world, that a primary goal of politics is to increase economic productivity. Under this assumption, the cycle of increased consumer desire and increased production is virtuous, and our political ingenuity ought to be directed towards setting such cycles in motion. I have attempted to call this presumption into question.

Given current patterns of climate change and resources depletion, it seems clear that increases in production and consumption are being secured today at the expense of future generations. A Rawlsian liberal would certainly be chagrined by this fact, and would insist that the interests of future generations must be counted on an equal footing when we assess the justice of our economic practices. I agree, yet I think that the problem is more immediate, and that liberal political theories do not have the resources to cast it in a genuinely revealing light. The problem with the current form of getting and spending is not merely that it is catastrophically bad for future generations and for life on this planet. Nor is the problem best captured in the language of rights, as a generalization of the kind of indirect infringement on liberty of conscience that some liberals see in the mandatory schooling requirements struck down in *Yoder v. Wisconsin*. It seems to me most illuminating to speak here of impediments to *eudaimonia* or human flourishing properly understood—understood, in particular, as a continuous and self-formative life activity involving a gradual elaboration and ever-further articulation of one's own evaluative outlook.

I have argued elsewhere (Brewer 2009) that desires, and the emotions in which they are often embedded, are vivid "seemings" of the evaluative contours of one's changing circumstance. They structure our pre-deliberative "take" on what it would be good to do or to be. If commercial advertising succeeds in reshaping our desires, it thereby succeeds in reshaping elements of our pre-deliberative sense of what it would be worthwhile to do or to be, along with those elements of our daily behavior that are controlled by this pre-reflective sense of value. It imprints someone else's interests on our sense of value. And while we are certainly capable of acting contrary to our desires, we cannot act *wholeheartedly* contrary to desire.

Hence even where advertising fails to produce conviction and fails to shape what we actually do, it might still determine what it comes naturally to us to do, and what we can do without inner reservation or resistance.

It would badly misconstrue the workings of the regime of advertising to suppose that what it does is merely to implant in us a set of isolated desires for particular goods and services. Rather, it works upon us largely by offering us a self, a way of being in the world, constructed by consumer tags. Indeed, the most valuable asset of many corporations is precisely the carefully sculpted social meaning of their brands, and a great deal of advertising has as its primary end the reinforcement and refinement of an instrument of symbolic expression. To consume these branded goods is to position oneself in a ready-made field of object-borne messages in such a way as to construct and communicate a social identity. It is arguably because consumption is in the end a form of symbol manipulation that our taste for it is basically inexhaustible. If we bought goods solely to use them, presumably we would keep them until we used them up. It is far better, from the advertiser's point of view, if we buy goods in order to express ourselves, particularly if we are likely to find that these expressions are never quite right, always in need of retouching. That is, it is best if we can be gotten to share the recurring thought of Eliot's Prufrock that "That is not it at all, That is not what I meant [to be], at all" (Eliot 1934, 1–9) without losing confidence that some other object might at long last make over our public personas and our lives so that they are aligned precisely with what we mean to be.

For advertisers, then, the game of consumerist identity-construction goes best if it permanently entices and yet forever disappoints us—if it leaves us, in other words, in the condition of Tantalus. On reflection, the game is almost perfectly calculated to work in just this way. The enticement of consumerist modes of identity-constitution lies in part in the fact that it offers us ready-made and instantly recognizable tools of self-expression, thus promising to spare us the hard work of bringing ourselves into a fully satisfying form and explaining the resulting idiosyncrasies to others. Yet this very fact arguably guarantees a certain measure of disappointment with the result. We might think of the true task of identity construction as involving the faithful articulation of our inchoate sense of how it would be good or valuable to live. The central activity here is the articulation of the intimations of value embedded in our existing feelings and desires. Here the word "articulation" is meant in both its common senses: we give a more fine-toothed and determinate shape to our intimations of value (that is, give them greater articulation) by bring them into the space of words (that is, by articulating them).[4] This activity requires faithfulness to our actual evaluative sensibility, but it also refines that sensibility by finding words for it that we are prepared to live by. This active sort of identity-formation continuously re-sculpts the self in line with a stance that it is able to affirm. The consumerist route to identity formation

---

4   I owe this idea of self-articulation to Charles Taylor, who sets it out in "Responsibility for Self" (1976).

leaves this work of self-sculpting entirely undone. It trades on an illusion about the nature of the self and its proper life tasks—an illusion that locates the self in its public self-presentation rather than in its characteristic way of apprehending and responding to value. And it takes the self to be a fixed entity in need of faithful public expression rather than a being called to take an active role in giving shape to itself. If we assume that most human beings have at least a liminal awareness that this self-understanding is illusory, we can expect consumerist forays in identity-formation to produce serial disillusionment and not satisfaction.

Viewed from another angle, we might trace the seduction of consumerism to the mistaken thought that the good is a state of affairs to be produced rather than a property wholly present in the activities and relationships that are most fitting for human beings, and that our activities should be calculated to produce the good rather than continuously to actualize it. Once we adopt this world-making conception of the good, we will be inclined to spend even our spare time reshaping the world so that it provides a fitting setting and fitting accoutrements for our lives. We will, for instance, begin to gather in large weekend crowds at home improvement megastores. Which is to say, we will find ourselves in the world we inhabit today.

One of the most illuminating insights of Aristotelianism is that the highest human good cannot be a state of affairs—not even an achieved state of the psyche such as a virtuous character—but must be intrinsically valuable activity arising from an appreciation of that very activity and continuously extending and sharpening that self-same appreciation. The self is forged continuously as the byproduct of its quest for words and actions that express its sense of the good, and refinements to the self open the possibility of more illuminating speech and more refined activity. Consumer pursuits are allied with a different conception of the self and its task in life, and by Aristotelian lights they leave the self comparatively superficial and unformed.

Changing Patterns of Work

In his early writings, Marx (1975, 329) argued that human beings are fully actualized—that is, they rise to their proper form of being—only when they freely and self-consciously contribute to the creation of a fitting environment for human life. Our laboring activity ought to move in a cycle between formulating a picture of how the world might be altered so as to accommodate more valuable activities, making over the world in accordance with our picture, then arriving through experience with the world so refashioned at another, yet more adequate picture of how the human world might be remade. Call this the Marxist, or materialist, conception of human self-elaboration.

In capitalist work conditions, Marx thinks, the proper cycle between practical thinking and labor is broken, and labor ceases to be a mode of self-elaboration. The laborer is called upon to put into action the plans of others. There is no opportunity for him to reshape his work in accordance with his evolving sense of what the product might contribute to human lives, or of what it is for a human life to go better rather than worse. The task of product design is assigned to specialists, as is the determination of production techniques. In order to minimize production costs, the production process is decomposed into simple constituent operations, each performed repetitively by a single worker along an assembly line. This tends to increase production speed while also permitting the employer to save money by replacing skilled craftsmen with unskilled workers.[5] The customer enjoys a lower price. But the worker comes to be employed only in his capacity as an unusually dexterous if not entirely reliable machine. It is in this sense that the worker is alienated from his laboring activity. The worker is obliged to treat himself as a rentable commodity whose value lies in its capacity for coordinated bodily motions, and must turn over the direction of these motions for most of his waking hours to other human beings whose interests lie in making these motions as repetitive and mindless as possible.

In the generation or two after Marx, some thinkers began to hope that technological advances in production would soon make it possible to defang the problem of industrial labor by greatly reducing the fraction of their time on earth that human beings would devote to work. Edward Bellamy expressed this hope in *Looking Backward*—a book that envisioned a nearly workless human future, to be achieved in the year 2000, and that inspired a nationwide utopian-socialist political movement when it appeared in 1888 (see Fromm 1960, vi). John Maynard Keynes envisioned a similar future in a little essay he published in 1930 under the title "Economic Possibilities for our Grandchildren." He projected that increased worker productivity would soon make it possible to sustain a decent standard of living for all while reducing the average work week to 15 hours. This prospect would bring human beings face-to-face with what Keynes regarded as their real and permanent problem: what to do with genuine freedom. This would require development of the art of liberty—the art of identifying and refining life activities that are genuinely valuable in and of themselves (that is, the "liberal arts" taken in their original and proper sense, and not in the fallen pre-careerist condition in which they limp along today). Keynes was pessimistic about the human capacity to meet this challenge. Looking around him, he observed that the wives of the wealthy were already faced with it and were failing badly. These women "cannot find it sufficiently amusing, when deprived of the spur of economic necessity, to cook and clean and mend, yet are quite unable to find anything more amusing" (Keynes 1930, 4).

Recent history suggests that Keynes's pessimism was well-founded. We seem inclined to evade our "permanent problem" even in conditions of remarkable prosperity. As Juliet Schor observes (1993, 2), the material consumption rates achieved in 1948 could have been sustained in the 1990s even if every single

---

5   For an excellent discussion of alienated labor and its relation to the fragmentation of laboring activity into simple mindless steps, see Harry Braverman 1974.

worker took every other year off. Yet the average American family contributed 16 *more* weeks of full-time work to the formal economy in 1988 than in 1967 (Bluestone and Rose 1997). This is not just a reflection of the entry of more family workers into the workforce. The trend holds good at the individual level as well as at the family level. The average US worker put in 148 more hours per year in 1996 than in 1973 (Berardi 2009, 78). Nor does this seem to be a function of economic need. The percentage of US workers putting in more than 49 hours per week grew from 13 percent in 1976 to 19 percent in 1998, while the percentage of managers working that many hours grew from 40 percent to 45 percent.[6]

This is the flip side of the vast increase in consumption experienced in recent decades in the US and Western Europe. We are working more and we are spending more—not now in the name of survival but as our first attempt to answer what Keynes called the permanent question of humankind. We have effectively refused the offer of increased free time in exchange for increases in paid work and consumption. Indeed, as noted above, in the United States our consumption patterns have become so lavish that they could be sustainably enjoyed by all of our fellow human beings only if we can somehow get our hands on five more planets that are roughly as well endowed with natural resources as the one we've got. Given this, our *de facto* answer to the permanent question of humanity is not available on a sustainable basis for humankind as a whole.

As noted above, this seems to me to ground both a practical and a moral demand to rethink our answer. A more difficult question is whether this answer would be a wise one even if our environment contained enough natural resources and waste sink capacity to make it sustainably available for all human beings. Is work in the postindustrial economy good for those who have it? This question opens up a crucial field of normative reflection. Like the question of the value of consumer plenty, so too this question is handled far too peremptorily in contemporary public debate, where GDP growth functions as a nearly fixed normative standard. Our *de facto* answer is clearly superior in this ascendant metric than the visions of Keynes and Bellamy.

The question is also handled badly by many of the more influential Anglo-American theories of distributive justice. Without doubt the most influential such theory is due to Rawls. Since higher productivity rates will presumably permit all members of society, including the least well off, to enjoy higher levels of income and wealth, schemes that encourage more rather than less work would seem to be favored by Rawls' principles of justice—provided of course that the extra work is not extracted coercively.

There is not much literature on the nature of work in what are sometimes called postfordist or postindustrial economies. What literature there is can be divided into two categories: sociological writings on work in the service economy, which generally requires a focused effort to manage one's own emotions (or at least one's public display of emotions); and sociological and philosophical reflections

---

6   These US Bureau of Labor Statistics figures are cited by Berardi 2009.

on work in those many sectors of the postindustrial economy that specialize in some form of symbol manipulation, and that therefore require the commercial employment of cognitive capacities. In other words, the literature can be divided into reflections on emotional labor and reflections on cognitive labor.

The first cluster of writings can be traced to Arlie Hochschild's 1983 book *The Managed Heart.* In that book, Hochschild seeks to show that service workers are called upon to represent the employer to the customer not only in speech and action but even in those semi-conscious projections of emotions that are achieved by subtle facial expressions and body language. It is a noteworthy fact about these intangible goods that they cannot conceivably be delivered impersonally and mechanically, in the manner of the assembly line riveter. As Hochschild puts the point, "Seeming to 'love the job' becomes part of the job; and actually trying to love it, and to enjoy the customers, helps the worker in this effort" (1983, 6). This leads Hochschild to claim that service economy work requires "emotional labor," by which she means engaging, in exchange for a wage, in "the management of feeling to create a publicly observable facial and bodily display" (1983, 7). For this reason, service work opens up the possibility of a distinctive and particularly insidious sort of alienation—alienation from those portions of one's own psyche and self-presentation that have been made over in conformity with the employer's profit interests. This basic problem is endemic in the modern economy. It extends well beyond "service work" narrowly construed, and encompasses many jobs that are highly paid and widely coveted.

Not surprisingly, sociologists (Grandey, Fisk, and Steiner 2005; Pugliesi 1999; Tracy 2000) have found that emotional labor is associated with high levels of stress and job dissatisfaction, a sense of inauthenticity in one's work life, and emotional numbness and other symptoms of depression. What is perhaps more interesting is that they have also found that the longer workers stay on the job, the more likely they are to make over their emotional registers so that they actually feel job-appropriate emotions (Tracy 2000, 115–16; Gross 1998; Brotheridge and Grandey 2002). What these findings suggest is that permitting one's emotions to be made over so that they express the evaluative standpoint of another person (that is, the corporation) is a common coping mechanism for those who engage in corporate forms of emotional labor. Within some corporations, professionals in "human resources" (a slightly ominous phrase) seek to promote this preferred outcome by exercising what they apparently call "cultural control" (a more decidedly ominous phrase) over the workplace, and by extension over those whose daily lives play out there. The idea is to use a combination of rituals, training programs, official dispensations of criticism and praise, internal publications, moderated discussions at employee retreats, financial rewards and promotions to establish a local currency of social esteem that tracks corporate profit interests (see Ashforth and Humphrey 1993, especially 102). The brilliant television show *The Office* gets a good deal of its satirical punch from its exploration of this process. It sets a rather pitiful attempt to breed a corporate culture against the backdrop of a work life whose aims and daily tasks are very nearly meaningless.

Dwight is the impossibly superficial but efficiently toady sort of man that emerges when corporate acculturation efforts succeed. Michael represents the crumbling of integrity visited upon semi-intelligent and vaguely good-willed managers who must represent corporate aspirations with an outward pretense of conviction; the rest are casting about for some way to keep a trace of integrity while paying occasional lip service to the aspirations and convictions prescribed for those who wish to remain in good standing in the office.

We can gain some insight into the psychodynamics of emotional labor from the writings of Sarah Tracy, a sociologist who worked on a luxury cruise ship for eight months in an undercover participatory study of this work environment. From the point of view of management, the single most important part of the job is attitudinal: the continuous ingratiating demeanor, the permanent smile. On Tracy's ship, these attitudinal standards were driven home by a corporate service credo posted in all crew bathrooms and on the walls of all crew cabins, just above the headboard of the bed, hence in an ideal position to be the last thing seen before dropping off to sleep and the first thing seen upon awakening. The credo included items like "We never say no," "We smile, we are on stage," and "We use proper telephone etiquette […] and answer with a smile in our voice" (Tracy 2000, 107). These elements of the credo were enforced not only by managers but by all passengers, via comment cards that weigh heavily in retention and promotion decisions. This practice, Tracy notes (2000, 105–9), has the effect of putting the customer in the position of a second boss, one whose gaze takes in nearly every nook of the ship. The effect is to deliver up, at a price within reach for upper-middle-class Westerners, a level of deferential personal service that has historically been a mere fantasy for anyone not to the aristocracy born. The enactment of this fantasy is affordable partly because cruise ships are able to broker a mid-ocean exchange between customers from the world's wealthiest countries and workers from impoverished countries (especially Indonesia and the Philippines). The result is a dramatic shrinking of the distance that ordinarily separates the world's "haves" and "have-nots," and a consequent exposure of the normally veiled relations that make it a routine matter for moderately well-to-do Western consumers to purchase several days of manual labor, congealed in an imported consumer product, with the net earnings of a single hour of work.

While this everyday, entirely routine arrangement is in its basic terms quite regal, these basic terms are rarely noticed by any of the parties engaged in it. Indeed, these parties are often quite literally oceans apart, and are rarely aware of each other's existence, much less of their roles in each other's lives. The anonymity of their relationship ordinarily prevents the wealthy consumer from seeing firsthand that he continuously enjoys the ministrations of what is in effect a small army of personal servants. He usually gives little thought to the remarkable fact that many other human beings are effectively obliged to place inordinate value on his smallest conveniences and comforts, and to impose great inconveniences upon themselves in order to supply these comforts. The cruise ship environment removes the cover of impersonality from these deeply inegalitarian arrangements.

One might hope here for a sudden moment of politicizing clarity. Yet luxury cruises are not known as seedbeds of radicalism. What apparently materializes, instead, is a new and distinct saleable commodity, one that cannot be delivered at a distance: inequality itself, served up in personalized and sometimes downright obsequious form.

One might think that the problem with this transaction lies solely in the self-deferential *content* of the self-image that these service workers are encouraged to internalize. While this self-image certainly is deeply objectionable, still I think that the case at hand represents a particularly damning form of a more general pathology of service economy work. Such work encourages the internalization of outlooks that one values only as a means for securing a wage. Like consumerism, so too this work threatens to disfigure the lifelong activity through which we human beings give shape to our understanding of the human good. We ought then to favor a complex analysis of the pathology at hand, one that highlights both its injustice and its unfriendliness to human flourishing.

As suggested above, a central part of the work of self-articulation is the effort to bring one's half-formed evaluative sensibility into words. The task is not to turn one's gaze inward, as if trying to describe something that has somehow lodged itself in one's psyche. The specification of an inchoate evaluative outlook does not call for *self-description*; it calls for an effort to look through the lens of that evaluative outlook and gain greater clarity about the goods or values that it brings into view. It is always possible that our words will fail to capture the appearance of value contained in our own incipient emotions and desires. There is, however, also the possibility that our articulation will "take"—embedding itself, so to speak, in our feelings, and giving a more determinate and perhaps more discerning character to the evaluative outlook mediated by these feelings.

There is a crucial normative aspect to the attitude I must take towards my incipient emotions and desires when I take them up as raw materials for the work of self-articulation. I must regard them as worthy of elaboration precisely because I rely upon them as the lens through which I discern the good. If I do not see them as valuable in this particular way, then I will not have reason to elaborate them by looking through them and trying to discern what is there to be seen. I might take myself to have reason to shape them in accordance with some other standard, dissociated from the faithful apprehension of goods that are there to be seen, but I will not recognize a reason to shape them by the sole standard of faithfulness to the values that they commend to my attention. Since I can hardly think it important for my feelings and desires to track the good unless I think it important for me myself to track the good and to think and act in its light, it follows that when I engage in self-articulation I am implicitly recognizing myself as a searcher after the good whose progress in that search genuinely matters. To the extent that service economy work induces us to sculpt our emotional register in order to excel and progress in our jobs, it induces us to compromise this conception of our value.

As we saw above, Marx (or, at least, the Marx of the *1844 Manuscripts*) found the *ergon* or characteristic activity of the human species in a cyclical form of labor through which we remake the world so as to accommodate our evolving sense of how human beings ought to live, then refine our sense of how human beings ought to live through sustained interaction with the world that we have fashioned for ourselves. I've set out a different, less materialistic conception of self-elaboration (or, as I've been calling it, self-articulation). Self-articulation shares the continuous cyclical structure of the sort of labor that interested Marx, but the cycle is both tighter and more personal—moving not between considered evaluative views and material objects, but only between considered and spontaneous elements of one's evaluative outlook. While I do not think that self-articulation so understood is an *exhaustive* account of the human *ergon*, it seems to me that it is an *essential* element of the kind of life to which human beings are called, and in which their best and highest potentialities are actualized. It is through the work of self-articulation that we are able to take responsibility for our characters by engaging in the daily task of giving determinacy to our conception of the good life. The most fundamental problem with emotional labor is that it tends to impart an alien evaluative outlook—one whose contours are shaped by the interests of the employer and not by the worker's own lifelong effort to see what is genuinely good.

The problem at hand extends beyond the service economy narrowly construed, and appears in a wide array of white-collar work. I recall that when I graduated from college, many of my classmates were vying for positions as management trainees in large corporations. Unemployment was high that year, so it was a real coup to get a job, and one of my close friends—a brilliant student who had majored in English literature—was among the elect. She was hired by Procter & Gamble to negotiate with supermarket and drugstore chains so as to secure more favorable shelf placements for the company's soaps, razors, and hair care products. The *summum bonum* of this human endeavor was eye-level positioning, and anything below the waist was considered grounds for dismissal. Thus my friend went, in the space of a couple of weeks, from interpreting Shakespeare's sonnets to haggling for advantageous positioning of bottles of Head & Shoulders shampoo. Her position was widely coveted and reasonably well paid, yet it would be obviously self-belittling to inhabit or even to become un-ironic about the outlook on value that its effective prosecution demanded. Again, the problem here cannot be fully diagnosed in the language of justice, at least in the austere usages to which that language is put by contemporary Anglo-American philosophers. It comes fully into view only when we take a more capacious concern for human flourishing.

I don't know how careers are seen in other countries, but in the United States we are exhorted to view them as the primary locus of self-realization. The question before you when you are trying to choose a career is to figure out *What Color is Your Parachute?* (the title of a guide to job searches that has been a perennial bestseller for most of my lifetime).[7] The aim, to quote the title of another top-selling guide to career choices, is to *Do What You Are*. These titles tell us something

---

7   First published in 1970, Richard N. Bolles' *What Color Is Your Parachute?* has been updated and reissued every year since by Ten Speed Press of Berkeley, California.

about what Americans expect to find in a career: themselves, in the unlikely form of a marketable commodity. This raises the question why we should expect that the inner self waiting to be born in each person corresponds to some paid job or profession. Are we really all in possession of an inner lawyer, an inner beauty products placement specialist, or an inner advertising executive, just waiting for the right job opening? Mightn't this script for our biographies serve as easily to promote self-limitation or self-betrayal as to further self-actualization?

We spend a great deal of our youths shaping ourselves into the sort of finished product that potential employers will be willing to pay dearly to use. Beginning at a very early age, schooling practices and parental guidance and approval are adjusted, sometimes only semi-consciously, so as to inculcate the personal capacities and temperament demanded by the corporate world. The effort to sculpt oneself for this destiny takes a more concerted form in high school and college. We choose courses of study, and understand the importance of success in these studies, largely with this end in view. Even those who rebel against these forces of acculturation are deeply shaped by them. What we call "self-destructive" behavior in high school might perhaps be an understandable result of being dispirited by the career prospects that are recommended to us as sufficient motivation for our studies. As a culture we have a curious double-mindedness about such reactions. It is hard to get through high school in the United States without being asked to read J.D. Salinger's *Catcher in the Rye*—the story of one Holden Caulfield's angst-ridden flight from high school, fueled by a pervasive sense that the adult world is irredeemably phony. The ideal high school student is supposed to find a soul mate in Holden and write an insightful paper about his telling cultural insights, submitted on time in 12 point type with double spacing and proper margins and footnotes, so as to ensure the sort of grade that will keep the student on the express train to the adult world whose irredeemable phoniness he has just skillfully diagnosed.

My conjecture is that we see here the surfacing of a normally buried tension in a widely accepted cultural self-understanding. If there is such a thing as a distinctively American culture, surely one of its central elements is an enthusiasm for authentic self-development. This focal value has been joined at the hip, in the popular imagination, with the pursuit of a fitting career. This is the source of our talk of careers as custom-colored parachutes that match our personal idiosyncrasies, and of finding jobs that permit us to "do what we are." Those who enter the white-collar workforce are expected to exhibit an extraordinary measure of personal identification with their jobs. If they withhold themselves, they are very unlikely to excel or advance. Partly for this reason, our jobs exercise a pervasive influence over post-adolescent acculturation, often marking us so deeply that within a couple of decades we have become inscrutable to friends from earlier stages of life. Yet they provide us with an extraordinarily fragile identity, especially given the demise of long-term relationships between employers and employees.

As I write this chapter the most recent edition sits at number 406 on the Amazon list of best-selling books in the United States, and at number one in the job hunting category.

Such an identity can crumble at any moment, with the arrival of a pink slip, and this fact must tend to cultivate a frantic show of unreservedness in one's identification with one's post. If we step back and view the passing show—in the spirit, say, of a perceptive but disaffected teenager like Holden Caulfield—the white-collar world can easily seem to be a place where personal ideals are compromised and aspirations betrayed. If we give credence to that view (and the staying power of Salinger's work suggests that at some level we do) then what comes into view here is another negative cultural externality of market behavior—a social practice of self-betrayal that arises unbidden as the cumulative result of individual choices made under a duress arising from the like choices of others.

In his highly influential 1976 work *The Cultural Contradictions of Capitalism*, the sociologist Daniel Bell argued that a radical disjunction had emerged in the United States between the prevailing culture and the functional demands of the social structure. In our capacity as consumers, we are encouraged to be undisciplined hedonists, and in our capacity as workers, we are required to be fastidiously self-controlled. We are to be organization men by day and pleasure-seekers by night. In the eyes of sociologist Richard Florida, this schizophrenic situation is rapidly being left behind due to a fundamental change that is taking hold in the workplace. According to Florida (2005, xix), the day of the "organization man" is done. Corporations are now dependent upon, and ready to handsomely remunerate, people who are "striving to be themselves, to find meaningful work." They are fostering a new "creative class"—a class whose personal creativity and idiosyncrasy can be expressed in a seamless way, both at work and at play. This, according to Florida, is the reason people are working longer hours: they view their paid work not as a burden but as the primary scene of self-actualization. More and more people are joining the cadres of artists, musicians, intellectuals, and scientists who "could never be forced to work, yet [...] were never truly not at work." For Florida (2004, 13), "this way of working has moved from the margins to the economic mainstream."

By this point it will come as no surprise that I have my doubts about Florida's sanguine picture of work in the "new economy." Where Florida sees a genuine restructuring of the workplace that brings it into alignment with the cultural celebration of authentic self-realization, I see a new ideological mask that decorates the sort of self-betrayal sketched above with the misleading veneer of self-actualization. One can begin to see fissures in Florida's picture of work life by querying his idea of creativity. Marketing and advertising are often referred to within business circles as creative work, and for Florida they are paradigmatic instances of such work. Yet they involve a very different sort of creativity from that which is manifest in, for example, the composing of a piece of music or the writing of a short story. In advertising and marketing, the creative effort has a standard of success that is entirely external and financial. In musical composition or short-story writing, the standards of success are internal to the art form itself: they are, respectively, musical and literary. Given this, I think it is at best highly misleading to say, with Florida, that "the shared commitment to the creative spirit in its many, varied manifestations underpins the new creative ethos that powers our age" (2013, 5). Crucially important differences are papered over by the mushy phrase "in its many and varied forms." These differences cast doubt on whether we can really speak here of a single coherent "ethos." An advertising copy writer who is moved ultimately by the demands of profit has a very different ethos than a short story writer for whom profit emerges, if it does, as a byproduct of an attempt to answer to literary ideals. The doubts become all the more pressing when the category of "creative work" is distended, as it is by Florida, to encompass the daily activities of nearly every contemporary white-collar worker, including bankers, investment professionals, doctors, lawyers, and knowledge workers of almost every stripe.

One crucial difference between the work of the new "creative class" and the work of the artist is this: in the case of the artist, but not in the case of the craftsperson or the cognitive laborer, consistent repetition of a single, formulaic kind of "creation" is a mark that something has gone wrong. (Pop art is the sort of counter-example that proves the rule, since its significance lies partly in the way that it casts doubt on its own status as art, thereby raising interesting questions about whether art has a sustainable place in a society marked by the mass production of commodities.[8]) If the point is to produce some result independent from the immediate product, repetition is perfectly sensible so long as it is getting good results, hence it need not mark any failure. But in artistic creation, the task is simultaneously expressive and self-formative, and formulaic repetition would mark a worrying personal stasis or a freezing of receptivity to the environment. If we think of art in this way, then intimate conversation is a candidate art form, while a great deal of professional conversation is not, since the use of a script in professional conversation would generally count as a deficiency only if it were ineffective in producing conceptually separate results. Nor does this professional sort of "creativity" make us visible to each other in anything like the way that artistic creative does. Through it we appear to each other only in the form of a gambit calculated to produce a desired result, and not in the direct and self-formative mode of self-revelation that we call artistic creation.

The contemporary Italian political philosopher Franco Berardi shares Florida's interest in postfordist labor patterns. Yet where Florida sees a new "creative class," Berardi see a "cognitive proleteriat" or "cognitariat"; and where Florida sees self-actualization on the job, Berardi sees "the subjugation of the soul to work processes." "Putting the soul to work: this is the new form of alienation," Berardi writes. "Our desiring energy is trapped in the trick of self-enterprise, our libidinal investments are regulated according to economic rules, our attention is captured in the precariousness of virtual networks: every fragment of mental activity must be transformed into capital." (Berardi 2009, 24) Maurizio Lazzarato (in Gorz 1999, 39) takes a similar view:

---

8   Here I follow Giorgio Agamben's discussion of Pop art and its significance in *The Man Without Content* (1999, Section 7).

> "Be active subjects!" is the new command echoing through Western societies
> today [...] You must express yourself, speak, communicate, co-operate [But]
> the communicative relationship is completely predetermined in both content
> and form [...] The subject is a mere coding and decoding station [...]
> The communicative relation has to eliminate the features which actually
> constitute [the subject's] specificity.

Viewed against the backdrop of the sort of factory labor that Marx denounced,
the rise of emotional and cognitive labor might be described as the humanization
of the working world. Yet, as Luc Boltanski and Eve Chiapello point out, these
new forms of work pose a special danger: "precisely because they are more human
in a way," they "penetrate more deeply into people's inner selves—people are
expected to 'give' themselves to their work—and facilitate an instrumentalization
of human beings in their most specifically human dimensions." (Boltanski and
Chiapello 2005, 98) This instrumentalization of our capabilities goes hand-in-hand
with the social choice to maximize consumption of goods and services. They are
two sides of the same coin. Considered in the collective, we can maximize our
consumption powers only by maximizing our productivity, and we can do this only
if we make an unreserved investment of time, mental energy and self-formative
capacities in enhancing our value as employable commodities.

Berardi agrees with Florida that the new cognitariat is deeply and almost
continuously absorbed in its work, but he has a different explanation for this.
Berardi pictures the workers of the cognitariat as the conductors of vast flows
of communication. In the name of efficiency, one must never permit this flow to
be interrupted; one must do one's part, in real time, in the decentralized group
activity of information-processing, or risk being marginalized or replaced. Since
one can always be reached by cell phone or laptop, there is no time or place in
which one can hide from these demands. According to Berardi (2009, 108), this
threatens a kind of alienation by overstimulation, in which we lose control over
our own train of thought and become incapable of an unimpeded experience
of our physical surroundings. And there is a vicious circle here. The psyche's
withdrawal from physical public space into the virtual communicative networks of
the new economy has the effect of impoverishing the shared lives of families and
communities, which makes it all the more tempting to immerse oneself in one's
work. This inclines us to sell more of our free time to our employers, which further
impoverishes the free time available to friends and neighbors, strengthening their
incentive to make a similar sale of their free time. Here again we see the outlines
of a strikingly negative market externality—one that might well constitute yet a
third tragedy of the cultural commons, this one consisting in the evacuation of
genuine human presence from public and communal life (Turkle 2011).

There is a striking affinity between the critique of cognitive labor found in such
thinkers as Berardi and Lazzarato and the critique of rhetoric set out by Socrates in
the *Gorgias*. For Socrates, the rhetorician misuses the distinctive human capacity
for thought and speech (*logos*) as a mere means of persuasion, which in turn is

bent to the task of furthering the rhetorician's quest for wealth and power. This alters the proper relation between the rhetorician and his own tongue, since he views his words as calculated instruments for re-making the world, and thereby cannot make use of them as the medium of the continuous effort of reflection through which humans can lend clarity and articulacy to their evolving idea of how best to live. Put another way, the practice of rhetoric effectively subverts the activity of self-articulation through sustained thought and dialogue aimed at clarifying and refining one's sense of what to believe and what it would be best to do with one's time on earth. The result, according to Socrates (Plato 1994: 481c–e), is that one is shaped instead by one's sense of what others would find flattering. This is precisely what Berardi and Lazzarato find troubling about the plight of the cognitariat.

Conclusion

In recent decades there has been a resurgence of interest in Platonic and Aristotelian ethics, yet the return to the ancients has not been nearly as pronounced in Anglo-American political philosophy as in ethics. To be sure, there has been considerable discussion of the political virtues. It seems to me, though, that what most needs to be retrieved is not ancient notions of the civic virtues but their reflections on different kinds of thought and action and their proper place in a well-lived human life.

This is a large topic, and in these concluding remarks I can do no more than give a glimmer of the riches to be found here. Aristotle regarded the highest human good as a distinctive sort of activity—one whose end or value is entirely present in each of its unfolding moments (that is, one that is *teleion* or *telos*-containing) and hence one that contains in itself a full realization of the proper activity of the human being (that is, an *en-ergeia*, meaning an *ergon*- or function-enacting activity). Such activity is contrasted with *poiesis* or (more generally) *kinesis*— that is, with action whose point lies in some separable product or state of affairs that it is calculated to produce. By Aristotle's lights, it is in the performance of *energeiai* that we human beings come fully into our own, honing our sensibility in such a way as to attain *phronesis* or practical wisdom. Taken in itself, engagement in *poiesis* serves by contrast only to hone technical knowledge (*techne*). Such knowledge differs from *phronesis* in that it does not itself determine our fundamental identity or core commitments, since we can stray intentionally from the dictates of a *techne* without showing ourself to lack it, while we cannot stray from the dictates of *phronesis* without manifesting some shortcoming in our wisdom.

I find these Aristotelian distinctions extremely helpful in articulating a plausible picture of the good life for human beings. And while they are quite abstract, and compatible with a large array of substantive conceptions of the well-lived human life, still I believe that they have enough content to ground a powerful critique of contemporary patterns of getting and spending. This is the sort of (broadly

Arendtian) return to the Greeks that most interests me, and while I have not used this terminology in the present chapter, I have been guided throughout by a wish to bring these Aristotelian notions to bear on the task of understanding contemporary economic life.

Since I have been exploring impediments to human flourishing that are presented by prevailing patterns of production and consumption, it might perhaps be fitting to close with some ruminations about the idea of consumption. The term is often used more loosely than perhaps it ought to be. We include under the heading of consumerism the acquisition of many goods that are not really consumed, at least in our lifetimes. At the same time we tend to omit what seems on reflection to be the consumable good *par excellence*—namely, time. This is one of the few goods that disappears without remainder as we make use of it. Its omission is curious, since it seems to be the most fundamental of human goods—the good of having a life to lead. It is the condition of all other goods.

Interestingly, the above-sketched Aristotelian typology of human doings is a categorization of active relations to time. They provide the rudiments, then, of an economy of time. If we are engaged in a pure case of *kinesis*—that is, in activity whose sole point lies in some intended product that it is calculated to produce—then we are related to the present as something wholly dispensable, and it would be rational for us to give away this stretch of time entirely if we could push a button and fast forward to the culmination of our task. An Aristotelian *energeia*, by contrast, contains its point in each of its passing moments, hence its moments are not similarly dispensable. Because each moment of an *energeia* is intrinsically valuable, we can complete these moments (that is, render them *teleion*) with a running appreciative attention that brings us fully into presence and makes our activity unreserved and pleasurable. To engage in *energeia*, then, is to savor time, while to engage in *kinesis* is to dispense with it. It seems clear that the working world as currently organized is rife with activities that ought really to be counted as *kineses* but that are dressed up in the ideological garb of *energeiai*, and that our most fundamental economic problem is that prevailing economic structures induce us to make poor use of that most important and most thoroughly consumable of goods: our time on earth. We misunderstand our good as something that lies not in the full actualization of our active powers but in some elusive state of mind or world that it is our task to bring about. This is a recipe for permanently postponing the arrival of the good.

If we consume our lives in unsatisfying work pursuits, we might perhaps feel a need for some compensatory satisfaction. For some thinkers, this would be the point of entry for a critique of religious belief in the afterlife. Such diagnoses strike me as more than a bit crude and reductive. A more modest and worldly point is that we might on reflection come to see that our compensation sometimes takes the form of a willed identification with workplace roles that are not wholly worthy of our allegiance. We might also see that we value certain things simply because they resist consumption—because they have the permanent vocation of remaining themselves—and that our desire for them is connected to an awareness that we ourselves are continuously consumed in time. We might then see such "keepsakes" as we place upon our shelves as offerings to the maw of time—offerings that appeal because time cannot readily digest them. What we call our taste for consumer goods might then be understood as a taste for consumption-proof goods that arises from our awareness of the inexorability with which we ourselves are being consumed. Here I can't help thinking of the following stanzas from "Calmly We Walk Through This April's Day," by aspiring philosopher turned poet Delmore Schwartz (1967, 66–7):

Avid its rush, that reeling blaze!
Where is my father and Eleanor?
Not where are they now, dead seven years,
But what they were then?
No more? No more?
From Nineteen-Fourteen to the present day,
Bert Spira and Rhoda consume, consume
Not where they are now (where are they now?)
But what they were then, both beautiful;
Each minute bursts in the burning room,
The great globe reels in the solar fire,
Spinning the trivial and unique away.
(How all things flash! How all things flare!)
What am I now that I was then?
May memory restore again and again
The smallest color of the smallest day:
Time is the school in which we learn,
Time is the fire in which we burn.

If this is our plight, and if our collective actions perpetuate this plight in ways that limit the possibility of an isolated individual recovery, then our condition might perhaps require a self-conscious politics of time. In other words, it might require a politics that gives proper recognition to the value of free time (which shows up all too often only as a lost opportunity for GDP enhancement) and to the creative activities and interpersonal relationships that might serve to enrich this time rather to erect a futile totemic fortification against its loss. A public reflection of this sort might perhaps help us to enhance the cultural environment while minimizing the depletion of the natural environment. Our recovery might also require a concerted effort, individual by individual, to vanquish habits of accumulation that are the lingering biological and cultural effects of a long human pre-history of genuine scarcity and need. I intend this chapter as a very small contribution to this long process, about whose fate I am deeply pessimistic.

References

Agamben, Giorgio. 1999. *The Man Without Content*. Palo Alto: Stanford University Press.

Ashforth, Blake and Humphrey, Ronald. 1993. "Emotional Labor in Service Roles: The Influence of Identity." *The Academy of Management Review* 18, 1: 88–115.

Baudrillard, Jean. 2006. *The System of Objects*. London and New York: Verso Books.

Bell, Daniel. 1976. *The Cultural Contradictions of Capitalism*. New York: Basic Books.

Berardi, Franco. 2009. *The Soul at Work: From Alienation to Autonomy*. Los Angeles: Semiotext(e).

Bluestone, Barry and Rose, Stephen. 1997. "Overworked and Underemployed: Unraveling the Economic Enigmas." *The American Prospect* 31: 58–69.

Bolles, Richard N. [1970] 2010. *What Color Is Your Parachute?* Berkeley: Ten Speed Press.

Boltanski, Luc and Chiapello, Eve. 2005. *The New Spirit of Capitalism*. London and New York: Verso Press.

Braverman, Harry. 1974. *Labor and Monopoly Capital: The Degradation of Work in the Twentieth Century*. New York and London: Monthly Review Press.

Brewer, Talbot. 2009. *The Retrieval of Ethics*. Oxford: Oxford University Press.

Brotheridge, Celeste and Grandey, Alicia. 2002. "Emotional Labor and Burnout: Comparing Two Perspectives of 'People Work.'" *Journal of Vocational Behavior* 60: 17–39.

Crawford, Matthew B. 2009. *Shop Class as Soulcraft: An Inquiry into the Value of Work*. New York: Penguin.

Eliot, T.S. 1934. "The Love Song of J. Alfred Prufrock." In *The Waste Land and Other Poems*. New York: Harcourt Brace Jovanovich.

Florida, Richard. 2004. *The Rise of the Creative Class: And How It's Transforming Work, Leisure, Community and Everyday Life*. New York: Basic Books.

Fromm, Erich. 1960. "Foreword." In *Looking Backward, 2000–1887*, edited by Edward Bellamy, v–xx. New York: New American Library.

Gorz, Andre. 1999. *Reclaiming Work: Beyond the Wage-Based Society*. Cambridge: Polity Press.

Grandey, Alicia, Glenda Fisk and Dirk Steiner. 2005. "Must 'Service With a Smile' Be Stressful? The Moderating Role of Personal Control for American and French Employees." *Journal of Applied Psychology* 90, 5: 893–904.

Gross, James J. 1998. "Antecedent- and Response-Focused Emotion Regulation: Divergent Consequences for Experience, Expression and Physiology." *Journal of Personality and Social Psychology* 74, 1: 224–37.

Hochschild, Arlie Russell. 1983. *The Managed Heart: Commercialization of Human Feeling*. Berkeley and Los Angeles: University of California Press.

Keynes, John Maynard. 1930. "Economic Possibilities for Our Grandchildren." Accessed August 22. http://www.econ.yale.edu/smith/econ116a/keynes1.pdf.

Institute for American Values. 2001. *Watch Out for Children: A Mothers' Statement to Advertisers*. New York: Institute for American Values.

Latouche, Serge. 2009. *Farewell to Growth*. Cambridge: Polity Press

Leach, William. 1994. *Land of Desire: Merchants, Power and the Rise of a New American Culture*. New York: Vintage.

Marx, Karl. 1975. *Early Writings*. London: Penguin Books.

Merck Family Fund. 1995. "Yearning for Balance: Views on Consumption, Materialism and the Environment." Accessed April 20 2014. http://www.iisd.ca/consume/harwood.html.

Plato. 1994. *Gorgias*. Oxford: Oxford University Press.

Pugliesi, Karen. 1999. "The Consequences of Emotional Labor: Effects on Work Stress, Job Satisfaction and Well-Being." *Motivation and Emotion* 23, 2: 125–54.

Rawls, John. 1971. *A Theory of Justice*. Cambridge: Harvard University Press.

Schor, Juliet. 1993. *The Overworked American: The Unexpected Decline of Leisure*. New York: Basic Books.

Schor, Juliet. 2005. *Born to Buy: The Commercialized Child and the New Consumer Culture*. New York: Scribner.

Schwartz, Delmore. 1967. *Selected Poems: Summer Knowledge*. New York: New Directions Publishing.

Taylor, Charles. 1976. "Responsibility for Self." In *The Identities of Persons*, edited by Amelie Rorty, 281–300. Berkeley and Los Angeles: University of California Press.

Tracy, Sarah. 2000. "Becoming a Character for Commerce: Self-Subordination, and Discursive Construction of Identity in a Total Institution." *Management of Communication Quarterly* 14: 90–128.

Turkle, Sherry. *Alone Together: Why We Expect More from Technology and Less from Each Other*. New York: Basic Books.

Twitchell, James B. 1999. "Two Cheers for Materialism." *The Wilson Quarterly* 23, 2: 16–26.

Chapter 8

On Being Human in a Consumer Society: Fashion Skirts the Ethical Agenda

Efrat Tseëlon

Introduction

The title of this chapter suggests that being "human" may not necessarily coincide with being a consumer, or that there can be a conflict of interests. Indeed, in a world of globalized businesses, where outsourcing has removed production from the field of vision of consumption, and where the sheer scale of mass consumption has short circuited considerations of welfare (of human and nonhuman animals) with considerations of profit and low retail price, the question is as relevant as in the height of the industrial revolution.

We can rephrase the question to ask whether we can have consumption (or fashion consumption) with a human face. The meaning of "human" in this reformulation refers to another ubiquitous assumption that "being human" is a positive attribute: it is, in fact, a shortcut term for ethical, compassionate, and kind.

The implicit subject of ethical consumption is the human as a legal category, but also as a compassionate one as in Levinas' ethical theory which reduces morality to the responsibility that is placed on us by the face of the Other. Face is used here both literally and metaphorically (as the "face-to-face encounter" but also as putting an individualized face on an abstract category). Together they refer to the sensibility and affectivity rooted in my being-for-the-Other, not being-with-the-Other.

The inherent paradox at the heart of the ethical project in a consumption context is its invisibility in a universe that relies so much on appearances: it is the antithesis of branding. In the context of fashion, for example, ethical practices don't invest the garment with any distinctive look or recognizable quality.

The Influence of Globalization

By the 1980s neoliberalism had effectively reigned in most parts of the global economy through trade liberalization and globalization. Globalization was hailed as a force of progress for world economies by way of closer integration through trade agreements that reduce barriers to the flow of goods, services, capital, knowledge, and to some extent labor.

Indeed, it heralded an era in which national governments were superseded by intergovernmental institutions (such as the World Trade Organization, the International Monetary Fund, the World Bank, the World Health Organization, the International Labor Organization and the UN), and by multinational corporations. As a consequence, economic regulation, in particular its ability to provide social buffers to the market economy and social inequality, has been undermined. The new global economic order has created a vacuum that replaced state regulation with voluntary industry regulation. The economic strategy of self-regulating free market economy adopted by the financial institutions led to repeated crises, culminating in the 2008 global economic downturn.

In his much acclaimed classic *Globalization and its Discontents*, Professor Joseph Stiglitz (who had previously worked at the World Bank and as an adviser to the Clinton administration) analyzed the dynamics and shortcomings of global economic policy. Though the book was published in 2003, it set the scene for the current crisis that started in 2008. Stiglitz explained that trade can be a positive force for development.

In an account from 2005 that seemed to preempt the notion of the self-regulatory market whose weaknesses were exposed in the 2008 crisis, he said:

> The notion that free trade unencumbered by government restrictions is welfare enhancing is one of the most fundamental doctrines in modern economics, dating back at least to Adam Smith in the 18th century and David Ricardo in the 19th century. But the subject has always been marked by controversy because the issue facing most countries is not a binary choice of autarky (no trade) or free trade, but rather a choice among a spectrum of trade regimes with varying degrees of liberalization. (Stiglitz 2005, 12)

The solution that the corporate world, international organizations, NGOs, activist groups, and human rights campaigners brokered to fill the vacuum left by lack of state regulation came in the form of an ethical agenda (Corporate Social Responsibility, or CSR). Its immediate goal was to limit the damage created by corporations' irresponsible conduct. This was seen mostly in the developing world, often with harmful human and environmental consequences, which lacked the regulatory infrastructure on issues such as employment and sustainability. CSR's long term goal has been to build a culture which puts social and environmental issues at the heart of corporate thinking. In fact, it appears to have addressed Stiglitz's main critique of globalization, that of neglecting the wider consequences, human and environmental, of corporate capitalism.

In this spirit, Ban Ki-moon, Secretary General of the United Nations, urged business leaders gathered at the World Economic Forum in Davos, Switzerland, in January 2009 to embrace "global co-operation and partnership on a scale never before seen" and to abandon short-term thinking in favor of long-term solutions to climate change and other pressing global challenges.

The Case for Business Ethics

However, "global governance without global government" fostered "globalization without a human face." Rather than becoming a force for good, it contributed to the undermining of cultural traditions, creating greater poverty, and more inequality. Anti-democratic practices replaced "the old dictatorships of national elites with new dictatorships of international finance." This version of globalization saw a rapid indiscriminant liberalization which had not been managed carefully. It did not leave sufficient time for adaptation, it showed lack of transparency and accountability of the global institutions, and it privileged the clients and users of the industrialized West at the expense of the producers. What is needed, Stiglitz reckoned, are "policies for sustainable, equitable, and democratic growth." Development, according to him, is not about making a handful of people rich, or creating a handful of protected luxury industries that only benefit the elite. He cautioned against mistaking the availability of luxury shopping for a societal development: "it is not about bringing in Prada and Benetton, or Ralph Lauren or Louis Vuitton for the urban rich and leaving the poor in their misery." Rather, he explained, development is about transforming societies, improving the lives of the poor, enabling everyone to have a chance at success and access to health care and education. Stiglitz also advocated reforms in the international institutions that govern globalization.

The corporate ethical agenda has ushered in a transition from a traditional bottom line approach to business (concern with maximizing profit levels, share value, and shareholder returns) to a notion of a wider range of "stakeholders" than just shareholders in the company. This approach is known as the triple bottom line (TBL) approach: people, planet, and profit (see Table 8.1). The TBL idea (Elkington 1994, 2004; Brown et al. 2006, European Competitiveness Report 2008) was that business and investors should link value with values and measure their performance against a new set of metrics, capturing economic, social and environmental value added—or destroyed—during the processes of wealth creation.

The emergence of CSR as an established trend for the corporate business world preceded the big corporate scandals in the USA caused by astonishing ethical lapses, and has become a major concern since. Many companies responded by increasing their compliance functions thus encouraging a *risk management culture* rather than an *ethics culture*. Ethics was externalized to compliance officers, risk managers and consultants and degenerated into a compliance exercise instead of being embedded in the companies' core business and values. Plender and Persaud, authors of *All you Need to Know About Ethics and Finance* (2005) warned that excessive regulation risks of transforming an ethical "personal integrity culture" into a "compliance culture." One cannot regulate people into good behavior as long as incentive structures are at odds with sound values. Writing in the *Financial Times* in August 2006 they pointed out that ethics do matter in business because they underpin trust, which is fundamental to business relations (Plender and Persaud 2006). There is a growing literature on the economic value of trust that comes from behavior driven by ethical norms. Lack of trust leads to higher compliance costs as more business behavior is subject to increased legislation and litigation. It is, they stressed, possible to run an organization efficiently without trust and without integrity, but it requires punitive management and control.

Table 8.1   From profit to holistic vision

	Profit oriented business	**Ethics oriented business**
Motivation	Compliance	Competition
Accountability	Non-transparent	Transparent
Technology focus	Product oriented	Function oriented
Corporate governance	Exclusive	Inclusive

Source: Adapted from Elkington 2004.

The 2005 Ethical Trading Initiative briefing paper "Bridging the Gap Between Commercial and Ethical Trade Agendas: Pioneering Approaches to Purchasing Practices" outlined the business case for reviewing purchasing practices and integrating responsible principles into the way supply chains are managed to make them more conducive to good working conditions. It pointed out that shorter lead times between concept and product, last minute changes, and fines for late delivery had adverse effects. They contributed to increasing pressure on workers, longer hours, shorter breaks, and short-term contracts, as Lucy Siegle documents in her book *To Die For* (2011).

Those who viewed the CSR as a marketing gimmick realized that while the ethical dimension does not necessarily bring consumers to swap their consumption choices, the reputational risks involved in bad publicity is a price too high to pay as Janet Dukerich and Suzanne Carter put it in "Distorted Images and Reputation Repair" (2009).

Skeptical voices doubted that the ethical trend would outlast the economic recession but it has proved to be a robust trend. Once seen as a fringe interest, CSR has morphed from an "add-on" to the core of the business enterprise and as a global mainstream business activity adopted by household brands.

In fact the business case for CSR has been voiced by the industry's many advocates. Business in the Community, one of the Prince's Charities, has carried out research (2008) that shows that companies consistently running their business according to responsible principles outperformed the FTSE 350 on total shareholder return between 2002 and 2007 by between 3.3 percent and 7.7 percent per year.

Stefan Stern, who writes for the *Financial Times* on management issues, reckoned at the end of 2007 that "In the inevitable life cycle of management fads CSR is now heading for the exit," and that the next rising trend would see CSR consultancies rebranding with the more contemporary "sustainability" label instead.

Indeed, as Bob Lurie wrote for Harvard Business Online (2009) society was undergoing a fundamental, permanent change and sustainability was "the epicenter of that change." The essence of this change was that sustainability has hijacked the CSR conversation, and marked a transition from *compliance* to *commitment*.

Evidence is accumulating that the ethical agenda matters. For example in 2003 Stokes, Tseëlon, and McMahon researched business executives' attitudes towards CSR in Ireland and showed clear preferences for companies known for their CSR practices.

In January 2004, a survey by Harvard graduate students[1] of more than 800 MBAs from 11 leading North American and European schools found that a substantial number were willing to forgo some financial benefits to work for an organization with a better reputation for corporate social responsibility and ethics.

Writing in *The Guardian* at the end of 2007 Yale Environment and Law Professor Daniel Etsy analyzed a shift of attitudes to ethical considerations from risk management to business opportunities.

The European Commission included for the first time a chapter on CSR in its 2008 "European Competitiveness Report." An overview of the effects of CSR on six different determinants of competiveness at firm level—cost structure, human resources, customer perspective, innovation, risk and reputation management, and financial performance—showed that it can have a positive impact on competitiveness even in a period of economic downturn. Specifically it showed that CSR influences three competitiveness factors: human resources, risk and reputation management, and innovation.

In fact, at CSR Europe's general assembly in Brussels on June 11, 2009, European Commission President José Manuel Barroso emphasized that "in the current exceptional circumstances, corporate social responsibility is even more crucial than ever." Calling for a "new culture of ethics and responsibility" Barroso stressed the importance of re-building trust in business. "People still want markets—but they want markets with a conscience."[2]

Sybil Goldfiner is the CEO of the high-end fashion label "comme il faut," a company that is exemplary in terms of its commitment to a whole range of ethical issues related to both production and consumption. Writing in *Critical Studies in Fashion & Beauty*, a 2011 volume dedicated to fashion ethics, Goldfiner shared

---

1   "MBA Graduates Want to Work for Caring and Ethical Employers". http://www.gsb.stanford.edu/news/research/hr_mbajobchoice.shtml. Accessed September 22, 2014.

2   http://optimistworld.com/Corporate-Social-Responsibility-Businesses-Conscience-re-build-market-economy/. Accessed May 22, 2011.

a thoughtful account of the implications of a genuine commitment to social responsibility in a profit-making context.

The paradigm change towards an ethical agenda was marked in recent years by a proliferation of professional and popular culture publications, in print and electronic media, as well as events such as conferences, educational and business initiatives, competitions, and exhibitions. These contributed to normalizing the ethical discourse on fair trade and sustainability as an unquestioned part of conversation, as Austin Williams critically argued (2008, 2011). The public appeared to be just as concerned with the presence of this discourse, as with its absence. This was manifest whenever a major retailer had been tainted with labor laws violations in one of their outsourced plants in the manufacturing economies.

The Case for Fashion Ethics

In the past decade ethical fashion has burst into public consciousness through many popular culture events and representations. Many of the activists (NGOs, column, magazine, and book writers) have been promoting ways of making fashion more ethical, using whatever definition of ethical they saw fit, or relevant. Through ethical fashion shows, through competitions for ethical initiatives at school, regional or state levels, ordinary citizens as well as entrepreneurs produced imaginative solutions on a micro or macro scale to increase a variety of "ethical" practices. These ranged from lobbying companies and legislators to creating local community or business initiatives that promote an ethical idea.

The following are a few examples: La Mode Éthique, an annual ethical fashion show started in Paris in 2004, the British Fashion Council founded Esthetica in 2006 as part of London Fashion Week to showcase eco sustainable fashion, in 2009 thekey.to launched an international event for green fashion in Berlin, and increasingly ethical collections feature in London Graduate Fashion Week. At the same time, there is a proliferation of young designers working ethically, focusing on either sourcing of materials or other aspects of the garment cycle. "From Somewhere," a London based ethical fashion brand of the Italian designer Orsola de Castro, uses waste material (cut-offs from clothing manufacturers, discarded clothes, stocks that don't sell and take up space in warehouses) to generate couture collections. Using raw material that has already been produced and processed, she reduces waste, and reduces the pressure to mine and harvest new material, as well as the energy to process it. Thus the brand provides an effective use of resources.

Similar popular expressions of the concept of ethics in fashion represent the first serious attempt on the part of the industry to engage with the social and environmental consequences of the fashion phenomenon on a global scale. In fact, fashion ethics fits in with a 200-year-old tradition of embodying consumption in a moral framework. From the Victorians through the Marxists, consumption has been viewed in terms of uses and abuses, where the characterization of virtuous productive or immoral unproductive was extended from the product to the consumer of such products (Hilton 2004). The contemporary "ethical" phenomenon is different from its predecessors in a fundamental way. It is a product of a consumer movement on the one hand, and supra state organizations (businesses, NGOs) that are part of neoliberal capitalism on the other. This type of grass roots movement championed by NGOs and big businesses themselves was, in a sense, an unlikely development at a time of increasing globalization and diminishing states. It emerged just when multinationals were getting richer and stronger than states, and social theorists from Stigliz to Bauman (2000) predicted the disintegration of community and the emptying of the nation state of all its protective functions.

What is meant by the use of the word "ethical" in trade, and in fashion trade, is not entirely clear-cut. "Ethical" in the sense of "ethical trade," means that companies, "take agreed steps to ensure their supplier companies respect the rights of their workers by adhering to national labor laws and the Conventions of the International Labor Organization (ILO)."[3] "Ethical" in the context of "ethical fashion" has come to mean "an approach to the design, sourcing and manufacture of clothing, which is both socially and environmentally sustainable"[4] as well as being a fashion "trend" in its own right, a segment of the market, like "petite" or "plus size" or "Goth."

According to Mintel, the global market and consumer research analyst, ethical clothing refers to clothing that takes into consideration the impact of production and trade on the environment and on the people behind the clothes we wear. At core, it rests on the principles of sustainability and responsibility.

A comment in Mintel's 2009 report on ethical clothing is telling. It says: "the issues surrounding ethical clothing are complex, and there is no universal agreement on what constitutes best practice in organics and Fairtrade." Hence it is using "organics and Fairtrade" and "ethical clothing" interchangeably. Indeed such usage reflects the industry's definition. The way most brands interpret "ethical" practice is through use of a range of sustainable fabrics in garment design.

In the context of beauty products Mintel's definition of "ethical" features a slightly different mix of categories from that which appears in the context of fashion. In particular, the role of animal welfare is more marked.

In its study of ingredients in beauty products, Mintel (2009) questioned consumers about attitudes towards the ethical positioning of new beauty product launches. The category people cared about most was animal welfare (56 percent), followed by environmentally friendly packaging (51 percent), environmentally friendly products (12 percent) and human friendly charity (11 percent).

The human rights group Labour Behind the Label published a report on unethical practices by the UK's biggest fashion retailers ("Who Pays for Cheap

---

3   Ethical Trading Initiative: http://www.ethicaltrade.org. Accessed September 22, 2014.
4   Ethical Fashion Forum: http://www.ethicalfashionforum.com/5.html. "What is Ethical Fashion?" Accessed September 22, 2014.

Clothes?" 2006).[5] In this report, Martin Hearson explained that while people use terms such as "eco fashion" "Fairtrade" or "values-led" interchangeably, for Labour Behind the Label, a company needs to ensure that workers throughout its supply chain can exercise their internationally-agreed labor rights before they can be called ethical. These include workers receiving a living wage, secure employment, working in safe and healthy conditions, not being forced to work excessive overtime, not suffering sexual harassment, discrimination, verbal or physical abuse and, most importantly, that they are able to speak out, defend and improve their own labor rights.

The remit outlined by different definitions, those that focus narrowly on "organics and Fairtrade" and those that include a broader scope is not insignificant. This will be discussed further below.

The work of various ethical organizations, as well as companies that have adopted various degrees of ethical commitment, however narrowly defined, as well as the expansion of the ethical market, are encouraging signs. The market for ethical clothing has grown fourfold over the first decade of the twenty-first century and though small, consumers' ethical beliefs are a central driver to companies' conduct. Sales of certified Fairtrade cotton products rose from £4.5 million in 2006 to £34.8 million in 2007, for example. Mintel estimates that ethical clothing is a growth sector which is currently worth around £175 million. However in reality it has more of a symbolic value than an actual value due to its tiny market share. According to a report by Cambridge University's Institute for Manufacturing, clothing and textiles represent about 7 percent of world exports. During the period 1997–2001, international trade in cotton products constituted 2 percent of the global merchandise trade value, but about 40 percent of textile production (with synthetic fibers taking up about 55 percent). The Délégation Interministérielle à l'Innovation, à l'Expérimentation Sociale et à l'Économie Sociale (DIIESES) reported that out of around €30 billion of sales in the French fashion industry in 2003, ethical fashion represented less than 1 percent. Mintel's figures show it to be about 0.4 percent of total market.

The good news is that ethical fashion is a real opportunity for market protection and development. Its standards of social and environmental care, as well as its intrinsic value, position ethical fashion in a segment of the middle-to-high range which generates higher profit. It thus permits a redistribution of riches to different participants in the textile chain, and creates a first-class economic lever.

The not so good news is that as with ethical consumption more broadly, ethical fashion is not the top priority when consumers are actually buying clothes. However, research findings suggest that while the demand for fast cheap fashion looks set to continue, especially among younger buyers, there is a considerable goodwill waiting to be tapped by the right combination of factors. But however

---

5   "Who Pays For Cheap Clothes? 5 Questions the Low-cost Retailers Must Answer". http://www.labourbehindthelabel.org/news/item/584-who-pays-for-cheap-clothes?-5-questions-the-low-cost-retailers-must-answer. Accessed September 22, 2014.

influential ethics is in purchasing decisions, *lack of ethics* creates a *reputational damage*. This serves as an added incentive for retailers to avoid the negative publicity in case of ethics-related omissions.

The following example is a case in point. It illustrates the ethical and commercial implications of outsourcing to countries with a poor record of labor or safety laws. This concern came into sharp focus with the collapse of a garment factory in Bangladesh, on April 24, 2013 killing more than 1,000 workers who labored under conditions of human rights abuse in unsafe working environments.

When such tragedies happen, retailers cannot get away with the neoliberal argument that outsourcing brings prosperity to poor economies. Failure to engage with compliance issues at the plants where clothes are sourced can generate risks—being perceived as complicity in the appalling human cost. Perceptions matter even if they are not immediately expressed in sales.

Shortly after the collapse of the Rana Plaza factory in the Dhaka suburb of Savar, campaigners for garment workers' rights have brokered a legally binding Bangladesh Safety Accord signed (in May 2013) by more than 30 brands and retailers, including H&M, M&S, Zara, Mango, and Primark, who sourced their cheap fast fashion in Bangladesh.[6]

They pledged to help finance fire safety and building improvements in the factories they use. On the anniversary of the tragedy, Primark contributed $10 million to the compensation fund for the victims set up by the ILO. Primark is one of those retailers whose cheap merchandise is almost recession proof. The fact that it considered it important to be seen as not walking away from a serious ethical breach is an indication of a trend.[7]

A year on, the NGO "Labour Behind the Label" report (April 30, 2014) showed that many companies surveyed by the campaign had codes of conduct committing them to a living wage. However, only Marks & Spencer, Inditex, Switcher, and Tchibo had actually done anything about it. In addition, several brands (for example Debenhams, Matalan and The North Face) were failing to live up to their responsibilities.[8]

Those high-profile efforts, though, were exposed as public relations moves in an investigation by the UK television channel ITV for a series *Fashion Factories Undercover* that was screened on February 6, 2014. It found that firms making cheap high street clothes were still using child labor, beating staff, ignoring fire safety rules, and threatening trade union members with murder.

6 "Fashion Chains Sign Accord to Help Finance Safety in Bangladesh Factories". http://www.theguardian.com/world/2013/may/13/fashion-chain-finance-safety-bangladesh-factories. Accessed September 22, 2014.

7 "Primark to Pay $10 Million More to Victims of Bangladesh Factory Collapse". http://www.businessoffashion.com/2014/03/primark-pay-10-million-victims-bangladesh-factory-collapse.html. Accessed September 22, 2014.

8 "Cheap Garments Carry a High Cost". http://www.independent.co.uk/voices/editorials/cheap-garments-carry-a-high-cost-9223561.html. Accessed September 22, 2014.

However, despite strong demands for sourcing in Bangladesh, the McKinsey & Company 2013 Apparel CPO Survey, "The Global Sourcing Map—Balancing Cost, Compliance, and Capacity," found the "Bangladesh effect." While many Chief Purchasing Officers (CPOs) still included Bangladesh in their list of top 3 destinations for apparel sourcing over the next five years, its popularity has declined over two years since the 2011 survey, from 80 percent to 52 percent.

Ethics or Aesthetics?

The predecessors of ethical fashion in the 1980s had to battle a folk or hippy image that was decidedly frumpy and non-stylish. Given the way ethics and aesthetics have been constructed as two ends of a continuum, both NGOs and retailers were keen to emphasize that ethical fashion no longer poses a dilemma between being ethically dressed and being fashionably dressed. The main ethical fashion events in the UK, for example, such as London Fashion Week catwalk Estethica, RE: Fashion awards, and the Fashion Conscience section at Clothes Show Live, all emphasize fashionable and stylish, often cutting edge, womenswear.

There is a certain irony in going to great lengths to demonstrate ethical fashion trendy credentials. The paradox is that there is very little interest in *up-to-the-minute fashion* in the British public (which is relatively ethically aware) compared with the interest in *style*.

Keeping up with the latest looks is less important to consumers than looking well dressed and stylish. When asked: How important is fashion? Both men and women attributed more importance to *style* than to *fashion*. In response to a statement about style 47.6 percent of men and 68.4 percent of women responded that what they want most is to look attractive/well groomed. Similarly, 50.5 percent of men and 60.2 percent of women endorsed the statement that "It is important for me to look well dressed." In contrast, questions about fashionability were ranked far lower. Only 18.2 percent of men, and 29.3 percent of women agreed with the statement: "I like to keep up with the latest fashions" (TGI survey of around 25,000 adults GB TGI, BMRB Q4 (July–June), 2008; base: adults aged 15+).

In the developed markets there is a move to a slower cycle and a growing demand for quality, stylish clothing with a longer-term appeal, especially among the older and more well off, who are free from the temptations of cheap fast fashion. This means great opportunities for producers of ethical fashion.

The Complexity of the Ethical Agenda

Another reason for the limited effectiveness of the ethical market is its simplistic way of defining "ethical," which reduces complexity to uni-dimensionality, and *values* to *objects*. It has come to be almost an accepted mindset that buying "organic cotton" amounts to saving the planet, or that having some code of practice in place can make a difference to the lives of sweatshop workers far from the prying gaze of journalists or inspectors. As I have elaborated in *Fashion and Ethics* (2014) such a narrow definition oversimplifies complexities and fetishizes them in concrete objects. It suppresses deeply unethical practices that the industry is in denial of, such as with regard to animal welfare (in the leather, feather, wool, and fur markets), or toxins in dyes and cosmetics. Further, it normalizes images of impossible perfection presented to young women as role models through the industry's offering of sizes, and choice of presenters on the catwalks or in photo shoots.

A group of researchers from the Institute for Manufacturing at the University of Cambridge conducted a scenario analysis (developed with three case study products, and analyzed according to the "triple bottom line") of various futures to meet the UK's future supply of clothing and textiles. In their report, Alwood et al. (2006) identified the following as the major contributors to environmental impact:

- *Carbon footprint*: the requirement for burning fossil fuels to create electricity for heating water and air in laundering. Other major energy uses arises in providing fuel for agricultural machinery and electricity for production.
- *Toxic chemicals*: used widely in cotton agriculture and in many manufacturing stages such as pre-treatment, dyeing, and printing.
- *Waste*: volumes from the sector are high and growing in the UK with the advent of "fast fashion." On average, UK consumers send 30 kg of clothing and textiles per capita to landfill each year.
- *Water use* (in production): the extensive use of water in cotton crop cultivation can also be a major environmental issue, as seen in the dramatic water depletion in the Aral Sea region.
- *Water footprint* (consumption based indicator): used in laundering over the lifecycle of the product. Overall the water footprint of a cotton shirt is 2,700 liters. The water footprint of a nation is defined as the total volume of fresh water that is used to produce the goods and services consumed by the people of the nation.

Thus, even pursuing ethics on the production side of the fashion cycle is multi-factorial and involves many contradictions. Table 8.2 illustrates some of those contradictions:

Table 8.2   Eco challenges and partial solutions to the materials economy

Fashion cycle	Challenges	Problematic solutions
Extraction	Water footprint, toxicity of pesticides	Organic farming eliminates toxicity but maintains water footprint in use
Production	Water and carbon footprint, toxicity of dyeing, finishing	Organic natural fibres + green manufacturing = low on toxicity but high on water footprint in use; man-made fibres such as non-woven or corn-based and wood fibre- (cellulose) based = low on water and energy footprint in use but high on carbon footprint for production
Distribution	Carbon footprint of transport	Buying locally contradicts Fairtrade aims
Consumption	Fast fashion, production of landfill waste	Keeping clothes longer; buying less and better quality slow down the fashion market, threatening jobs
Use	Water and energy footprints of cleaning, drying, ironing	Aiming to reduce washing and dry cleaning is defeated by the practice of re-using of clothes to create hybrid combinations containing mixture of fabrics (requiring specialist cleaning)
Disposal	Energy footprint and pollution from incinerators; energy footprint of carbon and transport from recycling	Recycling has high carbon footprint from transport and processing plants, while reducing carbon footprint in incinerators

To take just one example where values of sustainability and workers' wellbeing clash, I use the case of water footprint. Indeed the panacea of using organic cotton, except for the obvious health benefits of not using pesticides, differs from what it is made out to be. Cotton's consumption of water (in production and use) is unsustainable. Table 8.3, from the report of researchers at the Dutch university of Twente for UNESCO (Chapagain et al. 2005) clarifies this point:

Table 8.3   Global average virtual water content of some selected products, per unit of product

Product virtual water content (liters)	
1 pair of jeans (1 kg)	10850
1 single bed sheet (900 g)	9750
1 pair of shoes (bovine leather)	8000
1 cotton T-shirt (medium sized)	4100
1 cotton T-shirt (250 g)	2720
1 hamburger (150 g)	2400
1 glass of milk (200 ml)	200
1 glass of apple juice (200 ml)	190
1 bag of potato crisps (200 g)	185
1 cup of coffee (125 ml)	140
1 egg (40 g)	135
1 glass of orange juice (200 ml)	170
1 glass of wine (125 ml)	120
1 apple (100 g)	70
1 orange (100 g)	50
1 slice of bread (30 g)	40
1 cup of tea (250 ml)	35
1 potato (100 g)	25
1 tomato (70 g)	13

Source: Adapted from http://www.waterfootprint.org/Reports/Report18.pdf.

Due to the dilemmatic nature of ethical questions, those who try to create a fully ethical enterprise face an uphill task: a product can be simultaneously ethical and unethical in different ways. It may be made from organic cotton, but in a factory where trade union rights are not adhered to; it could be hand-stitched by a Fairtrade women's cooperative in an Asian country, but then flown or shipped to other markets, clocking air miles of carbon footprint.

An illustrative example is the Dove campaign for natural beauty that has taken on the issue of the industry's responsibility for promoting a range of body types and not just the stick-thin Western model. However, it is sourcing its products from palm oil. The expansion of palm oil plantations is currently a major driver of the clearing of tropical rainforests in South East Asia. Deforestation creates a fifth of the world's greenhouse gas emissions, and it is pushing species such as the orangutan and the Sumatran tiger to the brink of extinction. For this reason Greenpeace has been promoting a campaign "Stop Dove destroying rainforests for palm oil."[9]

---

9 "Stop Dove Destroying Forests for Palm Oil". http://www.greenpeace.org/international/en/multimedia/photos/stop-dove-destroying-forests-f/. Accessed September 22, 2014.

A Mindset or a Passing Trend?

On the surface, one can detect three types of companies in terms of their approach to issues of ethics:

1. *Passionate commitment* (specialist brands): at one end of the spectrum are companies whose whole ethos and *modus operandi* is suffused with ethical commitment to "doing things differently." They may not tick all the boxes, but for them it is not a marketing decision; it is a way of being. Their core values and vision are part of "the DNA" of the organization.
2. *Halfway house solutions* (main retailers with ethical credentials): some companies would adopt genuinely a number of trends or practices as a selling feature: stocking an organic range, or some Fairtrade cotton lines, or some initiatives, or a minimum standard.
3. *Jumping on the bandwagon* (value chains): on the other end of the spectrum are companies for which "ethics" is not high on the agenda, but more of a compliance issue. To the extent that they engage with it, they do it as a token form of greenwash: the minimum they can get away with without taking legal or reputational risks.

The difference between those groups cannot obscure the fact that the fundamental ethical question is if the role of ethics is to 1) *clean up* existing levels of fashion production and consumption, or 2) *reduce* its impact.

Most of the industry seems preoccupied rather selectively with the *first task*. It appears to offer ways to make existing consumption tick some boxes of sustainable production, and of concern with workers' wellbeing in the globalized garment industry.

At the same time the ethical fashion discourse advocates certain practices and represses others.

- Rather than engaging with all aspects of ethics, ethical fashion has adopted a narrow definition of "ethical" which materializes in selective concrete practices and products (organic, "natural," regulated, certified) ignoring the dilemmatic quality of ethical questions and reducing complex problems to oversimplified solutions.
- By displacing its concern with practices further afield the industry has allowed itself to assume a philanthropic role while avoiding looking too closely at its own practices at home. These include: home grown sweatshops of economic migrants in the EU, harming animals for the purpose of securing animal products (leather, fur, wool, feathers, ivory), or harming humans through the use of toxins in textile dyeing and in cosmetics, and offering publicity images of impossible thinness, and flawless perfection as role models for consumers.

- Targeting outsourcing is double-edged: philanthropic but also culturally patronizing (if not a form of cultural colonialism). The colonialist argument is detected in the discourse which positions ethical fashion's appeal as that of contemporary "high street fashion," unlike the "ethnic chic" version of the 1990s. It is a coded way of saying that Western models of taste have been brought to bear on whatever country production is located in, in order to make it "competitive" that is, conforming to Western taste.

However, focusing on the task of cleaning up the industry it manages to skirt the *second task* of reducing unsustainable consumption at current levels. In fact, the essence of the fashion industry is a built-in obsolescence, and striving to maximize output at every stage of the whole lifecycle of the product.[10]

Thus it disavows the paradigm of *excessive* consumption because to reduce consumption would create a conflict of interests for the fashion industry itself.

Can a niche market transform an industry not known for its ethical practices or is there a danger that the ethical discourse will remain the "conscience laundering showcase" for that industry?

In some ways ethical fashion appears to be moving from a niche position to a mega trend (in terms of image, rather than actual sales). As a "design trend" it appears to be a value-added optional extra. But it is the place it occupies in the public imagination that indicates a "mindset" more than just a style. For Martin Hearson from the charity Labour Behind the Label the solution cannot be a value-added optional extra but must be a fundamental change of outlook.[11]

There are many signs that while ethical fashion may be here to stay, the selective way in which it has been approached suggests that the industry is at least ambivalent about its motives and its desire for a comprehensive solution.

To summarize, what is needed is a paradigm change that requires, at minimum, to address the assumptions detailed in Table 8.4.

---

10   See www.thestoryofstuff.com.

11   "Who is the Ethical Consumer?" http://cleanupfashion.wordpress.com/2008/01/14/who-is-the-ethical-consumer/#more-17. Accessed September 22, 2014.

Table 8.4   Unexamined assumptions of ethical fashion

Assumptions	Counter arguments
1. Magic simple solution	Ethical problems are dilemmatic and cannot have a quick fix: they involve a balancing act of different footprints. Managing environmental impact is a trade-off between energy in production v. energy in use or disposal. Some paradoxical consequences occur because Fairtrade adds higher transport costs to the equation, biofuels create food shortage, organic cotton still has a high water footprint while man-made fibres use more energy in production but considerably less in use—to name just a few examples
2. Ethical is limited to (environmentally and socially) sustainable	Such a formula leaves out equally important and not equally "tangible" aspects of: • mind (normalization of certain homogenized fantasy models of beauty, and notions of the importance of the visual) • body (the influence of toxic chemicals found in cosmetic body care and fabric dye products) • wildlife (animal welfare and exploitation of animals for experimentation, and in products like leather, fur, and feathers)
3. Consumption is a given	Recycling, reusing, and restyling are still locked into the terms of the excess consumption paradigm. What is needed instead is a paradigm change: reduction and reflexivity

Perhaps a concise way of summarizing the ethical transformation that is required is captured by this cartoon by Paul Wood for *The Spectator* (Figure 8.1), depicting a couple in a despondent mood, with the caption: "It's depressing no longer being able to buy all those things we don't really need"

References

Allwood, Julian M., Søren Ellebæk Laursen, Cecilia Malvido de Rodríguez, and Nancy Bocken. 2006. *Well Dressed?* Cambridge: The Institute for Manufacturing at the University of Cambridge. http://www.ifm.eng.cam.ac.uk/uploads/News/UK_textiles.pdf.

Bauman, Zygmunt. 2000. *Globalization: The Human Consequences*. Columbia: Columbia University Press.

Brown, Darrell, Jesse Dillard, and R. Scott Marshall. 2006. "Triple Bottom Line: A Business Metaphor for a Social Construct." *Documents de Treball 06/2*. Bellaterra: Universitat Autònoma de Barcelona. http://www.recercat.net/bitstream/2072/2223/1/UABDT06–2.pdf.

"It's depressing no longer being able to buy all those
things we don't really need."

Figure 8.1   **"It's depressing no longer being able to buy all those things we don't really need"**
Source: Cartoon courtesy of *The Spectator* and the cartoon artist Paul Wood.

Business in the Community. 2008. "The Value of Corporate Governance & Responsible Business." Accessed   April 20, 2014. http://www.bitc.org.uk/media_centre/news/new_research.html.

Chapagain, A.K., A.Y. Hoekstra, H.H.G. Savenije, and R. Gautam. 2005. "The Water Footprint of Cotton Consumption." *Value of Water Research Report Series* no. 18. Delft: UNESCO-IHE.

Dukerich, Janet M. and Suzanne M. Carter, 2009. "Distorted Images and Reputation Repair." *Organization Studies* 30: 301–24.

Elkington, John. 1994. "Towards the Sustainable Corporation: Win-Win-Win Business Strategies for Sustainable Development." *California Management Review* 36, 2: 90–100.

Elkington, John. 2004. "Enter the Triple Bottom Line." In *The Triple Bottom Line, Does it All Add Up?*, edited by Adrian Henriques and Julie Richardson, 1–16. Sterling: Earthscan.

Esty, Daniel C. 2007. "Ride the Wave or Go Under." *The Guardian*, November 5. Accessed April 20, 2014. http://www.theguardian.com/environment/2007/nov/05/greenlist.comment2.

Ethical Trading Report. 2005. *Pioneering Approaches to Purchasing Practices.* London: ETI.

European Commission. 2008. *European Competitiveness Report.* Accessed September 22, 2014. http://ec.europa.eu/enterprise/newsroom/cf/_getdocument.cfm?doc_id=4058.

Goldfiner, Sybil. 2011. *"comme il faut*—Where Ethics is Not Just a Brand Image But a Brand Essence. Reflections of the CEO." *Critical Studies in Fashion & Beauty* 2, 1/2: 83–116.

Hilton, Matthew. 2004. "The Legacy of Luxury: Moralities of Consumption Since the 18th Century." *Journal of Consumer Culture* 4: 101–23.

Lurie, Bob. 2009. "A New Social Contract for Green Business." *Harvard Business Online*, May 12 2009. Accessed September 22, 2014. http://www.businessweek.com/managing/content/may2009/ca20090512_004263.htm.

Mintel. 2009. Consumer Attitudes Towards Beauty Product Ingredients—UK—May 2009; Accessed 22, September 2014. http://reports.mintel.com/display/393971/.

Plender, John and Avinash Persaud. 2005. *All You Need to Know About Ethics and Finance.* London: Longtail Publishing.

Plender, John and Avinash Persaud. 2006. "When Compliance is Not Enough." *Financial Times*, August 21. Accessed April 20, 2014. http://www.ft.com/cms/s/2/9c8374e0-3131-11db-b953-0000779e2340.html.

Siegle, Lucy. 2011. *To Die For: Is Fashion Wearing Out the World?* London: Harper Collins.

Stern, Stefan. 2007. "President Clinton, Google Grows, $100 oil, but No US Recession—This is 2008." *Financial Times*, December 30 2007. Accessed September 22, 2014. http://www.ft.com/cms/s/0/eb14b4b2-b6fe-11dc-aa38-0000779fd2ac.html.

Stiglitz, Joseph. 2003. *Globalization and its Discontents.* New York: W.W. Norton & Company.

Stiglitz, Joseph and Andrew Chariton. 2005. *Fairtrade for All: How Trade Can Promote Development.* Oxford: Oxford University Press.

Stokes, Paul, Efrat Tseëlon, and Léan McMahon. 2003. "BOBOS in Ireland: A Report of Attitudes in Ireland to the Social and Environmental Responsibilities of Business." Social Science Research Centre, University College Dublin.

Tseëlon, Efrat. 2014. "Introduction: A Critique of the Ethical Fashion Paradigm." In *Fashion Ethics*, edited by Efrat Tseëlon. 3–68. Intellect: Chicago University Press.

Williams, Austin. 2008. *The Enemies of Progress.* Exeter: Societas.

Williams, Austin. 2011. "Fashionable Dilemmas." *Critical Studies in Fashion & Beauty* 2, 1/2: 69–82.

Chapter 9

Framing Humanity Consumerwise: Embodied Consumer Selves and their Varieties

Roberta Sassatelli

Introduction

Humans are quite peculiar animals, as we have repeatedly heard from philosophers and social thinkers alike. Indeed, certain bodily characteristics (from adaptability to the capacity to articulate complex sounds; from opposable thumbs to a highly developed brain) have been associates to the human species which is also characterized as remarkably sociable. Human nature, in its turn, has been characterized by aggression as much as compassion, empathy, and altruism. Still, precisely because of humans' adaptability and relationality, what humanity is, must largely be seen as related to their conditions of living, which are, partly, of their own making. Certainly, fundamental to the human condition is the way bodies, selves, and material culture are socially arranged. And indeed, the relation between the body, self, and material culture in contemporary, postindustrial or late-modern societies has come to be largely defined through consumption. The *zoon politikòn* of Aristotelian memory has, in many ways, given way to the portrayal of the human being as "the only creature that consumes without producing" carved out by George Orwell in his dystopian novel *Animal Farm* just after the Second World War. In contemporary Western societies, we are increasingly attuned to a view of humanity which is defined by images, ways, and manners of consumption as much as other practices and thoughts. This occurs at least at three levels: the level of representation, of subjectivity, and of institutions. Firstly, at the representational level, the imagery associated with consumption is central to visual representation in promotional culture which simultaneously revolves around the display of the body as an object of desire and indicator of self. Secondly, at the level of subjectivity, how individuals realize themselves as embodied subjects—that is, how they manage corporeal identity participating in social interaction and how they experience and realize embodiment—happens largely via the use of commodities and against the backdrop of promotional imagery. Finally, at the institutional level, a variety of consumer spaces, contexts, and institutions increasingly address the individual as a sensuous, embodied subject in search of personal gratification and improvement.

In this chapter, I shall deal with all three levels, considering the broad literature that may be brought to bear on how representations, subjectivities and institutions converge and diverge in the shaping of consumers' embodied selves. The first level is, indeed, typically addressed by critical theories of consumer culture as advertising, image proliferation and promotional culture. Here the self is portrayed as being largely reduced to the (surface of the) body. The body in its turn features as "the most beautiful object of consumption"—to use Baudrillard's phrase—and its objectification contributes to the transformation of consumers themselves into commodities. When dealing with the second level we encounter at least two significant streams of work: one deriving from Bourdieu's notion of *habitus* and considering that embodied dispositions of tastes are mapped onto social divisions, class in particular, which consumers' lifestyles make visible; the other deriving from theories of reflexive individualization which stress the reflexive, strategic role of individuals in stylizing one's own selves through a variety of body projects. In both streams, body and self are posited as in a dialectical relation mediated by commodities and mediating social reproduction (responding, respectively, either to class/gender divisions and hierarchies or to individualization and cultural de-classification). Reaching the third level we will then come across a quite varied set of suggestions, theories, and even disciplines: just as contemporary marketing is very aware of the sensory and situational component of consumption, we find a number of studies of how, particularly in the leisure sphere, institutions of consumption address individual consumers as embodied selves. Places such as the restaurant, the spa, the beauty center, the tourist village, the theme park, and the gym are becoming key institutions for the production, consumption, and display of legitimate embodied selves. These places address a public of consumers, offering varieties of fairly standardized products to accommodate what are described as individual wants and desires.

Taking stock from this discussion, the chapter proceeds by looking more deeply into two different ways of constructing the consumer as an embodied subject: fitness culture on the one hand and critical consumerism on the other. I consider fitness culture as promoted by commercial health and fitness centers which, in a Simmelian fashion, as a fragment of reality revealing broader cultural trends as evident in mainstream Western consumer culture. Fitness culture revolves around a particular vision of the self as strong and rational, commands practices that negotiate between fashion, variety and obsolescence (of one's own body, of cultural forms, of body techniques), and provides forms of polite sociability which are sufficiently spick and span to be functional to individual goals. Fitness culture is thus used to illustrate the dominant normative notion of the consumer as an autonomous, high-speed, flexible, self-centered, and self-possessed being. This view is thereby juxtaposed with another portrayal of the consumer, a view which places weight on personal relations, social and environmental responsibility, slowness and care, whereby the individual body is less a purely individual project and is placed in the context of generations to come and nature as endangered environment. Thus the portrayal which emerges from critical consumerism locates ethical and sustainable consumer initiatives as places where the embodiment of consumer humanities is rendered *vis à vis* nature, other human beings (both in the present and in the future), and the materiality of commodities. The chapter thus concludes with a discussion of the normalization of consumers, dealing with how the humanity of consumers as embodied selves has been articulated in contemporary Western consumer culture and offering some exploratory remarks on the different renderings of individual autonomy which may now be detected in different cultures of consumption.

Representation, Subjectivity and Institutions

> Without taking things out of nature's hands and consuming them, and without defending himself against the natural process of growth and decay, the animal laborans could never survive. But without being at home in the midst of things whose durability makes them fit for use and for erecting a world whose very permanence stands in direct contrast to life, this life would never be human. (Arendt 1958, 116)

Within these words Hannah Arendt adumbrates an important existential human dilemma: we need to produce and use up stuff we extract from nature, but we also need to provide this stuff with lasting meaning in order to produce ourselves as human. A society dominated by consumption, like ours, was in the eyes of Arendt a wasteful society, which may not provide enough durability for selves to become human. That goods and commodities have a function to fix our world, is a crucial tenet of cultural anthropology: "the main problem of social life is to pin down meanings so that they stay still for a little time"; the acquisition and use of objects is therefore a way of "mak[ing] firm and visible a particular set of judgments in the fluid processes of classifying persons and events" (Douglas and Isherwood 1979, 65 and 67).

Societies saturated with commercially-led normative injunctions have been described as displacing the solidity of material culture, promoting cultural de-classification and the ceaseless obsolescence of objects and meanings. In such conditions, there is greater pressure on the self to perform not only flexibility—the capacity to master swings and changes—but also durability. As Simmel (1990, 283) wrote, people's lives become dominated by a "deep nostalgic desire to confer new meaning to things" and still appear as the I who performs the bestowal. A well-governed body may be particularly helpful in such a performance and, in the face of a shifting world, self-durability is very much played upon the individual's own body. This is matched by a promotional imagery and a health and beauty market which invites individuals to joyfully take responsibility for their bodies and to invest in body maintenance in order to perform culturally appropriate self-presentation.

To be sure, the proliferation of commercially circulated visual culture (movies, photographs, and so forth) increases individuals' awareness of external appearance and bodily presentation. For example, the burgeoning film industry has legitimated public bodily display and participation in leisured bodywork (from sunbathing to fitness training). Contemporary advertising has made full use of the human body to promote the most diverse goods and services, contributing to turning the body into a public place, stressing the shapes, sizes, and texture of its parts, representing both body maintenance routines and sexual arousal, playing with fantasies of body transformation, and opening even its invisible interiors to public scrutiny via the fictional representation of medical practice and the arts. In all societies, certain physical characteristics are publicly celebrated and associated with high status, but they are also very often acknowledged as exclusive to the privileged or the fortunate. In contemporary consumer culture, bodies which are more accessible to the privileged are coded as both a matter of individual will and proof of personal and social success for all. In such circumstances, the body is viewed as a site of domination through commoditization, which ultimately leads to the reproduction of gender, ethnic, and class biases (Wernick 1991; Wykes and Gunter 2005). Indeed, women in particular are targeted by advertising and commercially-provided goods and activities aimed at the body, and the diffusion of illnesses such as anorexia and bulimia among young females are evidence of the particular investment of female subjectivity (Bordo 1993). Commercialization extends to the body; the outer body as a carrier of the self is emphasized. The outer body, the "look" is both "the finest consumer object" and an "object of salvation" (Baudrillard 1998; Featherstone 1991).[1] The rationalized emphasis on performance which is dominant in the sphere of work has extended into the domain of consumption. The consumer is expected to assume responsibility for his or her appearance; that is, to engage in bodywork where failing to do so becomes a sign of moral failure. Conversely, consumer culture is codified through leisure and pleasure, thereby giving way to a rather complex mix of asceticism and hedonism.

Rather than being seen as merely productive of a pathological consumer, the particular and ever-changing mix of asceticism and hedonism which characterizes contemporary consumer culture is best seen as offering visions of normality which people are asked to engage with. It is through the appropriation of otherwise fairly standardized, distant services and goods that consumers may cope with, and thus effectively come to terms with and reframe, body ideals that are inevitably incumbent upon them. This brings us to the issue of the underlying

---

1   Following Marcuse, Baudrillard considers that the liberation of the body promised by advertising in fact amounts to an intensification of power relations; anticipating Lasch ([1979] 1991) the reward for ceaseless bodywork is no longer spiritual salvation, but a more marketable physical appearance. This resonates with recent works that consider investment in self-presentation via consumption an instance of a deeper "corrosion of character" (Sennett 1998) or of the transformation of consumers themselves into "sellable commodities" (Bauman 2007).

moral framing of consumers. Rather than removing ideologies of asceticism and self-abnegation and replacing them with ideologies of liberation and hedonism centered on imperatives of display, a rapidly escalating promotional culture has promoted the combination of hedonism and asceticism offering commodities, and their institutional settings of provision and use, as balancing devices (Sassatelli 2001). It is through the appropriate, tamed but joyous enjoyment of certain goods that consumers can demonstrate their command of themselves and their bodies. In doing so, consumers fight with and against promotional culture, with different degrees of success—and they do so to fix their relational world and identities and to counter the objectifying tendencies of commodity circuits. The characteristically modern combination of asceticism and hedonism has indeed been considered central to understanding the development of the consumer as social persona. Colin Campbell (1987) has notably suggested that modern hedonism may be rooted in Romantic teachings, while Chandra Mukerji (1982) sees a mixture of hedonism and asceticism as characteristic of the kind of materialist culture which has fostered commercial modernity. Many consider that it is from the dawn of the twentieth century that signals have become stronger. Writing on the commercially mediated leisure spaces of the US, for example, Mrozek (1989, 20) suggests that after the First World War in particular, "it became a virtual duty to 'have fun,' to enjoy yourself. Having fun meant using your body as a vehicle of gratification and pleasure."

As George Vigarello (1978) has demonstrated in his *Le Corps Redressé*, together with the concept of the body as the locus of the unconscious, where the latter found expression and external demands which repressed it, a number of commercially mediated objects and techniques developed which aimed to rediscover the body in all its aspects. The body thereby became an arena that can and must be explored, visualized and appropriated to new profit, something that gradually took hold of bourgeois strata. A "quest for disciplined vitality" and "for intense experience" (Lears 1983) was expressed and favored by the massive arrival on the market of a variety of goods (cosmetics, deodorants, make-up, and so on) and services (hairdressers, beauty salons, gyms, and so on). Indeed, in increasingly rationalized capitalist economies, in ever more "unexciting" societies as Elias would say, the "compensatory" role of "pleasurable excitement," itself organized in specialized institutions and focalized in specific practices as a form of "controlled de-control" of emotions, may have greatly increased (Elias 1986, 36). As is the case with amateur practices, such as wine tasting and collecting or music playing and listening (Hennion and Tèil 2004), the continuous, often strenuous, and never-ending disciplining of a taste *vis à vis* the physical and symbolic engagement with objects and places is intrinsic to the pleasure of consumption rather than its opponent.

The strategic dimension of identity constitution through goods has been foregrounded in the age of what authors such as Beck (1992) or Giddens (1991) have called "reflexive individualization." In Giddens, the notion of "body projects" summarizes again the idea that the self today has become a reflexive and secular project which involves unremitting, if creative, self-monitoring, self-scrutiny, planning and ordering of bodily practices and choices into a coherent display of identity, which may have its costs, but may allow consumers to enact resistance to the tyranny of the marketplace. Yet, the absence of a stable social and cultural order in a post-traditional society, rather than the drive of capitalist economy, makes choice into a burden as much as a possibility. Just as it was for Simmel (1990; see also Sassatelli 2000), consumer choice, and the choice to master one's own embodiment, is not an option for consumer subjectivity; rather, it is obligatory. We have "no choice, but to choose"—writes Giddens (1991, 81): late modernity confronts the individual with a complex diversity of choices which is "non-foundational," produces anxiety and offers "little help as to which options should be selected." The solution to such risk and anxiety to be found in consumer culture is internal to such culture and "technical": it solves the problem of the durable and coherent self in the face of incessant non-foundational complexity by treating all problems as solvable through specific commodities (Baumann 1992, 200). Each of them may be highly functional to a precise task, but they still have to be arranged in a coherent, credible whole.

Lifestyle, as a reflexive attempt at consumer coherence, can be seen as a way in which the pluralism of post-traditional identity is managed by individuals and organized (or exploited) by commerce. Lifestyle orders things into a certain unity, reducing the plurality of choice and affording a sense of "ontological security." This may bring us to conceive of the self as a commodity itself, with "self-actualization [being] packaged and distributed according to market criteria" (Giddens 1991, 198).[2] These observations reflect the fact that in contemporary late-modern societies, various techniques of body modification and body marking are being commercialized as a potent symbols of both status and character, inviting people as consumers to adopt quite conscious strategies of self-management which extend to one's own intimate embodiment and disposition. While we try, reflexively, to govern our choices in order to shape our embodied selves as adequate projects fitting ideals and situations, tastes nevertheless, as socially structured embodied dispositions, orientate us towards the world of goods (Bourdieu 1984) with an unconscious movement. Although it is expressed in the apparently neutral and innocuous language of individual preference, taste is about relationships: "gates and bridges" as Douglas (1992) would say, and therefore power and hierarchies. To Bourdieu, the individual *habitus* stands in a relationship of homology—

---

2   Even more polemical are Bauman's observations, which appear to resonate precisely with Hannah Arendt's (1958) criticism of consumer society in *The Human Condition*: for Bauman, in fact, "to consume means to invest in one's social membership, which in a society of consumers translates as 'saleability' […] the crucial, perhaps the decisive purpose of consumption in the society of consumers […] is not the satisfaction of needs, desires and wants, but the commodititization or recommoditization of the consumer" (2007, 56–7). For a discussion of how we can conceptualize embodiment in different traditions, from Giddens to Bourdieu, from Bourdieu to Goffman and Foucault, see Sassatelli (2003a).

that is, of "diversity within homogeneity"—with respect to the class *habitus* defined by structural forms of capital derived from one's own professional position, education and social networks. Embodied disposition, indeed, works as "symbolic power," naturalizing the existing system of power differences. If the state of each individual body—its size, its volume, weight as well as gesture, posture, looks, and so on—is the realization of an "unequal distribution among social classes of corporeal properties" realized concretely through "working conditions" and "consumption habits," its "political mythology" is perceived through "categories and classification systems which are not independent" of such distribution (Bourdieu 1977, 51). These categories are however, I believe, increasingly available to consumers as the bases of self-elaboration, even though this reflexive process is uneven, and articulated in terms of consumer subjectivities and consumer spaces.[3] When we consume, we can gain a measure of reflexivity from market relations, but precisely because we act in practical ways, we do not reflect on everything; on the contrary, the meanings we attribute to our practices and the narratives with which we reflexively create our trajectory of consumption and present ourselves at least partly reflect (and thus blindly constructed upon) the conditions in which we find ourselves and act.

Such a form of bounded reflexivity characterizes the dialectic between material culture and embodied subjects. It corresponds to the fact that people not only express but also constitute themselves through what they get from the market, and use. Consumption not only expresses but also performs identity: through making objects their own, social actors make themselves, both as consumers and as embodied selves with specific and different roles linked to different identity markers such as ethnicity, gender, sexuality, and so on, which are loosely coupled with specific styles of consumption. More broadly, scholars of consumer practices have focused on their internal complexity, on their creativity and on their capacity to generate classifications, styles and ultimately contribute to the continuous structuring of *habitus* in their own right (Sassatelli 2007). Whilst they are far from being the direct expression of natural individualities or of self-interested agents, domains or cultures of consumption may consolidate identities and dispositions which are relatively disarticulated from structural division (class, profession, gender, ethnicity, and so on). As I shall suggest below, in some well-documented cases at least—for example youth sub-cultures or amateur practices—it is the

---

3 Cultural de-classification allows for increasing possibilities of re-appropriation partly disarticulated from long-established social hierarchies. Yet, re-appropriation is not equally accessible to all. Also, commodities still act as markers of social distinction. But this happens in local ways, pointing to the specific, highly dynamic domains of consumption where bodies, selves and goods come together. Thus, reflexive body projects are linked to the particularly stringent self-presentational needs of the new middle-class (Bourdieu 1984; Featherstone 1991) while some consumer fields such as sporting activities or fan cultures require participants to work reflexively on dispositions as to self and body and purposively reframe them (Noble and Watkins 2003; Sassatelli 2007).

practices of consumption themselves that create a structure for the standardization of taste. Bourdieu's *habitus* helps us consider that it is not enough to postulate a relationship between embodied taste and the world of things, since the second doesn't generate the first, or vice versa. Still, to approach consumption we need to qualify the homological effects of class, gender, and other structural positions on individual taste, and consider that, in diverse contexts, the encounter between embodied subjects and objects is indeed creative: understanding how tastes and material culture find correspondences and are mutually shaped requires attention to the local contexts of consumption, and in particular to the institutions which mediate acquisition and use, organizing interaction and manners in ways which we consider appropriate and proposing narratives for the constitution of accountable, morally acceptable selves. This amounts to realizing that consumption does contribute to the constitution of human embodied subjectivity. The bounded reflexivity of the actor as consumer can be pinned down by taking seriously the idea that consumption is a "relatively autonomous and plural process of cultural self-construction" and "stands for the diversity of 'local' social networks" (Miller 1995, 41). As such, consumption is a fundamental social activity which realizes the market in a variety of ways, which inevitably mixes economic rationality (instrumental) with affects and emotional coding (Zelizer 2008).

The diversity of local networks is realized in the many consumer spaces and institutions that have come to populate contemporary urban realities. The rise of consumer culture is linked to the spread of urban living and its many consumer spaces—from cafés to theaters, from cinemas to tourist villages, from restaurants to fitness centers. As I have suggested elsewhere (Sassatelli 2007), these spaces offer situated, embodied experiences of locally relevant structured variety, drawing people into relatively separated realities where they can engage with a specific set of goods, activities, manners, and identities. They offer the possibility of entering into organized contexts of involvement which arrange a world of internal rewards that is partly decoupled from broader social rules of relevance. They thus provide for learning experiences which may mobilize bodies and selves quite profoundly. These places are indeed vessels for bounded reflexivity with their ceremonies, meanings, and narratives for self-constitution. They are domains of action mediated by commercial relations where participants must not only command reflexive choice to account for participation, but also draw on the specific domain's internal and largely taken-for-granted repertoire. Such repertoires may be more or less encrusted with class and gender distinctions as are standard outside, in the broader social structure. A similar line of thought may be seen as according with a micro-sociological tradition—from Goffman to Becker—which considers that different degrees of involvement within a relatively separated social world (fan cultures, sub-cultures, sport cultures, music cultures, and so on) be as important as external determinants in understanding meanings and differentiation in a given field, place or institution. Indeed, the many works which have conceived of consumption as a form of appropriation looking at rituals of consumption or at sub-cultural styles have largely responded to a similar research agenda.[4] Collectors or amateur circles effectively work to create relatively separated "small" worlds sustaining specialized tastes, meanings and hierarchies (Bromberg 1998; Fine 1998; Hennion and Tèil 2004). Likewise, youth and sub-cultural styles are constituted precisely through the choices of consumption; they do not always reflect the other social identities belongings of the individual (in the guise of class, gender, or age), and they are increasingly practiced even by actors who are well past adolescence. Within such cultures a form of capital (knowledge and assets) develops. It is "consumer capital" (Sassatelli 2007), something cannot be traced back directly to external resources, but is locally produced, and as Sarah Thornton (1995) has suggested, may be conceived of as "sub-cultural capital" to all effects. Still in other cases, such as the burgeoning development of self care, body care and even spiritual care cultures and organizations, typically mediated by some sort of commercial nexus, what is at stake is the very transformation of the *habitus* (the self, the body, the embodied self). While a certain (middle-class) *habitus* may be more attuned to change and transition, these cultures are effectively engines for the formation of taste with creative powers. All in all, therefore, consumption practices participate in the generation of *habitus* being differently articulated or coupled with broader social structures and hierarchies—sometimes more loosely, sometimes more stringently.

Varieties of Practices, Varieties of Consumers

Let us look at how consumer practices, as mediated by institutions, subjectivity, and representation, contribute to the generation of embodied dispositions and ultimately selves and bodies. I shall start by discussing a characteristically late-modern consumer space such as the fitness gym. I have long studied these mainly commercial institutions across both Italy and the UK, using both ethnographic methods and discourse analysis (see Sassatelli 1999, 2002, 2010). Arguably, it is institutions such as the fitness gyms that are on the rise in contemporary Western culture, namely institutions which address participants as self-oriented consumers, expressing participants' subjectivity in a consumer vocabulary. And consumer culture as such expresses its dominant or hegemonic traits in typically promotionally-led institutions such as the fitness gym. Drawing on the telling example of fitness culture, therefore, it is therefore possible to explore the ways in which people are invested with what may be called "hegemonic" consumer

---

4   This obviously tends to happen with the mediation of different "experts" (from fashion journalists to architects, from chefs to environmentalists) who try to orient our choices in particular socially recognizable and relevant directions. On cultural intermediaries, see Negus (2002).

subjectivity.[5] To this variety of embodied consumer selves others are juxtaposed, thereby foreshadowing a palette of consumer subjectivities. To explore such variety, we need to consider alternative, critical or marginal practices of consumption, whereby the very notion of the consumer is embraced and put into question. This section will thus end with a discussion of the variety of consumer subjectivity which is embodied by critical consumers and their attempts at re-dressing contemporary consumer culture and its shortcomings.

Fitness gyms or health centers are clearly diverse, and they offer different body techniques and facilities. Still, on the whole, certain traits characterize the fitness gym as a commercial institution that epitomizes dominant consumer culture, as against other recreational clubs or sports centers. Instructive is the comparison with another, quite peculiar and much less market-driven contemporary site dealing in body practices and physical activity, the boxing gym. The boxing gym has been studied ethnographically, notably by Loïc Wacquant (2003). The boxing gym is an important space of leisure and consumption in working-class neighborhoods, it is typically managed through charities or public provision rather than commercial relations and it offers its mainly male clients an "antidote to the street," a "dream machine" and a sub-culture of "controlled violence" whereby the boxing *habitus* appears in clear continuity with the (lower) class *habitus* (Wacquant 2003, 239–40; 85). Precisely because the fitness gym is part of a rather blurred mainstream cultural formation such as commercial body modification techniques (from cosmetics to plastic surgery), promotional imagery, and the representational needs of fashionable urban living, it promotes a *habitus* that is far less class bound. The carnality promoted by the fitness gym is sanitized, managed excitement: whilst the boxer has to resist the excitement of violence, learning to control very immediate fears and dangers, fitness fans have to become "excited to resist," embracing the joyous strenuousness of a practice that is all training (Sassatelli 2010, 125–9). In both cases, though, the control of embodied emotions—the capacity to generate pleasure in danger or pleasure in discipline—is crucial, and narratives of self-revolve around this. While boxing *habitus* is the result of training which has mythical status and produces bodies which, within the boundaries of the sub-culture, are valued in themselves, fitness *habitus* is very much about being ready to change and try out new training options in order to keep going: body work is instrumental to the fit body, which in turn is instrumental to a better, fuller, living in everyday life. In other terms, fitness *habitus* is very much about learning to find pleasure in repetition and routine which testifies to one's own capacity to "take care of oneself," this capacity in turn allows the self to command the body towards greater flexibility and capacity to work and consume. More generally, the comparison between fitness and boxing gyms illustrates the different ways institutions or spaces of consumption articulate more or less loosely different structural aspects, for example being loosely or tightly

---

5   I here borrow the idea of hegemonic views of identity developed by Connell (2005) for hegemonic masculinity and apply it to consumer subjectivity.

coupled with class codifications or mainstream fashion dynamics. It also allows us to consider that bounded reflexivity is a feature of such spaces: by attending, participants purposively acquire knowledge and capacities and yet, typically, the more they acquire the more their embodied knowledge becomes an *illusio*, to use Bourdieu's term, which sets the cognitive and moral limits to what they can see and feel. Boxing gyms and fitness gyms do tell us of the powers of locally realized resources within institutional settings of consumption and offer a perspective on the mechanisms which are at work in places which are aimed at changing the subject, body and self. In both places, regular participants come to shape their *habitus* and come to view themselves as subjects of discipline. Both places thus invest participants with subjectivity, and yet the subjectivity at stake stands in a different relation to the social persona of the consumer. Embodied selves are variously constructed by consumer practices, and such variety stands in different relations to commoditization and consumer culture. Indeed, what Raymond Williams wrote a few decades ago still holds: "to say *user* rather than consumer is still to express a relevant distinction" (Williams 1976, 70). While fitness culture is very much about the translation of participants' subjectivity into a consumer vocabulary, the boxing gym appears distant if not alien to it.

It should feel natural now to move back and tackle more directly the issue of the constitution of human subjectivity within contemporary consumer culture. The rendering of subjectivity through a consumer vocabulary is what I call *consumership*. Consumership, like citizenship, may certainly corroborated by a number of formalized rights such as those promoted by consumer protection organizations (Hilton 2009; Sassatelli 2003b). However, consumership is, above all, a *cultural frame* which attributes to people, their bodies and selves, certain qualities and capacities as "consumers." In this final section I shall start by looking again at fitness culture and address the view of subjectivity promoted therein. As suggested, and as many social theorists (including Baudrillard, Giddens, and Bauman) have briefly noted, fitness culture illustrates well the dominant tendencies of contemporary consumer culture. To me, the fitness gym is a particularly telling fragment of contemporary consumer culture because it is a site where people, bodies and selves, are addressed as consumers, and *human embodied subjectivity is framed consumerwise*. In particular, gym-goers are typically addressed as individuals who choose among different commodities and, through the consumption of certain goods, take control of themselves, their bodies, and the market (Sassatelli 2010). Fitness culture highlights individual choice. The services of a fitness gym as well as the efforts of a personal trainer are truly legitimate and successful, so goes the dominant script in fitness expert discourse, only when clients "really want" to train, when they "have made a true choice for themselves," "opting for the exercise that suits them," "taking advantage of all the possibilities on offer." In many ways a fitness participant is a consumer, and a good one. This is not just a matter of selling jargon, even though gym-goers are often referred to as "clients," "customers" and "consumers" by gym staff. It is neither a purely economic circumstance, even though regular gym-goers often buy a variety of commodities associated with keeping fit. Fitness fans are consumers, primarily as they themselves use a consumer vocabulary and tend to portray themselves as choosers—and they are good ones—because they are subjects capable of making their own individual choices, deriving pleasure from choice, and making pleasure coincide with the incessant search of the perfect option for themselves.

Let us explore this further. In fitness gyms, gym-goers are addressed as consumers who want to take control of themselves and do so in what could be potentially a very challenging environment, packed with ever-new techniques, options, and a crowd of participants. As it is frequent in contemporary consumer culture, fitness culture solves the problem of competition among participants by offering non-competitive gratification predicated on an infinite and pluralistic horizon of happiness and growth. Contrary to what happens in athletic sports, fitness gyms deny scarcity of desire, ability, honor, and so on. Instead, this field of action is founded on the generation of a pluralistic abundance. Trainers strive to suggest that there is always something more, something else, something new in fitness, something which can be adjusted to clients' needs to make them feel better. The lack of challenge with external opponents and the difficulty to get one's own achievements recognized in an official hierarchy is replaced by novelty and an emphasis on self-experimentation, again two major desire management devices within contemporary consumer culture. Regular clients maintain that, in order to continue training when exercise capacities improve, they constantly need to get new incentives, try more difficult things and explore modern techniques and new trainers. Pluralistic abundance, novelty and self-experimentation are as many desire management techniques which make the gym into a desire-producing machine revolving around personalization and standardization. Fitness trainers and managers insist that clients should consider their gym as a place where one has to find a personal way of training by using the array of standardized techniques available and by making the most of all standardized novelties as introduced by the industry. The creation of thus personalized and continuously renovated training programs is itself a major device for the provision of non-competitive satisfaction that can accommodate both genders, different ages, and varied social identities without limiting the market to provide for cohesive communities. Fitness gyms commercialize both *fun* and *discipline*. Staff, trainers, and official fitness discourse portray clients as people who have learned to like what is best for themselves and display a joyous commitment to the task. Regular clients stress that engagement with routine may indeed become "fun," a "pleasure": it allows them to "detach from everyday duties," it offers a task whereby "improvements" can be "obtained" and "appreciated," it provides for a form of "light," "uncommitted but positive" "togetherness" with other participants. Still, cheerfulness in training clearly has a normative slant as evidenced by the continuous positive incitements which are a feature of trainers' instructions and comments. The good client not only has fun, but also demonstrates it while working hard. Fun and self-discipline point to the joyous pursuit of self-sufficiency on the part of a rather strong self. The fit body, so I heard over and over again, is essentially a body that is "more ready for everything" and "an effective resource" for the self. Fitness fans associate the energy produced by training with the possibility of living a fuller life and using the body to the fullest: fitness provides the body with energy that helps them to "do everything better," to have "more drive," to "get more done." Adumbrated in these words is the polite, instrumental, and tamed hedonism that contributed to the diffusion of mass leisure in the twentieth century. It is a script which resonates with the cult of individual autonomy as self-control which is crucial to Western consumer culture. "Ready for everything," the fit body is a powerful, docile universal utility. It illuminates an allegedly infinite horizon of potentiality adumbrating the existence of a self that is not confined to different social roles: a self which is able to master and govern roles and contingency by self-control operated, quite dualistically, via body control. Such body control has itself to be controlled—giving way to what appears as an endless individualistic exercise of self-control, which can be relieved only via the comfort offered by the possibility of detaching oneself from previous choices and choosing ever-new options from a institutionally guaranteed set of alternatives. Fitness participants thus distinguish between "normal" fitness fans, and "addicts" or "maniacs" who can't do without their set routine for a day. Fitness consumption, like other forms of consumption, is normalized. That is, fitness participation is not predicated on unconditional increases, uncontrollable desires or untamed pleasures. It is, rather, conditional upon self-governed appropriation demonstrated by the embrace of commercially-led variety as locally proposed by the gym. Fitness fans are good consumers in that they are "autonomous," they choose what they like, in order to do good to themselves, and possess their desires by shifting their preferences over body techniques to continue pursuing what is best for themselves. As suggested, while there may be particular gyms and trainers that try to follow an alternative path, fitness culture as a whole works well as the epitome of mainstream consumer culture, producing a particular variety of consumer. It fits nicely with the dominant normative rendering of consumer subjectivity as defined by a psychological, individualistic view of autonomy as self-control dualistically predicated on the body.

Such a dominant rendering is not undisputed, though. There are other views of what consumption is and ought to be as well as other capacities, duties and rights attributed to the consumer. As suggested, a fertile terrain on which to explore this, is that of critical consumption. While critical consumption initiatives are diverse and varied, on the whole they illustrate how consumers may be politically invested in ways that are potentially linked to a reappraisal of individualistic consumer choice predicated on autonomy as self-control. Indeed, under the banner of critical (as well as ethical, political, or alternative) consumption, a diverse assortment of initiatives, movements and practices which try to critically address contemporary late-capitalist ways of consuming is gathered (Harrison et al. 2005; Lewis and Potter 2011; Miller 2012; Sassatelli 2004, 2006, 2009). A variety of actors (both individual and collective, economic and political, oriented towards profit maximization or towards collective goods) are contributing to shaping alternative views of what consumers may do and of the market in which they may move. This variety is reflected in the many nuances of the discourses on the critical consumer, their uneven resonance, and the varying economic and political effectiveness of attempts to approach commodities as bearers of environmental, ethical, and political concerns. Still, as I have elaborated more widely elsewhere (Sassatelli 2006), a fundamental cultural move characterizes these initiatives, namely a political problematization of consumer choice. Individual consumer choice is portrayed as neither universally good nor a private issue. People are typically asked to consume better. As a source of power, consumption is not to be given up altogether, but consumer choice is framed as a practice with direct and momentous consequences for the common good. The common good in turn is seen as inevitably linked to personal well-being. Thus consumption practices express consumer sovereignty only if consumers take full responsibility for the environmental, social, and political effects of their choices and are ready to reconsider their consuming life on those grounds.

Critical consumption initiatives have attracted much attention recently, becoming a more urgent object of research in times of environmental crisis and the painful re-structuring of global economic relations. While the effectiveness of critical initiatives on mainstream market relations is disputed, it is important to consider which cultural frames are taken up and developed by self-defined critical and alternative consumers. Clearly, the discourses surrounding critical consumption delve into a consumer vocabulary, but how do they delineate the consumer? To answer this question and to consider if and how critical consumption initiatives amount to an alternative rendering of consumer subjectivity, I shall draw on a large qualitative research project conducted in Italy among engaged consumers as well as activists from a variety of organizations (Sassatelli 2008). Different initiatives share a distinct notion of consumer sovereignty, which critically elaborates, and sometimes overturns, *laissez faire* wisdom. Three themes in particular seem to emerge in varying degrees and combinations: redistribution and interdependency, collective goods, and the pleasures of frugality. Most informants put forward a civic vision of the market, contending that market relations thrive among equals, and indeed that to realize itself the market's social potential requires a pacified social space, which places value on redistribution and sees the powerful consumer as the prime motor behind this. They also share the view that goods which transcend individual, exclusive enjoyment (in particular, the environment) are of the essence for consumers' quality of life, but are all too often neglected by capitalist market relations: here again, consumer choice is seen as a way to internalize environmental factors. Finally, the liberal view of the relationship between consumption and happiness is regarded as simplistic. Happiness does not come from increasing the pace of consumption, but from slowing it down, so as to appreciate both our process of learning to use goods and good's potentialities as sustainable, adjustable items, rather than opting for a high-waste, high-discarding, as well as compartmentalized and ultimately hyperfunctional forms of consumption. Critical consumers are living again in a world of scarcity (quite often in a perceived and self-imposed scarcity, given that they mostly have a middle-class profile): scarcity of uncontaminated natural resources, of fair relations, of craftsmanship and creativity. Theirs is a world in which the ever-shifting, fashion dominated merry-go-round of novelties with its ethics of self-experimentation are largely indicated as futile, false indulgences which are not so much immoral as ineffective in bringing about happiness. Theirs is a world where personalization of standardized commodities is quite different from personalized circuits of commodity provision where commercial logic is forever intertwined with personal trust. Their views match a growing body of literature in philosophy and the social sciences which argues that people's well-being might be understood in terms other than their expenditure, and which starts from notions of "quality of life" which will often add environmental or communitarian depth to a short-term, individualist, and private vision of individual choice.

The discourses surrounding critical consumer practices provide a set of specific criteria of choice drawing on "regimes of justifications" (Boltanski and Thévenot 1991) which have been taken beyond the dominant mode of legitimating markets in Western culture. As suggested (Sassatelli 2006), themes mainly associated with the promotion of consumption as a legitimate sphere of action *per se*: "taste," "good taste," "pleasure," "fantasy," "comfort," "distinction," "happiness," "refinement," and so on, are replaced by themes predominantly associated with the definition of a democratic public sphere and with production. The vocabulary of critical consumerism draws either on social and political activism (to purchase is to "vote," "protest," "make oneself heard," "change the world," "help the community," "mobilize for a better future," and so on) or on production (to purchase here becomes "work you do for the community," "effort done for yourself and the other," "creative," "productive," and so on). Alongside this, a new set of criteria for measuring quality of life and pleasure is slowly evolving which draws on spiritual themes, de-rationalization and even a communitarian worldview. What is more, from empirical research conducted in Italy, there is evidence that actual practices are structured so as to enhance a different variety of consumer embodiment: one where the now is related to the future, there is an emphasis on slowness as the embrace of bodily limits, and a return to "solidity" as an embracement of social interdependencies. This is articulated, for example, in the diffusion of self-production practices, car sharing, local provisioning, and so on among critical consumers (see also Sassatelli 2013).

It is not the purpose of this chapter to evaluate the extent to which the phenomena collected under the banner of critical consumption may be effective in facilitating cultural change and assisting alternative ways of organizing the market. Yet critical consumption initiatives point to a different vision of consumer choice based on a different, relational rendering of individual autonomy, one in which self-government does not spiral in on itself or work dualistically on the body, but is arguably geared towards common goods which provide paths for individual pleasures and which need to be publicly addressed, discussed and worked upon. All in all, critical consumption initiatives adumbrate a view of subjectivity and self-autonomy as the capacity of giving oneself norms and learning to like what is "good."

Happiness is less an individual business, and more a matter of nurturing a space for relationships that are expressed, notably, in a more responsible and aware use of goods and commodities. In this rendering, critical consumers are good consumers in that they choose what is good and they educate their desires to like what is good, questioniong goodness against the backdrop of a personal network of relations engaged directly with the ethical and political questioning of choice.

Conclusion

> For a long time, the individual was vouched for by the reference of others and the demonstration of his ties to the commonweal (family, allegiance, protection); then he was authenticated by the discourse of truth he was able or obliged to pronounce concerning himself. (Foucault 1976, 58)

Michel Foucault thus expresses what is otherwise called modern individualization. His well-known remarks certainly stress the cognitive aspect of identity constitution, but, as he demonstrate in his constant interest in discipline, body management and demeanor are fundamental in sustaining self-authentication. In most cultures throughout history a variety of body practices are fundamental to mark social identity. In our culture, which is largely a consumer culture, whereby our relation to objects and our own body is largely mediated by market processes, promotional culture and the cash nexus, a variety of subjectivities are constituted consumerwise. In contemporary societies, we not only satisfy our most elementary daily needs through commodities; we also conceptualize the purchase and use of goods as acts of "consumption" and we are arguably increasingly happy, or at least accustomed, to be addressed as "consumers." That of the "consumer" has become a crucial social persona, addressed by a plethora of scientific disciplines, public discourses, and social institutions which contribute to the delineation of what kind of relation to body and self-consumers do and must perform. From early modern times in Europe, the human being has increasingly been portrayed as a consuming animal whose needs are infinite and undefined (Brewer and Porter 1993). The characterization of life as a merry-go-round of production and consumption becomes dominant, with consumption in a rather ambiguous position: it represents desire but, as desire, it is dubious at least morally. Indeed, from modernity consumption often takes on a paradoxical guise: a private vice which is good for the nation and thereby a passion which needs to be tamed into accepted, rational forms of capitalization or self-improvement. Various forms of tamed hedonism, typically predicated on dualistic premises, have represented the main way out of the paradox, with emphasis being placed on the capacity of the self to govern the self, on autonomy as self-government (Sassatelli 2007). Commercialized fitness clearly fits nicely within this paradigm.

In more recent times, what we may call late modern or postindustrial societies, this view exists at least side by side with another—one which sees consumption as perhaps innocent at a private level and bad when it comes to common goods (from community relations to the environment). This view is today epitomized by initiatives and practices which go under the banner of critical consumerism. In broader terms, a focus on the creative, slow appropriation of commodities resonates with the growing body of literature in philosophy and the social sciences which suggests that people's well-being could be reformulated on grounds other than increasing expenditure, starting from notions of "quality of life" which will often thicken up a short-term, individualistic, competitive and private vision of individual choice with environmental or communitarian contents. This may imply some form of "voluntary simplicity" or "downshifting" in consumption, rejecting upscale spending and long working hours, to live a simpler, more relaxed life and to enhance personal fulfilment, socio-economic equality and environmental awareness (Sassatelli 2013). The emphasis on simplicity is in many ways all but regressive: it is an emphasis on slowness and embeddedness which amounts to the deepening of consumers' knowledge, where the redundancy that allows for the elaboration of taste as a reflexive, critical practice does not come from sophistication or distinction but from the embrace of the relational nature of commodities. An emphasis on slowness may take place in order to discover new pleasures and enhance personal satisfaction, as well as to further socio-economic equality and environmental awareness. Clearly, seen in this light, critical consumption practices do have potential for social change. While such potential needs to be considered case by case, it is evident that critical cultures of consumption of different varieties represent a crucial reservoir for political mobilization, but should not be equated with it, partly because they are broader and much more mundane than political consumerism strictly speaking (Sassatelli 2004, 2006, 2009). Critical or ethical commodities and commodity circuits embody a critical dialog with many aspects of consumer capitalism, including the notion of consumer sovereignty. But they do not throw this notion away. Rather, they consider consumer subjectivity and consumer sovereignty to be a political project larger than the market as narrowly defined. They thus attempt to modify consumer capitalism from the inside, the starting point of these initiatives being that consumer choice is not universally good and it certainly is not a private issue.

Of course this view has its own genesis, but here I want to stress that rather than emphasizing autonomy as self-government, it emphasizes autonomy as the capacity to give oneself rules, and do so in accordance with visions of the public good that may call into question received visions of consumer choice. This much stronger notion of autonomy is thus potentially critical of the processes upon which commercial consumer culture is currently based. This is evident in the debates within critical consumption, a phenomenon which is different from, and yet sits side by side, the growing market for beauty, health, and fitness. To be sure, radically critical lifestyles may be a minority phenomenon, and the road to a different organization of commercial relations and commoditization is long and uncertain. Still, as cultural framing critical consumption points to rather different views of consumer subjectivity. Its point of reference is not individual happiness as predicated on individual maintenance, pleasure and enhancement, but a social notion of individual well-being whereby the good life for the individual entails a vision of the common good. Choice is fundamental but it is as much a duty as it is a right: a good consumer must not only choose according to desires so long as he or she is not a slave to them, he or she has to make reasoned choices. As private decisions and preferences have an impact outside individual life, consumers have power and responsibility not only towards themselves but also towards the social and natural world. This means a duty, of course, but also a chance, to realize more stable paths towards well-being. All in all, this points to the fact that while humans are increasingly framed consumerwise in contemporary societies, how wise the consumers are is a matter of dispute and the notion of the consumer is itself a frenzied battlefield.

References

Arendt, H. 1958. *The Human Condition.* New York: Doubleday Anchor Books.

Baudrillard, J. [1970] 1998. *The Consumer Society: Myths and Structures.* London: Sage.

Bauman, Z. 1992. *Intimations of Post-modernity.* London: Routledge.

Bauman, Z. 2007. *Consuming Life.* Cambridge: Polity.

Beck, U. [1986] 1992 *Risk Society: Towards a New Modernity.* London: Sage.

Boltanski, L. and L. Thévenot. 1991. *De la Justification. Les Économies de la Grandeur.* Paris: Gallimard.

Bordo, S. 1993. *Unbearable Weight. Feminism, Western Culture and the Body.* Berkeley: University of California Press.

Bourdieu, P. 1977. *Outline of a Theory of Practice.* Cambridge: Cambridge University Press.

Bourdieu, P. [1979] 1984. *Distinction: A Social Critique of the Judgement of Taste.* London: Routledge.

Brewer, J. and R. Porter, eds. 1993. *Consumption and the World of Goods.* London: Routledge.

Bromberger, C., ed. 1998. *Passions Ordinaires.* Paris: Bayard.

Campbell, C. 1987. *The Romantic Ethic and the Spirit of Modern Consumerism.* Oxford: Basil Blackwell.

Connell, R.W. 2005. *Masculinities.* Second Edition. Berkeley, CA: University of California Press.

Douglas, M. 1992. "Wants." In *Risk and Blame: Essays in Cultural Theory*, edited by M. Douglas. London: Routledge.

Douglas, M. and Isherwood, B. 1979. *The World of Goods. Towards an Anthropology of Consumption.* New York: Basic Books.

Elias, N. and E. Dunning. 1986. *The Quest for Excitement: Sport and Leisure in the Civilizing Process.* Oxford: Basil Blackwell.

Featherstone, M. 1991. *Consumer Culture and Postmodernism.* London: Sage.

Fine, G.A. 1998. *Morel Tales. The Culture of Mushrooming.* Cambridge, MA: Harvard University Press.

Foucault, M. [1976] 1978. *History of Sexuality*, vol. 1. Harmondsworth: Penguin.

Giddens, A. 1991. *Modernity and Self-Identity.* Cambridge: Polity.

Harrison, R. et al. 2005. *The Ethical Consumer.* London: Sage.

Hennion, A. and G. Téil. 2004. "L'Attività Riflessiva dell'Amatore. Un Approccio Pragmatico al Gusto." *Rassegna Italiana di Sociologia* 44, 4: 519–42.

Hilton, M. 2009. *Prosperity for All: Consumer Activism in an Era of Globalisation.* Ithaca, NY: Cornell University Press.

Lasch, C. [1979] 1991. *The Culture of Narcissism.* New York: Norton.

Lears, T.J.J. 1983. "From Salvation to Self-realization: Advertising and the Therapeutic Root of the Consumer Culture 1880–1930." In *The Culture of Consumption. Critical Essays in American History 1980–1980*, edited by W. Fox and T.J.J. Lears, 3–38. New York: Pantheon Books.

Lewis, T. and E. Potter. 2011. *Ethical Consumption.* London: Routledge.

Miller, D, ed. 1995. *Acknowledging Consumption. A Review of New Studies.* London: Routledge.

Miller, D. 2012. *Consumption and its Consequences.* Cambridge: Polity.

Mrozek, D.J. 1989. "Sport in American Life: From National Health to Personal Fulfilment." In *Fitness in American Culture*, edited by K. Grover, 18–46. Amherst, MA: University of Massachusetts Press.

Mukerji, C. 1983. *From Graven Images: Patterns of Modern Materialism.* New York: Columbia University Press.

Negus, K. 2002. "The Work of Cultural Intermediaries and the Enduring Distance between Production and Consumption." *Cultural Studies* 16, 4: 501–15.

Noble, G. and M. Watkins. 2003. "So, How did Bourdieu Learn to Play Tennis? Habitus, Consciousness and Habituation." *Cultural Studies* 17, 3/4: 520–38.

Sassatelli, R. 1999. "Interaction Order and Beyond. A Field Analysis of Body Culture within Fitness Gyms." *Body and Society*, 5, 2–3: 227–48.

Sassatelli, R. 2000. "From Value to Consumption. A Social-Theoretical Perspective on Simmel's Philosophie des Geldes." *Acta Sociologica* 43, 3: 207–18.

Sassatelli, R. 2001. "Tamed Hedonism: Choice, Desires and Deviant Pleasures." In *Ordinary Consumption*, edited by J. Gronow and A. Warde, 93–106. London: Routledge.

Sassatelli, R. 2003a. "Corpi in Pratica: Habitus, Interazione e Disciplina." *Rassegna Italiana di Sociologia* 3: 429–58.

Sassatelli, R. 2003b. "La Politicizzazione del Consumo e l'Evoluzione dei Movimenti dei Consumatori." In *Consumi, Genere e Generazioni*, edited by P. Capuzzo, 63–92. Rome: Carocci.

Sassatelli, R. 2004. "The Political Morality of Food. Discourses, Contestation and Alternative Consumption." In *Qualities of Food*, edited by M. Harvey et al., 176–91. Manchester: Manchester University Press.

Sassatelli, R. 2006. "Virtue, Responsibility and Consumer Choice. Framing Critical Consumerism." In *Consuming Cultures, Global Perspectives*, edited by J. Brewer and F. Trentmann, 219–50. Oxford: Berg.

Sassatelli, R. 2007. *Consumer Culture. History, Theory, Politics*. London: Sage.

Sassatelli, R. 2009 "Representing Consumers; Contesting Claims and Agendas." In *The Politics and Pleasures of Consuming Differently*, edited by K. Soper et al., 25–42. Basingstoke: Palgrave.

Sassatelli, R. 2008 "L'Investitura Politica del Consumatore. Modelli di Soggettività e Mutamento Sociale." In *Il Consumo Critico*, edited by L. Leonini, and R. Sassatelli 144–69, Laterza: Bari.

Sassatelli, R. 2010. *Fitness Culture. Gyms and the Commercialisation of Discipline and Fun*. Basingstoke: Palgrave.

Sassatelli, R. 2013. *"Creativity Takes Time, Critique Needs Space."* In *Culture of the Slow: Social Deceleration in an Accelerating World*, edited by N. Osbaldiston, 154–77. Basingstoke: Palgrave.

Sennett, R. 1998. *The Corrosion of Character*. New York: Norton.

Thornton, S. 1995. *Club Cultures. Music, Media and Subcultural Capital*. Cambridge: Polity.

Vigarello, G. 1978. *Le Corps Reddressé*. Paris: Delarge.

Wacquant, L. 2003. *Body and Soul*. Chicago: Chicago University Press.

Wernick, A. 1991. *Promotional Culture: Advertising, Ideology and Symbolic Expression*. London: Sage.

Williams, R. 1976. *Keywords*. London: Collins.

Wykes, M. and B. Gunter. 2005. *The Media and Body Image: If Looks Could Kill*. London: Sage.

Zelizer, V. 2008 *Vite Economiche*. Bologna: Il Mulino.

Index

Page numbers in **bold** refer to figures and tables.

acculturation 129, 149
addictions 69, 75
Adorno, T.W. 46
advertising
    child-aimed 129–30, 136–7
    creativity 150–51
    function 77
    human body 180
    identity-construction 140–42
    impact on consumption 79, 132–4
    impact on desires 140–41
    persuasion 71
    political responses 137–8
    proselytism 134–6
    values 136–7
agency, human xv, 5–6
airports 29
alienation 38, 145, 151, 152
All you Need to Know About Ethics and Finance (Plender and Persaud) 161
Amazon 38
ambivalence 99, 135
America (Baudrillard) 13
Animal Farm (Orwell) 177
Apple Corporation 41, 60
Archer, Margaret S. 72n2, 77n5, 78
Arendt, Hannah 179
Aristotle 153
art of liberty 143
asceticism 132, 180–81
authenticity 77, 87, 89, 91, 97
autonomy 138, 179, 189, 191–2, 193

Ban Ki-moon 160
Bangladesh 167–8
Bangladesh Safety Accord 167
Barroso, José Manuel 163
Baudrillard, Jean 4, 13, 77, 134, 178, 180n1

Bauman, Zygmunt 77, 182n2
Bell, Daniel 150
Bellamy, Edward 143
Berardi, Franco 151, 152
Bernstein, Elizabeth 89
the Bible 11, 20
The Blackwell Dictionary of Sociology (Johnson) 47
Boltanski, Luc 152
bounded authenticity 89
Bourdieu, Pierre 178, 182–3
boxing gyms 186–7
"Bridging the Gap Between Commercial and Ethical Trade Agendas" 162
business ethics 161–4, **162**; *see also* fashion ethics

"Calmly We Walk Through This April's Day" (Schwartz) 155
Campbell, Colin 69, 72–3, 75–6, 81, 181
capitalism 25, 38, 39, 75, 132, 142–3, 193
careers 148–51
casinos 29
Castro, Orsola de 164
Catcher in the Rye (Salinger) 149
cathedrals of consumption 29–31
de Certeau, Michel 25
charisma 8
Chiapello, Eve 152
children
    acculturation 149
    advertising aimed at 129–30, 133, 136–7
    coming-of-age struggles 129
    consumer socialisation 114
    food placement in stores 31
    moral development 12–13
    pathway consumption 88

relationships 94–5, 96–8
    shopping at Gekås 113
choice
    in consumerist discourse 91, 96
    critical consumption initiatives 190, 191
    illusion of 5–6, 31
    in liberal theory 137
    obligatory 182
    "opt out" 6, 13, 15, 17
    and responsibility 194
Christianity 83, 132
civilization 17–18
cognitive labour 148–53
The Comfort of Things (Miller) 74
coming-of-age struggles 129
Comme Il Faut 163–4
commoditization 71, 180
communications technology 138–9, 152
communitarianism 139
conformity 13, 116, 118, 121, 138, 145
conspicuous consumption 4, 60–61
    classes of 41–2
    conscious awareness 51–2
    defining and identifying 46–9
    differing views of theory 43–5
    evidence for 53–6
    habitual 52–3
    "I Am Rich" app 41, 60
    intentions 53, 56–9
    plausibility 59–60
    sociological meaning 51–3
    sociological understandings 49–51
    theory of 43, 59–60
    and waste 19–20
consumer capital 75, 132, 185, 193
consumer culture 103–4, 180, 184,
        187, 189, 192, 193; *see also*
        fitness culture
consumer culture study
    ambivalence and insecurity 88–9
    ambivalence in relationships 91
    consumerist discourse 98–9
        in intimate life 94–5
        language use 95–6
        and raising teenagers 96–8
        at work 91–4
    methodology 90
consumer practices 80, 185–92

consumer socialization 114
Consumer Society (Baudrillard) 4
consumer sovereignty 134, 190, 193
consumer spaces 27, 177, 178, 184, 186–7
consumerism
    commoditization 71
    consumption decisions 79–81
    critics of 70–72
    discourse of 69–70
    and distaste for consumerism 135
    and identity 141–2
    materialism 73–4
    motives and values 75–6
    narcissistic 19
    narratives 79–80
    needs, wants, desires 72–3
    problems 69, 71
    religion's role 82–3
    responsible 19
    strength of system 76–8
    vice-promotion 74–6
    see also consumption
consumerist discourse 88, 98–9
    in intimate life 94–5
    language use 95–6
    and raising teenagers 96–8
    three tenets 91
    at work 91–4
consumers
    abilities 77–8
    beliefs 9
    consumer socialization 114
    control of 27, 28, 29–31
    defining 16
    dehumanization 26
        cathedrals of consumption 29–31
        fast food restaurants 27–8
        globalization of nothing 31–4
    embodied selves 178, 182, 183, 185,
        187
    as embodied subjects 178–9
    manipulation of 6
    moral framing 180–81
    narcissism 4–5
    peer comparisons 59–60
    position in capitalist structure 3, 6
    power 77–8
    putting to work 35–6

reflexivity 78
see also prosumers/prosumption
consumership 187
consumption
    consequences 70, 75–6
    conspicuous, *see* conspicuous
        consumption
    consumers' views 135
    critical consumption initiatives 189,
        190–92, 193–4
    functional status 70
    good–bad paradox 192–3
    goods and virtues 83
    "human" 79
    and identity xv–xvi, 57, 181–2,
        183–4
    and meaning 179
    nature xv
    patterns, changing 132–42
    rationalization 27–8
    as self-expression 141–2
    and social comparison 103
    and social inclusion 111
    socially necessary 116
    sustainable 42–3
    of time 154–5
    views of humanity 177
    see also consumerism
consumption decisions 70, 71, 79–81
consumption settings 27, 184
contracts, commercial 6, 13–15
control
    in boxing 186
    centralized 32–3
    of consumers 26, 27, 28, 29–31
    consumer's 26
    continuum 25
    in fitness gym 187, 188, 189
    on Internet 39
    prosumer's 37
    in workplace 145
cooperation 12, 18, 19
Corporate Social Responsibility (CSR)
    160, 161–4
Le Corps Redressé (Vigarello) 181
Creative Commons 39
creativity 150–51
credit card company contract 13–15

critical consumption initiatives 189,
    190–92, 193–4
Critical Studies in Fashion & Beauty
    163–4
cruise ships 29, 146–7
The Cultural Contradictions of Capitalism
    (Bell) 150
cultural de-classification 183n3
cultural externalities 130
The Culture of Narcissism (Lasch) 4
customer relations 118, 120

Darwin, Charles 18
Davis, Arthur K. 50
dedication 78
dehumanization 25, 26, 27–34, 38, 71n1,
    73–4
deliberation 78
Democracy in America (Tocqueville) 7
department stores 31; *see also* Gekås
    Ullared study
dependence 82, 87–8, 99
desires 18, 72–3, 135, 140–41, 147
development 161
difference principle 139
discernment 78
Disney, Walt 30
Disney World 30
Disneyland 30
distinction 116, 118, 120, 121, 122
The Division of Labor (Durkheim)
    11, 18
division of labour 20–21
Donati, Pierpalo 71n1
Dostoevsky, Fyodor 7
Douglas, M. 179, 182
Douglas, Mary 80
Dove 171
Durkheim, Emile
    division of labour 20–21
    economic sphere 16, 17–18
    education 17–18
    government 18
    needs and wants 18
    optimism 8
    the sacred 8
    solidarity 10–11
    warfare 20, 21

"Economic Possibilities for our
Grandchildren" (Keynes) 143
Edgell, S. 44n1, 46
education 16–17, 18
emotional dissonance 16–22
emotional labour 21, 145–7, 148
emotions 6, 7, 8, 144, 145, 147, 181, 186
environmental concerns 69, 70, 71, 79,
160, 169, **170**, **171**
ergon 147–8
Escrivá, Josemaría 83
Esthetica 164
ethics
Aristotelian 153–4
business ethics 161–4, **162**;
see also fashion ethics
defining "ethical" 165, 168–9
Etsy, Daniel 163
eudaimonia 131, 140
European Commission 163
The Evolution of Educational Thought
(Durkheim) 17
experiments in political possibility 131
exploitation 3, 9, 10, 25, 26, 38

families
child's moral development 12
consumer socialization 114
decision-making 112–14
post-industrial changes 88–9
shopping 108, 111, 112
fashion 47, 57, 73, 82, 116, 168
Fashion and Ethics (Tseëlon) 169
fashion ethics
and aesthetics 168
approaches 172
assumptions **174**
case for 164–8
complexity 168–71, **170**, **171**
duration 172–4
Fashion Factories Undercover (ITV) 167
fast food restaurants 27–8, 32, 33–4, 35
Fauconnet, Paul 11–12
Featherstone, Mike 103
fetishism 73–4, 91
Financial Times 161
fitness culture 178, 185–9
fitness gyms 185, 186–9

Florida, Richard 150–51
force 3
Foucault, Michel 192
Frank, Robert H. 116
fraud 3, 6
From Somewhere 164
Fromm, Erich 4
future research 111, 122

the Gap 29–30
Geis, Gilbert 10
Gekås Ullared study 104, 120–21
baskets and trolleys **110**
Christmas merchandise **123**
conformity 116, **119**
customer relations 120
customer socialization 114
distinction 116, 118, **119**, 120
entrance **106**
family decision-making 112–14
family shopping 108, 111
future research 122
location 104, **105**
loss leaders **119**
market in Strängnäs **121**
merchandise in trolleys **117**
outside fitting room **113**
overview of Gekås Ullared 104–8
price awareness 111
queue **109**
role specialization 112
shopping as social activity 108, 112
shopping strategies 108
trolleys **115**
Giddens, Anthony 5, 181–2
gift giving/receiving 82
globalization 31–4, 71, 159–60, 161
Globalization and its Discontents (Stiglitz)
160
The Globalization of Nothing (Ritzer) 31,
32–3
glocalization 31
Goldfiner, Sybil 163–4
the "good" 80–82, 134, 142, 148, 154
the good life 72, 130, 132, 133–4, 148,
153, 194
Gorgias (Socrates) 152–3
governance, global 161

governments
    control of dangerous consumption 76, 83
    economic productivity 140
    global 161
    political postemotionalism 7
    position in capitalist structure 3, 10, 18
    sacredness 9
    trade 160
grobalization 31–4
The Guardian 163

habitus 31, 182–3, 184, 185, 186, 187
happiness 75, 190, 192
Hearson, Martin 166, 173
hedonism 74, 150, 180–81, 189, 192
Higher Learning in America (Veblen)
    16–17
Hjort, Torbjörn 116
Hochschild, Arlie 145
Hoover, Herbert 133, 139
human body 177, 178, 179, 180–81, 182,
    186, 188–9
human, defining 5, 25, 87, 159, 177
human flourishing, obstacles to 130, 131,
    140
humanization 25, 26, 34–9
hyperconsumption 29; *see also*
    overconsumption
hypergoods 81

"I Am Rich" app 41, 60
identity xv–xvi, 57, 78, 97, 149–50, 181–2,
    183–4, 192
identity-construction 141–2
IKEA 30
inclusion/exclusion 111
individualization 89, 178, 181, 192
industrial revolution 34–5
inequalities 70, 76, 146–7
insecurity 87–8, 88–9, 93, 98–9
insincerity 7
Institute for American Values 136–7
Institute for Manufacturing study 169
institutions of consumption 177, 178, 184,
    185; *see also* fitness gyms
intentions 11, 49, 53, 56–9
Internet 6, 26, 36–7, 38–9
iron cages 27–8

irrationalities 28
Isherwood, B. 179

justifications 191

"keeping up" 43, 51–2, 114
Keynes, John Maynard 143

La Mode Éthique 164
Labour Behind the Label report 165–6, 167
language 70, 78, 95–6
Lasch, Christopher 4
law
    as business enterprise 15
    Fauconnet's analysis 11–12
    Veblen's analysis 9–10
    see also morality
lawyers 9–10
Lazzarato, Maurizio 151–2
Leach, William 132, 133
Lennerhov, Boris 104, 118, 120
lifestyles 60, 75, 112, 178, 182
Lipovetsky, Gilles 73, 75
The Lonely Crowd (Riesman) 4
Looking Backward (Bellamy) 143
Lurie, Bob 163

MacIntyre, Alasdair 79, 81, 82
The Managed Heart (Hochschild) 145
Marcuse, Herbert 73
Marx, Karl 25, 38, 73–4, 142–3, 147–8
Mason, R.S. 46, 53, 54
materialism 69, 73–4, 80, 83, 122
Mauss, Marcel 82
The McDonaldization of Society (Ritzer) 8,
    9, 27, 35
McDonald's 34; *see also* fast food
    restaurants
Mead, Emily Fogg 133
meaning of goods 69, 81, 179
Merton, Robert K. 50, 51
Meyer, Dick 48
Miller, Daniel 69, 74, 76, 78, 80–81
Mills, C. Wright 4, 43, 46
Mintel 165, 166
Moral Education (Durkheim) 17
The Moral Judgment of the Child (Piaget) 12
morality 11–13, 17, 19, 80–82

Mrozek, D.J. 181
Mukerji, Chandra 181
Murray, Andrew 57

narcissism 4–5, 19, 20
narratives 79–80
nationalism 21–2
Natural Law, doctrine of 10
needs 18–19, 72–3, 81, 192
NGOs (non-governmental organizations) 165
Nietzsche, Friedrich 8, 18
non-human technologies 28, 31
non-humanness 71
Notes From the Underground (Dostoevsky) 7
nothing, defined 32–3
novelty, love of 75

The Office television programme 145–6
"On Sabotage" (Veblen) 9
open source software 38–9
Orwell, George 6, 177
overconsumption 29, 43, 70, 71, 111, 144
overwork 70

patriotism 21–2
peer comparisons 50, 59–60, 103
Persaud, Avinash 161
Piaget, Jean 12–13
Plender, John 161
political philosophy 130–31, 137–40
postemotionalism
    defined 6
    emotional dissonance 16–22
    illustration 13–15
    issues of being human 5–8
    and Ritzer's *McDonaldization of
        Society* 8–9
postindustrial society 87
postmodernism 6–7
power
    of consumers 26, 77
    of corporations 14, 15, 132
    and humanness 25
    of prosumers 26, 37, 38
price 45n2, 50, 106, 111, 116, 118
Primark 167
production 26, 27, 34–5, 37, 139, 140, 143,
    169

Professional Ethics and Civic Morals
    (Durkheim) 16
prosumers/prosumption 26, 34–9
*The Protestant Ethic and the Spirit of
    Capitalism* (Weber) 132
Prufrock, Eliot 141

quality of life 190, 191, 193

Rana Plaza factory, Bangladesh 167
Rand, Ayn 5
rationalization 27–8, 29
Rawls, John 134, 139, 144
Reagan, Ronald 10
reflexivity 78, 181–2, 182–3, 184, 187
regulation, economic 160, 161–2
relationships 182–3
    and consumer culture 91
    consumerist discourse 87, 98–9
        employer–employee relationships
            91–4
        intimate life relationships 94–5
        language use 95–6
        parental views of teenagers'
            relationships 96–8
    with things and people 74
religion 11, 21, 82–3, 132, 137–8
replaceability 91, 98
representation 177–85
La Responsabilité (Fauconnet) 11–12
responsibility 11, 12, 180, 190, 194;
        see also Corporate Social
        Responsibility (CSR)
Riesman, David 4, 7, 9, 43
Ritzer, George 8–9, 77

the sacred 8, 9, 82–3
Salinger, J.D. 149
Sassatelli, Roberta 71, 77, 79
Schor, Juliet B. 44, 55, 143–4
Schwartz, Delmore 155
self-articulation 147, 148, 153
self-betrayal 150
self-development 149
self-realization 148–9
selfishness 69
service workers 145–7
Shakti mat 118, **119**

Shirky, Clay 26
shopping, *see* Gekås Ullared study
shopping malls 30
Siegle, Lucy 162
Simmel, Georg 116, 179
simplicity 193
Slater, Done 103
sociability 77
social hydraulics 77
social status
    conspicuous consumption,
        see conspicuous consumption
    emulation 116
    inner-directed consumers 4
    meanings 58
    peer comparisons 50, 59–60, 103
Socrates 152–3
something, defined 33
something–nothing continuum 33–4
The Spectator 174, **175**
Stern, Stefan 163
Stiglitz, Joseph 160, 161
style 168
subjectivity 177–85, 186–7, 189, 190, 191,
    193–4
Suicide (Durkheim) 8, 17–18
supermarkets 30–31
sustainability 42–3, 163, 165, 170
Sweden 104; *see also* Gekås Ullared study

Taylor, Charles 80, 81
technology 28, 37, 138, 143
teenagers 96–8
Theory of Business Enterprise (Veblen) 10
The Theory of the Leisure Class (Veblen)
    19, 46, 50
The Third Wave (Toffler) 34
Thornton, Sarah 185
time 154–5
To Die For (Siegle) 162
Tocqueville, Alexis de 7
Toffler, Alvin 34
tourism 70
Tracy, Sarah 146
Trigg, A.B. 44, 50
triple bottom line (TBL) approach 161
trust 161–2, 163
The Tumbleweed Society (Pugh) 92

values
    of businesses 161, 172; *see also*
        Corporate Social Responsibility
        (CSR)
    of consumers 75–6, 79, 80
    predatory 17, 22
    teaching children 136–7
    of upwardly mobile 58
Veblen, Thorstein
    Age of Enlightenment 7
    conspicuous consumerism 19–20
    conspicuous consumption theory 46,
        49, 50–51, 60
        economists' views 44–5
        other writers' views 44–5
        sociologists' views 43–4
    corporate-government barbarism 3, 4
    economic sphere 16–17
    education 16–17, 18
    influence 4
    law and lawyers 9–10
    needs and *wants* 19
    past–present coexisting 10–11
    warfare 20, 21
    waste 19, 20
vices 74–6
Vigarello, George 181
virtues of acknowledged dependence 82
visual culture 180

Wacquant, Loïc 186
Wall Street film 16
wants 18–19, 70, 72–3
Ward, Scott 114
warehouse stores 30
warfare 20–21
waste 19, 20, 48, 164, 169
"Watch Out for Children" report 136–7
water content **171**
Web 2.0 26, 36–7, 38–9
Weber, Max 8, 25, 27, 132
well-being 140, 190, 191, 193, 194
What Color is Your Parachute? (Bolles) 148
"What's Wrong with Consumerism?"
    (Campbell) 69
"What's Wrong with Consumption?"
    (Miller) 69
Wikipedia 38, 39, 47

will to power 18
Williams, Raymond 187
Wood, Paul 174, **175**
work
    cognitive labour 148–53
    consumerist discourse 91–4, 98
    of consumers/prosumers 26, 35–9
    emotional labour 145–7
    goodness 144–5
    identity 149–50
    postfordist 131
    sociological literature 144–5
    utopian views 143
workers
    careers 148–51
    cognitive workers 148–53
    consumers as 35–40
    cultural control of 145–7

    defining 27
    emotions 145–7
    fashion industry 165–6
    insecurity 88, 91–4, 99
    Marxist view 25, 38, 142–3, 147–8
    overworking 143–4, 150
    postemotional dissonance 20–21
    relationship with employer 91–4
    self-articulation 148
    self-betrayal 150
    service workers 145–8
Wright, Bradley 48

Yoder v. Wisconsin 137–8
young people, *see* children
YourDictionary 47

Zola, Émile 31

For Product Safety Concerns and Information please contact our EU representative GPSR@taylorandfrancis.com Taylor & Francis Verlag GmbH, Kaufingerstraße 24, 80331 München, Germany

Printed and bound by CPI Group (UK) Ltd, Croydon, CR0 4YY

01/05/2025

01858450-0002